I Got
THUNDER

I Got THUNDER

Black Women Songwriters on Their Craft

LaShonda Katrice Barnett

Thunder's Mouth Press
New York

I Got Thunder:
Black Women Songwriters on Their Craft

Copyright © 2007 by LaShonda Katrice Barnett

Published by
Thunder's Mouth Press
An imprint of Avalon Publishing Group, Inc.

AVALON
publishing group incorporated

Thunder's Mouth Press books are available at special discounts for bulk pur-
chases in the United States by corporations, institutions, and other organizations. For more information, please contact the Special Markets Department at
the Perseus Books Group, 2300 Chestnut Street, Suite 200, Philadelphia, PA
19103, or call (800) 255-1514, or e-mail special.markets@perseusbooks.com.

First Printing October 2007

Library of Congress Cataloging-in-Publication Data is available.

ISBN-13: 978-1-56858-331-0
ISBN-10: 1-56858-331-1

Book design by Bettina Wilhelm

Printed in the United States of America
Distributed by Publishers Group West

For, the *first* voice,
Brenda Jean Williams Long

In the fall of 1973, my mother made the difficult decision not to return to Baker University for her junior year, forfeiting her full scholarship in music. Pregnancy and impending motherhood, she deeply felt, warranted all of her attention. So begins the litany of sacrifices my mother would make for me, and so earns her this dedication. If you are ever in the area, stop by St. Thomas Missionary Baptist Church in Kansas City, Missouri, to hear my mother, a dazzling contralto, rock the house on her solo of "Order My Steps."

I am a Black woman
the music of my song
some sweet arpeggio of tears
is written in a minor key
and I
can be heard humming in the night
Can be heard
        humming
in the night

            —Mari Evans, excerpted from
                "I Am a Black Woman"

CONTENTS

Acknowledgments

Early in the process of this inspired project that I often referred to as "the dream job" in conversation with family and friends, I received the following e-mail from my friend, poet Kamilah Moon:

> This book is going to be SO tight!!!!! . . .
> What a treasure to spend time with and document
> the gifts of these divine songbirds. Their songs have
> saved/save lives—what would this world be without
> a black woman's song riding the wind??? I never want
> to know. . . .

The highlight of this work has of course been the opportunity to have intelligent conversations with creative black women who contribute so much love, in the way of music, to the planet. Kamilah said it best when she pondered the state of the world if not for these voices, voices that bring joy, solace, and inspiration to countless millions the world over. It has surely been one of my life's greatest experiences to capture these artists, in their own words, on topics of special significance to me—creative process, influence, and inspiration. I am first and foremost thankful to all of the artists presented here who not only gave graciously of their time and thoughts, but who welcomed me so warmly and who enthusiastically encouraged this work.

Sooner or later in the creative world, most undertakings are at the mercy of collective commitment, so that I am deeply indebted to Lukas Volger and senior editor Anita Diggs, both formerly of Thunder's Mouth Press, for their sincere interest and hard work in bringing this work to fruition. Lastly, it is my great fortune to have been born into a culture and a family that loves music; to have close friends and colleagues who match me in music obsession is an added boon. Their input along the way bolstered me when I felt too exhausted to make another phone call or type another e-mail in an effort to secure a date to sit and chat with the divine ones you will come to know more intimately in these pages. Thank you: Abbey Lincoln, Ruth Heit, Lonnie Plaxico, Blanche White, Elaine Marshburn, Kate Scott, Malinda Walford, April Reynolds-Mosolino, Suzanne Gardinier, Mary Porter, Karma Johnson, Rachelle Sussman-Rumph, Z&S, Hermine Pinson, Shirley Smith, Nancy White, Phylicia Rashad, Mari Evans, my lovely PKO sorority sisters (of Alpha Kappa Alpha) and my bloodfolk, especially my sister, Lisa Long-Searcy. My heartfelt thanks to you all for sharing in my interest, my love.

Introduction

In my childhood home one particular scene ocurred often enough that when I envisioned this project, it seemed a fated undertaking. Often the women in my family would squeeze together on the living room sofa to watch some music awards show, music videos (when they lent themselves to viewing by parents and their children—of all ages), or an interview with a *serious* musician. Implicit in my mother's idea of a serious musician was not only one who gave a memorable performance, but one who created as well as interpreted the music of others. Watching black female singers win audiences and please legions of fans employing voices not very different from those of our family members or soloists from the church choir was, in my home, a special communal activity equivalent to Sunday dinners and birthday celebrations. We exalted, almost to the point of deification, those artists possessed of voices my mother accorded with "truth-telling" (in the black religious tradition of testifying), and exemplified by powerful and original phrasing embellished with soft humming, scatting, wailing, moaning, and, especially, the hollering reminiscent of early classic blues.

As vocalists, lyricists, and composers, black women produce an astonishing body of work documenting their individual artistic development while collectively highlighting the dynamic nature of black music and cultural representation. For over a century now, their music has dominated the airwaves. Yet, despite the wealth of music they have created, songs written and performed by black women have never been the primary subject of any book published in the United States, or anywhere else. Intellectual interest, as manifested in scholarly research, is only now, after a century, beginning to match the commercial interest that black women's music has generated in American culture and globally. The dearth of published material on black women's songs derives in part from the perspective that singing is physical and songs are emotional, and that both its practice and its product are accessible to everyone. Additionally, the absence of analysis of black women vocalists in particular stems from the ephemeral nature of music combined with what many (myself included) perceive to be a God-given talent for singing. It is widely thought that describing musical experience is impossible. No matter how elegantly a writer writes, there is something fundamentally untranslatable about the power of musical experience, placing an even greater premium on documenting musicians' experiences and thoughts on their own work.

While I am the first to contend that many a songstress has held my listening heart in thrall, and that certainly the women musicians within and outside this book are conjurers of a sort, casting spells on audiences worldwide; intellectual practices and cultural traditions play a part in the magic. Black women's songs are a tool for deciphering both the individual experiences, beliefs, and deepest feelings of their orginators, and the African diasporic experience in general. For though they are usually informed by a personal experience, these songs signify the ideas and values of the singer's community. However, it is not my aim in this book to highlight the common qualities that drive the music and particularly the lyrics written by these women, but rather to ascertain what impels the creative act and what practices maintain this commitment.

That small field of study, wherein black women's lyrics are mined for their cultured and gendered values, begun by people like Hazel V. Carby ("It Jus Be's Dat Way Sometime: The Sexual Politics of Women's Blues" and "They Put a Spell on You") Angela Davis (*Blues Legacies and Black Feminism*), Tricia Rose (*Black Noise*), Gwendolyn Pough (*Check It While I Wreck It*), and Kyra Gaunt (*The Games Black Girls Play*) welcomes the contributions of others.

Nevertheless, I assert that the presence of a distinct philosophical tradition among black women singer-songwriters is borne out by original lyrics that display the themes of spirituality, freedom, relationships, motherhood, romance, sexuality, and social activism. What is distinct about the lyrics (to say nothing of the voices interpreting those lyrics) is their dialogic nature; they are conversations about the singer's individual and personal life that also reflect the experiences of her community and heritage. Furthermore, the commercial success of music by these artists certifies these songs as legitimate expressions of communal sentiment. Notwithstanding this music's ability to bring previously occluded experience to light, no book has dealt with black women singer-songwriters and the actual mechanics of writing lyrics, composing music, and performing in their own words. However, that *I Got Thunder* is without precedent is but part of what motivates this work. My connection to these artists underscores my awareness of the subjective power of music, for in this music I see reflections of the experiences and meaning of my own life. My goal, then, in these conversations, which were undertaken as oral histories, was to illuminate for music lovers and would-be students of this art form a crucial but understudied and underappreciated component of black women's music-making: the role of the creative process.

Often recognized in only one musical idiom or genre, most of the singer-songwriters highlighted here are beyond singular categorization. That is to say, they work and record within multiple idioms—folk, R&B, jazz, gospel—sometimes over the course of the same album. For this reason, it was more fruitful, when talking to these artists, to discuss the process of songwriting and music-making in general terms of who they are rather than what forms of music they sing. The result was an organic emergence of multiple themes of great significance to the artists themselves on topics such as inspiration, the origin of a song, and the state of black music today. The artists' responses to the aforementioned topics often bore striking resemblances to each other. To begin with, on the subject of inspiration, Abbey Lincoln responded, "I am inspired by a holy muse and my ancestors, and I don't take it for granted. I lead a very quiet life and I work hard to cultivate peace so those spirits will feel welcomed." Similarly, Chaka Khan described her state of inspiration as one where she is "naked of spirit, with no other intention but to be of service to the music and to tell the truth." Explanations of the origin of a song, and whether the lyric or the music comes first, were as varied as the artists presented here. Angélique Kidjo stated, "For me, the song comes and brings everything at the same time." Independent artist Narissa Bond echoed this experience, saying, "The two [lyric and music] usually come to me at the same time." The song process of Abbey Lincoln and Oleta generally begins with "the story," the lyric, and for other artists, such as Brenda Russell, Chaka Khan, and Tokunbo Akinro, the method of song origin is varied. Conversations about black music today invariably included recollections of a time when the music was more intergenerational, as evidenced in Dianne Reeves's quote: "I remember growing up and the music that I was listening to my mother was also listening to. The generations weren't so separate. She loved the Temptations and Aretha Franklin and I did, too." Similarly, Brenda Russell reflected, "When I was growing up the music was still loved by the parents and kids alike. There wasn't a big separation in the musical taste. So the kids would be grooving at the party with the parents playing the same music, which is very rare now. Back then there was more family participation to be enjoyed while listening to the music."

Over time, these conversations revealed important trends that mapped the trajectory of a singer-songwriter's path. Common strands included the intense level of musical dedication and devotion of all in their youth, in most cases before age ten, which saw them singing in church choirs as little girls, forming their own high school bands, and launching solo careers or performing in Top 40 bands long before the first record company executive appeared. Because many of the artists were called to music at a young age, and even though as adults they play their instruments with marked study and impressive ability, many of their initial experiences with said instruments were atypical. Consider Oleta

Adams, who recalled, "My first lessons were not on a piano. I had one of these things that had piano keys on it—a photocopy of the keyboard folded into sections." To the subject of unusual formative musical habits, indie artist Pamela Means added, "When I was about eight years old I got a hand-me-down toy guitar. It only had four strings on it and I didn't know you could restring. . . . I remember playing that guitar with a broken pick and three little strings." The shared belief that making music is a calling united all of the interviews. As Nona Hendryx said, "The work you do in a sense is not a chosen work, but a vocation. You come to it because you're prepared for it in some way"; or, as expressed in a reminiscence of Patti Cathcart Andress (of Tuck and Patti): "I felt this voice move through me and it said to me, 'You will sing, and everything will be all right.'" Not surprisingly, all of the artists I spoke with find strict adherence to one particular sound or genre in direct opposition to creativity and antithetical to the practice of music. Consequently, they voiced strong opinions about being labeled by record companies or even their fans. Along these lines, Dionne Warwick remarked, "I have always thought the singer is whatever the listening ear decides. . . . The music industry couldn't decide if I was R&B or what. The only reason they would even put that label on me is because I am a black woman." Also drawing a parallel between race and labeling, the late Nina Simone commented, "I have always resented the label because jazz is not what I play or how I live. Duke Ellington resented the label, also. So did Bessie Smith. I play black classical music, which I feel includes all of the forms I experiment with—the classical tradition, gospel, rhythm and blues, popular music." None of the singers I spoke with set out to become famous; nor does fame creep into these conversations even as a subtopic. By and large, these songbirds are linked by their devotion to music for the sake of music. This commitment enables them to endure hectic tour schedules and to put up with the unsavory side of the music industry, all the while endearing legions of fans. Every artist in this book speaks about the healing power of their own music and the ways in which performance "saves" them, "mends a broken heart," and helps them to "rectify the issues in [their] lives."

Representing the musical genres of blues, jazz, folk, gospel, and rhythm and blues, the following conversations, then, are best read in the broader context of a tradition of black women's original music. These women speak of their initial calling to music and give examples of their creative process and the ways in which it changes in the context of a project. They recall insight they gained from working with and listening to other artists, and lessons they learned from the music industry. They reminisce about creative inspiration and its sometimes uneasy manifestation.

Whether it is the virtuosic range exhibited by Chaka Khan or Tramaine Hawkins; the dramatic depth and emotional message found in the music of Abbey Lincoln, Shirley Caesar, and Nina Simone; the insouciant vocal delivery of Odetta, Patti Cathcart Andress, or Miriam Makeba; or the talents displayed in the mellifluous sound structures employed in the work of Oleta Adams and Brenda Russell, these artists, and many more, give voice to spiritual and cultural needs. Moreover, the success of international singer-songwriters such as the United Kingdom's Joan Armatrading, Germany's Tokunbo Akinro, France's (by way of West Africa) Angélique Kidjo, and South Africa's Miriam Makeba, make us aware of the global reach and profound impact of music created by black women, while independent artists such as Narissa Bond, Pamela Means, and Toshi Reagon remind us that despite the often bleak impression given us by radio disc jockeys and music corporations, somewhere very near you someone has her shoulder to the wheel (or in this case, the guitar) making *serious* music without the support of a major label.

For me, finding music that hits home is a pleasure imbued with great significance. It has been this way since I left the home of my childhood, the place where special memories like the one that began this introduction were born. Thinking of this early in the throes of this project one afternoon, I paused to savor every note of a voice as familiar and intimate to me as one of Big Mama's recipes. In her stylistic enunciation, wherein she stretches out syllables, and in slow tempos that often draw on melodic embellishments like slides and bends, this voice soothes me. I take great comfort in her ability to draw me in to tell a story that enables me to contemplate and celebrate my own life. This voice delivers me home. Along the way, I am moved and I delight also in thinking about the words she sings:

> 'Cause love is an emotion,
> It'll move you to do things
> Do things, do things
> Love is an emotion,
> It'll move you to do things
> I got thunder and it rings!

The lyric and music belong to Abbey Lincoln, an artist whose work has inspired me in numerous ways. The sentiment "I got thunder and it rings!" belongs to a great lineage of black women singer-songwriters gifted with distinctive vocal technique, composing achievement, and stage presence. Resounding like thunder in the atmosphere, these voices carry our truth to the world with powerful expression that will ring forevermore.

One
ABBEY LINCOLN
also known as AMINATA MOSEKA (AUGUST 6, 1930)

Actress, singer, songwriter, painter, poet Abbey Lincoln was born
Anna Marie Wooldridge on August 6, 1930, in Chicago, Illinois.
The tenth of twelve children, Lincoln grew up on a farm in the
township of Calvin Center, Michigan. In interviews the artist
recalls the freedom with which she "picked out melodies" at the
family piano where she began to experiment with music at age
five. As a youth Lincoln also sang in the choir at the AME church
her family attended. At age fourteen she was deeply affected by the
recordings she heard of Billie Holiday and Coleman Hawkins.
After winning an amateur singing contest in 1949, Lincoln traveled
to California with her brother. Following a brief stint as a night-
club performer in Los Angeles, in 1951 she moved to Honolulu,
where she sang with the Rampart Streeters at the Trade Winds
Club. During this time she met jazz performers Louis Armstrong
and Anita O'Day. In Honolulu, Lincoln attended several Billie
Holiday performances at the Brown Derby. Reportedly, Holiday
also attended two of Lincoln's shows, though the two never met.
Performing under the names Gaby Lee and Gaby Marie at various

supper clubs such as the Moulin Rouge, upon her return to California in 1954 Lincoln joined the company of José Ferrer, Rosemary Clooney, and Mitch Miller, who introduced her to lyricist Bob Russell. Russell later became her manager and suggested the singer change her name to Abbey Lincoln. In July of 1956 *Abbey Lincoln's Affair: A Story of a Girl in Love*, the singer's first recording with the Benny Carter Orchestra, was released on the Liberty imprint of the Riverside label. Lincoln recorded three consecutive albums for Riverside, including *That's Him* (1957), *It's Magic* (1958), and *Abbey Is Blue* (1959). In 1956, the year she landed a singing role in the film *The Girl Can't Help It*, Lincoln moved from California to New York. In New York City she performed regularly at the Village Vanguard and met many leading musicians, including Max Roach, Thelonious Monk, Dizzy Gillespie, and Charles Mingus. These artists, whose music addressed racial inequality, influenced Lincoln so that she too began to draw on cultural and political content in her songs. More important, however, than the reflection of social causes in their music was the fact that these musicians were also composers. In many interviews Lincoln has credited Thelonious Monk with encouraging her to compose, although it would be more than a decade before she fully embraced this aspect of her artistry. Lincoln collaborated with Max Roach and Oscar Brown Jr. on the landmark civil rights recording *We Insist! Max Roach's Freedom Now Suite*. The 1960 work featured the piece entitled "Tryptich: Prayer/Protest/Peace," in which Lincoln's vocal obligatos depart from traditional jazz singing and scatting. Here, words are replaced by hums, chants, and sighs, which are followed by screams, roars, screeches, and pants. The performance transformed Lincoln's reputation from supper club chanteuse to "social" singer. That same year, Lincoln also appeared in the off-Broadway production of Jean Genet's absurdist drama *The Blacks*, which boasted the stellar cast of James Earl Jones, Maya Angelou, Billy Dee Williams, Roscoe Lee Browne, and Cicely Tyson. The following year Lincoln provided vocals and lyrics for two songs, "Garvey's Ghost" and "Mendacity," on Roach's 1961 Impulse album *Percussion Bitter Sweet*. She also released her own album, *Straight Ahead*, on the Candid label, which featured four of her own lyrics, most notably "In the Red," which spoke to black America's economic plight. In 1962, Lincoln married percussion giant Max Roach. She also founded the Cultural Association for Women of African Heritage. According to Lincoln, the association was organized for the sole purpose of exploring the cultures of the African diaspora. The group's activities included promoting African hairstyles (during this time Lincoln herself began to wear an Afro and braids and was quoted in *Ebony* magazine for coming out against black women who straighten their hair), producing Afrocentric fashion shows, and protesting the assassination of Patrice Lumumba at the United Nations. In the midsixties, Lincoln's acting career gained new impetus when she appeared in several films, including *Nothing but a Man* (1964) and *For Love of Ivy* (1966). Following her divorce from Roach in 1970, Lincoln returned to California, where she taught drama at California State University in Northridge; painted; composed songs; and wrote essays, poetry, and a play. That year author Toni Cade Bambara edited and published the first anthology of nonfiction, fiction, and poetry by African–American women. To *The Black Woman*, Lincoln contributed an essay on black women's moral, economic, and sexual victimization entitled "To Whom Will She Cry Rape?" That year Lincoln's play, *Pig in a Poke*, was also produced at the Mafundi Institute, a black cultural center in the Watts section of Los Angeles, and she appeared on several television shows, including *Mission Impossible, Name of the Game*, and *The Flip Wilson Show*. She did not record again as a lead until 1973's *People in Me*, the only album she made in the seventies, recorded in Japan on the Philips label. During this period, however, Lincoln traveled extensively throughout Asia, Europe, and, most significantly, Africa. In 1975 the South African singer Miriam Makeba invited Abbey Lincoln to Africa as her guest. For Lincoln, the highlights of the trip involved meeting the leader of Guinea, Ahmed Sékou Touré, who named her Aminata ("trustworthy"), and the Zairean minister of information, who gave her the name Moseka ("God's image in the form of a maiden"). Lincoln has since commented in many interviews that immediately following that trip "[she] discovered songs coming out of [her]. . . . It was the biggest surprise. I started writing them down when I was about forty-two. . . . In a way it's like catching the rain in your hand. It's everywhere." A 1980 collaboration with tenor saxophonist Archie Shepp culminated in the album *Painted Lady* (Blue Marge, also reprinted as *Golden Lady* on the Inner City label in 1981). For the German label Enja, Lincoln released *Talking to the Sun* (1983) and three Billie Holiday tribute albums (1987). The latter compilation, *Abbey Sings Billie*, signaled a comeback for the singer. Lincoln moved back to New York in 1989, where she was signed by Verve at the behest of French record producer Jean-Philippe Allard, and cast by Spike Lee to appear in his 1990 jazz drama *Mo' Better Blues*. (Lincoln appears briefly in the opening scene as the mother of the young trumpeter protagonist, Bleek Gilliam.) In what most would consider a late flowering of her career, Lincoln has recorded nine albums—of primarily original compositions—to great critical acclaim. They include: *The World Is Falling Down* (1990); *You Gotta Pay the Band* (1991); *Devil's Got Your Tongue* (1993); *When There Is Love* (1994); *A Turtle's Dream* (1995); *Who Used to Dance* (1997); *Wholly Earth* (1999); *Over the Years* (2000); *It's Me* (2003); and *Abbey Sings Abbey* (2007). Writing about Lincoln's voice, jazz writer Stanley Crouch noted, "[She] sings with a dark sound and a small range which she has exploited with such cunning that you could say her virtuosity is homemade. . . . Through gradations of intonation and inflection she seems to pick at a pitch, or worry it into a broader emotional world, especially on those long notes Lincoln flares and narrows with chest and head tones." Characterized by her behind-the-beat phrasing and diction, distinctive features of Lincoln's singing are her ability to alter tone color, the voice production, and emphasis on word syllables she chooses to stress in any given song. Her combination of pitch and time is what linguists and philologists call "significant tone." Significant tone or tonal semantics as demonstrated in Lincoln's singing include elongating vowels, staccato phrasing, and talk-singing to lend special meaning to a particular word or phrase. Hers is an African-based aesthetic that also draws from spirituals and work songs. Lincoln performs in the tradition of the griot or the African-American preacher; that is, she has made vernacular sermonic performance the central element of her artistic expression. In the vocal performances of original songs such as "Talking to the Sun," "I Got Thunder (And It Rings!)," "Devil's Got Your Tongue," "Wholly Earth," and "Throw It Away," her interpretations are dramatic and instructive in language, tone, theme, and gesture. Describing her own approach to singing in

2003, Lincoln told interviewer Wayne Enstice, "I'm a storyteller. I don't have any confusion about it in my mind at all. I tell stories on the stage set to music." The recipient of several honorary doctorates, in 2001 Lincoln was the subject of a two-day symposium, For Love of Abbey, at Columbia University, where critics, musicologists, musicians, writers, and literary and film scholars gathered for panel discussions and other events devoted to the artist's work. In 2002, her original compositions were honored by Jazz at Lincoln Center in New York City with a three-evening concert program. Abbey Lincoln: Over the Years—An Anthology of Her Compositions and Poems featured vocalist Freddy Cole, saxophonist Joe Lovano, and tap dancer Savion Glover. Abbey Lincoln, the 2003 recipient of the National Endowment for the Arts Jazz Master Award, lives in New York City's Morningside Heights neighborhood.

Selected Discography

Abbey Is Blue (Riverside)

Straight Ahead (Candid)

Talking to the Sun (Enja)

The World Is Falling Down (Verve)

You Gotta Pay the Band (Verve)

Devil's Got Your Tongue (Verve)

A Turtle's Dream (Verve)

Who Used to Dance (Verve)

Wholly Earth (Verve)

Over the Years (Verve)

It's Me (Verve)

Abbey Sings Abbey (Verve)

Abbey Lincoln

LKB: Abbey, I've seen you perform in different venues all over the United States and even abroad. When I attend one of your live performances, I am always struck by your ability to bare it all onstage. You give very much of yourself during a performance.

Abbey: That's the way it is in the arts. If you don't know how to do that it's better if you just stay away.

LKB: With the grueling pace of a professional musician's life—especially one who has been at it half a century—and the level of intensity in all of your performances, I wonder if you have a method or source of inspiration that enables you to create such rich and full work.

Abbey: This is holy work, LaShonda. I sing to please my ancestors. There's no emptiness there. This is not about me. It's about the people. My people.

LKB: During a performance, Abbey, I'm wondering if you are consciously educating?

Abbey: It's not that I am intentionally educating.

LKB: Yet, I take so much from your songs, and I know I'm not alone. Your songs are like lessons.

Abbey: People may get something from it, but that is not what I'm doing. You know what I'm doing? I'm having therapy before thousands of people. [*laughter*] Okay? I'm singing about my life, and it helps me to live. After I finish a performance I can see her—my spirit—shining all in my face and everything. Yes, that's exactly what I'm doing. If somebody gets it, it's all right with me. But it's for myself, darling, that I do this. To save Abbey here on this planet!

LKB: What makes one a good singer, Abbey?

Abbey: I've always been concerned with the story I'm telling. This music is social. Our music is social. Nobody cares whether it sounds pretty or not. Can you tell the people what it's like to be here? To live here? That's what the people care about. Can you be honest in your singing? Look at Billie Holiday. She had a wee-bit voice that cracked. But she sang about black bodies hanging from trees and about the child who has his own and the people loved her for that. She'll always be remembered. Armstrong had a funny, squeaky voice, and there would be no jazz singing if not for him. So you see, we don't come from a tradition that worries about pretty singing. Good singing is in the way you use your voice. It's in what you are saying and how you say it.

LKB: Abbey, before a performance or a recording date, are there certain exercises or vocal practices you go through to prepare?

Abbey: No. I'm not an opera singer. This musical tradition doesn't require that necessarily. For the last ten, fifteen years, I've allowed my voice to do what it will knowing that any way it comes out is okay because I'm telling a story. My audience knows this about me. I'm a storyteller.

LKB: Can you describe your songwriting process?

Abbey: I am blessed by a muse that visits me. I don't go looking for songs. Sometimes I hear the melody first, sometimes the lyric. More often the lyric comes to me first because I am also a poet. But I learned early on that this work is not about me. I am inspired by a holy muse and my ancestors. And I don't take it for granted. I lead a very quiet, very peaceful life, and I work hard to cultivate peace so those spirits will feel welcomed.

LKB: I have made a list of some of my favorite songs that you wrote. I'd like to go down the list and find out the inspiration behind some of these songs, beginning with the wonderfully philosophical "Throw It Away," which has been covered by many singer-songwriters, most recently Cassandra Wilson on her 2003 album, *Glamoured*.

Abbey: That song helped to save me. I had left the marriage that I had and I had left my career as well. I was an actress. I had made two films, *For Love of Ivy* and *Nothing but a Man*, but I didn't like what I had to put up with in Hollywood. So I went to my mother's house. She lived over a garage. And I thought, *Well, if it's good enough for Mama, it's good enough for me*. I moved over the other garage. And one day, I was thinking about my life. I wouldn't say that I was miserable. I was painting and writing songs and things, but I was living low on the ground. So, Oscar Brown Jr. called me and asked, "Abbey, are you hip to the I Ching?" I wasn't. It's a Chinese oracle. So I got the I Ching and I learned to throw the changes. One day I threw the changes and it said to me, the oracle, "You cannot lose what belongs to you even if you throw it away." So I thought, *I'm going to develop this and make a song out of it*. And I did. "I think about the life I live / A figure made of clay / And think about the things I lost / The things I gave away / And when I'm in a certain mood / I search the halls and look / One night I found these magic words in a magic book / Throw it away / Throw it away / Give your love live your life each and every day." I'm saying you don't have to be bothered with none of this. Throw it away! If it's yours you'll know it 'cause you can't lose what's yours, even if you throw it away.

LKB: "The River"? [*singing*] "There's a river on the freeway." What inspired that song?

Abbey: I was living in the same building. I finally had the whole house. I had moved my bedroom to the front of the house right on Venice Boulevard. And I heard this sound every night and every morning. The cars—it sounded just like a river—the people driving on the freeway. I just described that. I described myself as somebody who is observing everything from a spaceship. She wasn't on the river; she was up there in the sky. And everywhere she'd gone she'd seen this sight—people on the freeway, in a mad scramble to go somewhere and make some money! [*singing*] "There's a river on the freeway / Where the four winds blow / From the city to the countryside / Winding to and fro / In the morning and in the evening the tide begins to swell / And the river runs and races / And it's signaled by a bell / A hollow metal vessel / And it vibrates and it rings / And the river runs and races to bring the many things / It carries on the surface / Of a running racing tide / There's a river on the freeway / You can take it for a ride." She's telling her betters, her elders, that if you wanna take this out, you can definitely take it for a ride. They'll go for anything in a capitalistic society.

LKB: I love the imagery in "The Merry Dancer." The song begins and continues in the vein of oral tradition, a bedrock of African American culture. "Mama told me—"

Abbey: "—of a beauty that is made of purest gold / One the weather will not tarnish / One that never will grow old / She said beauty comes from understanding / Looking at the things we see / Beauty of the human spirit / Beauty that will set us free." I talk like her. I look like her. I sound like her. My mother, Evalina Coffey. She's always here with me. Yeah, she taught me to see God when I look in the mirror. That's the problem today with youngsters, and adults, too. Nobody knows how to see God in themselves, and how to draw on that as the only source of energy you need. Everybody's so quick to call God's name, but as a people we've really lost sight on who God really is. I deal with this in a poem that I wrote. I'm planning to record it one day. It's called "Where Are the African Gods?"

LKB: Will it be on the album you're recording now?

Abbey: No, it won't be on this one. But I want to share it with you: "In a life a searching soul is looking for the key / For the answers to the questions that are plaguing you and me / Stories of enchantment say that we came from the sod / Fashioned by the spirit in the likeness of our God / Pictures of the gods are painted / Names intended to restore / The image of the glory of the ones who came before / Named and called upon for action / For protection on the way / Gods whose heads and forms are human / Gods who are the light of day / Where are the African Gods? / Did they leave us on our journey over here? / Where are the African Gods? / Will we know them when they suddenly appear? / The ones dismissed with voodoo, rock an' roll an' all that jazz / And jungle mumbo-jumbo . . . And a-razz-a-ma-tazz / Where are the African Gods / Who live within the skin? / Within the skin, without the skin, and in the skin again / Do they hide among the shadows while we stumble on the way? / Or did they go with heaven to prepare another day? / Where are the African Gods? / Who'll save us from this misery and shame? / Where are the African Gods? / Will we find them while we pray in Jesus's name? / Where are the African Gods / Who live and set us free? / We are the African Gods / We are / You and me."

LKB: Abbey, that is beautiful, and more than beautiful, it's true. It puts me in the mind of your song "You Made Me Funny," which reads and sounds more like a prayer-poem than a song in that you are speaking it rather than singing. When I listen to that song I hear it as though it's a one-sided conversation with God.

Abbey: Yeah, I was talking to the holy spirit about what we're going through. The reputation that we have.

LKB: Black women?

Abbey: Women and men and everybody else. The human being, period. Ain't nobody got it good here. The Europeans don't see themselves in the light of God. They're more pitiful than anybody else because they claim to be the only one and they know it's not true. They don't believe in nothing. Santa Claus, indeed! The Easter bunny. Everybody knows better than this. [*laughter*] They'll say anything. Naw. This is just a pile of lies. So, this tune is my complaint. But, on the other hand, the creator gave me everything. He made me perfect.

LKB: What inspired "When I'm Called Home?"

Abbey: I wrote that with a feeling of grief. When I think of all that the African woman has gone through with the African man, and what little respect he has for his mother, sister, and lover, it saddens me. Black men think that all of the women belong to them. They have no loyalty. If they make any money a white woman usually is the recipient of it, and she inherits everything he has. He doesn't know how to be a polygamist, so he becomes a monogamist and throws his first wife away and takes himself strange women. Yeah, I was confronted with that. The musicians in my band, their companions and I were on tour. And there I was with three black men, and I was the only black woman. And, I thought, *Okay, when I'm called home I'll tell them about this.* I recorded it with Stan Getz who said, "I don't want to jinx it, but, Abbey, this is a great song." A lot of people feel that way about this world. It's full of holes and craters of lies that don't help you to live. The song goes, "When I'm called home, I will bring a book . . ."

LKB: ". . . that tells of strange and funny turns . . ."

Abbey: ". . . and of the heart it took."

LKB and Abbey: "To keep on living in a world that never was my own. A world of haunted memories of other worlds unknown."

Abbey: "I'll tell them of the trouble here when they call me home." I will. I'm talking about what it costs to set your spirit free.

LKB: Some people believe you are singing about the effects of slavery on recent generations of blacks.

Abbey: My life didn't begin with slavery and neither did yours, you hear? That's what they'd like you to believe, but don't go for the okeydoke, LaShonda. You're too smart for that. Our lives, African-American lives, began with the pyramids, with mathematics, science, and the philosophy the Greeks eventually stole and passed off as their own. I'll tell you, my continent is Africa. That's mine.

LKB: There are many African Americans who don't identify with Africa, Abbey. Do you feel that it's important for black artists to identify with Africa?

Abbey: I know there are a lot of people like that. They're unfortunate. They're the ones who've been brainwashed. They don't understand. Roach said to me something once when we first started to see each other. He said, "Abbey, they talk about pretty and ugly and everything, but everything that the creator made is beautiful." There is no human being that is not beautiful and that is really a reality. So if you get hung up on the texture of somebody's hair and the color of their skin, you're just pathetic. After all, character is not in the way people look, it's what they do and what they think and what they believe. I know there are many people who disclaim Africa. Whoopi Goldberg says she's not African, and many more say this. God bless them. They don't have to claim Africa—the less the better. It's mine.

LKB: Going back to your comment about the challenge of black men and women maintaining love relationships, is this part of what inspired you to write the very personal song celebrating your union with Max Roach?

Abbey: Yes, "The Wedding Song" is a lyric that I put to music Roach composed called "Prelude." I wrote the lyric to cement the joy I felt and to express the gratitude I felt for having found a companion, someone to work together with and to exchange ideas with. Although I grew up in a house with both my mother and father I had never really thought about marriage for myself. I didn't have anything against it, but I knew black men and women have a hard time together. My parents did, and eventually Mom divorced Dad. But when Max asked me to marry him, I was really thrilled because I believed in him and myself. I thought we could build something together and we did. Even though the marriage didn't last, what we made together did. We created something lasting—and it wasn't a baby neither [*laughter*]—something else lasting, the music. That's what a black woman and man can do together—really build something—if the world would let them.

LKB: Do you feel that you are bearing witness to your African ancestors during a musical performance?

Abbey: Of course I am. How else are you gonna live? We live through one another. We live through our ancestors. We carry the very look of them—their genes and everything. We come from them. We don't come from the void, you hear? Bojangles came from a people. And we are definitely the music that comes from America. We're invited to go everywhere in the world. We are the music in this hemisphere—the African in North America, in South America, in the Caribbean. Yes, I'll say it again, we are the music of the world today! Now, why would anybody want to play that down? You know why they would? Well, you'd have to be more than ignorant. You'd have to be a damned fool.

LKB: Well, with jazz in particular, Abbey, you know that historically the art form has been associated with an unseemly lifestyle. Even though everybody recognizes its genius, in some circles striving to become a jazz singer is not necessarily looked upon as pursuing a high calling.

Abbey: Yes, I know this and I wrote a song about this. Do you know how the song "The Man with the Magic" came to me?

LKB: The song that is also titled "Dorian," and on your *People in Me* album?

Abbey: Yes. Roach wrote the music; I wrote the lyric. Well, I was sitting in the dressing room with Roach and another musician, whose name I won't mention, when this musician asked Max,

"Where's the man with the magic?" Later on, when I had some privacy with Max, I asked him who the man with the magic was, and he told me the cocaine dealer. Now tell me, LaShonda, with all this magic why would you be looking for the cocaine man? I'll tell you why you would—you'd be crazy and confused. You can't worship God in other people's images and have anything here. If you constantly look to other people—who you've been taught to believe are greater than you—for a directive, you'll be lost here. Lost and empty. As a people, we have always practiced the arts for the sake of our spirits. We didn't get into doing this for recognition or a dollar—at least not until they started lying and stealing from us. Haven't you ever wondered why there are so many unsigned spirituals, so many unsigned songs that they refer to as Negro spirituals or "traditional"? We wrote them because it is who we are and what we do. But it was not for recognition or fame. Over time, though, we learned that we better sign our shit, or they'll lie and say they created it.

LKB: Who were some of your earliest musical role models?

Abbey: When I was first coming to the stage there were composers like Duke Ellington, Mary Lou Williams, and Nat King Cole to follow. Later on, through Roach, I met Monk, Charlie Parker, Charles Mingus. I have always been surrounded by greatness. I worry about the children looking for musical role models today. Most of the rap artists that they listen to are competing with pimps and hos for a place in the sun. Where are youngsters supposed to take a musical tradition like that? How far do you think they'll get?

LKB: Your song "Devil's Got Your Tongue" addresses this issue. I'm reminded of the verse: "Tell a dirty story of a lowly jerk / Even though the joke's on us / It's supposed to work / Tell a dirty story / Show it on the screen / That's the combination for a jelly bean."

Abbey: Yes, I was talking about the video that they make that goes along with the rap song, where the woman has her ass hanging out and everything. And these young women don't know any better? We don't know any better than to degrade ourselves like this while the whole world is watching? [*long pause*] The youngsters will do anything to get paid. So there we are, dancing for a jellybean.

LKB: Just like the character Topsy in *Uncle Tom's Cabin.*

Abbey: You see. Yeah, I talk about them in the song: "Dancing with the devil / Drawing from the lip / Curses for yo' mama / Getting down is hip / Dancing with the devil / Curses for the sun / Got yourself a partner / Devil's got your tongue . . . love is made forever / Ever is the sun / You got holy magic / But the devil's got your tongue!"

LKB: In general, Abbey, what do you think of rap music?

Abbey: Well, I am proud that the people who brought the art form are African and know how to bring music to the world, and how far to take things eventually. It's a new form. It's still experimental, and they've taken the world with it, but at the same time they need to reexamine what they're talking about and how they talk about it. [*pause*] Yeah, they're brilliant like everybody who's brought the music before them—just like the African who brought the spirituals, gospel, jazz, R&B, and rock and roll.

LKB: So rock isn't Elvis Presley?

Abbey: I don't know why you said that. You know better than that, LaShonda. Humphh. Everybody knows better than that. That's a pathological lie, and it won't help anybody to live here.

LKB: It amazes me that lies like this are perpetuated, and eventually passed off as fact.

Abbey: These kinds of lies are perpetuated by the same ones who pretend that they made Jesus. They claim the creator's work, let alone ours.

LKB: Do politics ever influence your songwriting process?

Abbey: I wear the world like a loose garment, like my mother taught me. I don't fret over political things. I write songs about the things I think about, but I wouldn't say that I spend time thinking about politics.

LKB: Were you thinking about relationships or a particular romance when you wrote "Should've Been"?

Abbey: More and more I'm above everything. I'm very much influenced by the writers of that work they call the Bible. The approach they had to language. I know it's been translated many times, but the usage of metaphors is critical to those stories. So I write in metaphor and black vernacular . . . how we talk. Like in this song. I used to hear my mother say, "Shoulda been, coulda been, woulda been." One day I decided to use that. I was thinking, *Yeah it coulda been this and woulda been that, but what it is is what it is.*

LKB: You might not recognize this, but when you write songs like this you are furthering the cultural traditions of our language. Capturing your mother's sayings and committing them to music helps to create a cultural memory, and I appreciate it very much.

Abbey: Thank you.

LKB: When I hear your songs "And It's Supposed to Be Love" and "Love Has Gone Away," I think about domestic violence.

Abbey: That's what I'm talking about. O. J. Simpson—people who beat their wives, black their eyes and shit. There's a whole bunch of people who do this behind closed doors. Sometimes they leave her for dead. Um-hum. This is what goes for love here. "Well, I just call you 'Bitch' 'cause I love you, Bitch." It's really sad.

LKB: Just as you explore victimization, you also celebrate women's power in songs like "I Got Thunder (And It Rings)," where the opening verse is: "Some folks talk about my power / Some folks say I'm wild and strong / Others say my style of living makes a man go wrong / I'm a woman hard to handle / If you need to handle things / Better run when I start coming / I got thunder and it rings!"

Abbey: When I was growing up, when I was a young woman, people used to always say to me, "Anna Marie, you talk too much." I did talk a lot, but I also knew the value in listening. You couldn't be brought up by my parents and not know the value in listening. What they were complaining about was the fact that I'm a woman who speaks her mind. I've always been this person—that's who the artist is here. The artist is the one that tells it like it is for all time. I tell you, I don't know what I would've done without the arts. I'd probably be scrubbing somebody's floor. I'm grateful for the stage. It does me good to have someplace to take all of my thoughts and my feelings.

Two
ANGÉLIQUE KIDJO
(JULY 14, 1960)

By the time Cotonou, Benin–born Angélique Kidjo was six, she was performing with her mother's theater troupe, which fostered in the singer-songwriter an early appreciation for music and dance. Influenced by childhood musical idols Bella Bellow, Aretha Franklin, Miriam Makeba, James Brown, Carlos Santana, and her older brothers who formed a band of their own, Kidjo became enthralled with music and began to envision herself a singer. Torn between pre-law and music during her college career, she studied both courses for one year before deciding to focus on music. In 1982, continuing political conflicts in Benin led her to relocate to Paris, France, permanently. There she performed as a backup singer in local bands before establishing her own group. By the end of the 1980s, she had become one of the most popular live performers in Paris. Kidjo's music, which has garnered her three Grammy nominations, cross-pollinates the West African traditions of her childhood in Benin with elements of American R&B, funk, and jazz, as well as influences from Europe and Latin America. Throughout her career, she has collaborated with a diverse group of international artists, such as Cassandra Wilson, Gilberto Gil, and Santana. Her duet with Dave Matthews on the song "Iwoya," which appeared on the album *Black Ivory Soul*, was a critical success that helped diversify her fan base. The third part in a trilogy that previously explored African roots in music from the United States (*Oremi*) and Brazil (*Black Ivory Soul*), her most recent album, *Oyaya!*, fuses African and French lyrics to music that draws upon musical traditions of the Caribbean diaspora. With her husband, musician and producer Jean Hebrail, Kidjo penned the album's thirteen original songs in a variety of indigenous Caribbean styles, including salsa, calypso, merengue, and ska. Recently, Kidjo was featured in Martin Scorsese's *Lightning in a Bottle: A One Night History of the Blues*, a documentary about blues music that features live concert footage of other rock, rap, and blues greats. A UNICEF goodwill ambassador, Kidjo, who is fluent in English, Fon, French, and Yoruba, writes and sings songs in all four languages. She often utilizes Benin's traditional Zilin vocal technique and jazz vocalese. Angélique Kidjo is based in Brooklyn, New York.

Selected Discography

Logozo (Mango)

Ayé (Fontana Island)

Fifa (Mango)

Oremi (Polygram Records)

Black Ivory Soul (Sony)

Oyaya! (Sony)

Djin Djin (Razor & Tie)

Angélique Kidjo

LKB: Do you come from a musical family?

Angélique: I would say that my family is very creative, very liberal, very open. My dad used to play banjo, but he worked for the post office. When my mom went to school she was trained for theater, singing, and clarinet. My mom started the only theater group that ever existed in Benin so far. Most of the actors that come out of Benin, my mom trained them.

LKB: Were you influenced by your mother's life in the theater?

Angélique: Yes. I started working with her when I was six years old.

LKB: Acting?

Angélique: Acting and singing.

LKB: Your mother gave you vocal training?

Angélique: Yes.

LKB: Did you receive other vocal training outside of home?

Angélique: Yes. Once I decided I really wanted to pursue music. After high school, I had decided that I wanted to be a human rights lawyer so I went to study in France, where I was going to a music school part-time and also the university part-time for pre-law. After a semester it was killing me. It was very hard to jump from one to another. Also, after three months of law courses I decided that I was better off making music than practicing law. You see, law is written by us with the intention of balancing the unfairness of life. But it doesn't take a genius to look around to see that most of the laws written don't serve any real sense of justice. And if you are going to be a human rights lawyer, you cannot afford having to fight with your conscience. For me it seemed impossible to achieve what I wanted to achieve if I had to deal with the politics. If I had to deal with

politics while trying to save a human being's life, it would
never work. So I went back to music school thinking that
music would be the better—

LKB: —way for you to reach people.

Angélique: Yes. To touch people directly without using any, oh,
what you call that—we say in France *voile*—

LKB: Veil . . . or artifice.

Angélique: Absolutely. Artifice. I don't want that standing between
me and the people. We can disagree. People can dislike what I
say, that's okay. I've got no problem with that as long as it's not
in a spirit of malice or hatred. But I want the opportunity to
communicate to people exactly how I feel and what I think.

LKB: How old were you at the time you decided to focus on
music school?

Angélique: Seventeen. And I had classical and jazz training for four
or five years.

LKB: Was your time as a student in France your first time away
from home?

Angélique: No, because I had already recorded an album while I
was in high school and I had gone to the Ivory Coast and
Cameroon to promote it.

LKB: The album you're referring to is *Pretty*, which was produced
by the Cameroonian singer Ekambi Brilliant?

Angélique: Yes. I don't like to talk about it because it was a horren-
dous experience.

LKB: Perhaps some young artist who will read this book, though,
will learn something from your misfortune.

Angélique: We recorded the record in Paris. I recorded all of the
vocal tracks in one day. I had to because my parents did not

want me missing any school. So after the travel time, it only left me with one day to do all of the vocal tracks. And I was back home and did not miss any school at all. I had taken out a student loan, which I was supposed to use for my first year in the university and used it for the album. And Brilliant ran away with all of my money.

LKB: Well, did the album do well? Did you collect any royalties?

Angélique: Nope. Nothing. I have no idea how well the album sold. That was my "welcome to the business." In this business you can get screwed right or left anytime. But I remembered what my mom and dad said about a person who steals money from you. . . . It's just money they've taken; it's not your power or anything. I accept that now as just part of my path. It was something I had to go through in order to grow. He isn't the only one who has stolen money from me, but it doesn't matter. Thieves won't stop me from singing.

LKB: Were you ever daunted by the lack of security that sometimes comes with choosing the artist's path?

Angélique: No, because I grew up in a family that believed in one humanity. I truly believe that I am connected to others—despite color or race. If I don't speak your language I can make myself understood somehow. This kind of belief has spared me from a lot of fear and worry. I also grew up believing that whatever you decide to do, if you give yourself over to it completely, you can achieve it. I wanted to practice music so badly there are only two things that I would not have done—drugs and prostitution. For an opportunity to sing and be heard, I would've swept somebody's floor or cooked or sewn clothes . . . any kind of work as long as it did not call my integrity into question. My integrity has never been for sale and never will be. I don't believe in the power of money. I believe in the human being. In time money's power is very limited. But if you are fortunate enough to have one person on this earth that is your friend, a person that you can call up and it doesn't matter what you ask them for they will say yes, and if you are in trouble they will jump into that trouble with you, well, that is worth more than money.

LKB: Who or what were some of your early musical influences?

Angélique: Traditional music, because of my aunt. My aunt was a traditional singer.

LKB: When you say "traditional," what do you mean?

Angélique: Traditional singers are for me people who teach you who you are through songs. The traditional musician in my country is the one that is the memory of the people. I am saying that for me to be able to do the kind of music that I am doing today is because of my mom and my aunt. I was attracted to the purity of their voices—the honesty and sincerity.

LKB: Does your mother still sing?

Angélique: No, she's ruined her voice by not caring for it, by screaming and such. She has too much empathy and that kills you very fast in Africa. I am very much like her. I cannot feel indifferent, which is why I live here now.

LKB: What is your earliest memory of music?

Angélique: The earliest I can recall is being in my mom's womb. I remember hearing my mother's and my aunt's voices. My mom said I sang before I spoke—songs that no one taught me, but songs that I'd somehow remembered.

LKB: When did you start listening to other genres of music, beyond the traditional Zilin music of Benin?

Angélique: When I was about nine years old, I was listening to Aretha Franklin, James Brown, the music of Motown. Also when I was nine, my older brothers decided to put together a modern musical group. My dad bought all of the instruments and gave them a room in the house to rehearse. I am never going to forget coming home from school one day and finding all of the big boxes in the middle of our house, plastic everywhere and the whole place smelling like new stuff. I was jumping up and down asking, "What is that? What is that?" They said, "Instruments." And I must've said, "Traditional instruments? They don't come packed like that." I'm telling you, when I saw those instruments, I didn't want to go to school anymore.

LKB: What instruments had your father purchased for your brothers?

Angélique: Electric bass, Fender bass, Farfisa organ, a drum kit, and the conga.

LKB: Who were some of the first singers that you were listening to, apart from your mother and aunt?

Angélique: Bella Bellow. She was from Togo. She died in 1973 in a car accident. Damn, she could sing. She was my favorite vocalist growing up. I also liked Miriam Makeba and Aretha Franklin. These women not only had great voices; they had power. In Africa, if you are a little girl who dreams of making a career as a vocalist, it is very hard on you because the singing profession is considered like prostitution. So it was very important for me to have them as models.

LKB: Really. A woman onstage is stigmatized as loose?

Angélique: Yes. That happened to me a lot as a teen. The whole sex, drugs, and rock-and-roll mentality hit Africa, too. For a while all of the relationships I was having failed because I was singing. The last person that I was dating before I left Benin, we stayed together four years. In four years he came to my show one time. He had the nerve to come to the house after the show and say, "It was cool, but I'm not going to marry a singer." He was really working my nerves so I told him to just take the same door he used to come in to go back out. My mother was so shocked, but I was dead serious. I was through. And I really was.

LKB: When did you write your first song?

Angéligue: I wrote it for the death of Bella Bellow. She really meant so much to me.

LKB: And that's on your first album, *Pretty*.

Angélique: Yes, but I wrote it when I was thirteen.

LKB: What was the process like?

Angélique: The moment they announced the death the song was born in me. It just came out, and it was mature. It was ready. I told my brother the melody and he found the chords on the guitar, and I wrote the lyric from start to finish in one sitting. It came quickly and easily.

LKB: Since *Pretty* you have recorded eight more albums, with *Oyaya!* being the most recent. You cowrote all thirteen tracks on *Oyaya!* with your husband, Jean Hebrail. Tell me what the experience of cowriting has been like for you.

Angélique: Before I met Jean I wrote all of my songs alone. *Pretty*, *Ewa Ka Djo*, *Parakou*, I wrote all of those albums by myself.

After *Parakou*, Jean and I started to write together. He cowrote some of the songs on my first international album, *Logozo*. Jean cowrites the music. He listens to me when I'm singing and he's very sensitive to the words, he builds the music around the words. The special thing that it does for me, when Jean and I work together, is that it forces me to go deeper into the language. Words that I don't use usually, I will take them and try to make associations with them. I have learned a lot about how when certain words are sung they can make sounds that create powerful emotions. In my songwriting, I rely a lot on proverbs. Like the duet with Dave Matthews, "Black Ivory Soul," it's based on a Yoruba proverb that says: a bird that is burned today will not die unless the faith of the bird ceases.

LKB: Did Dave Matthews participate in the creation of that song?

Angélique: I wrote the song while I was on tour with him as his opening act. The last day of the tour I gave him the lyric. I think we were playing an arena in Dallas. He took the lyric from me, and he said, "So, where's the music?" So I gave him the music, too. Then I went on touring by myself. A few weeks later I was in Calgary recording—about to go to Seattle—when I received a call that Dave Matthews was in Calgary and wanted to come to the studio to do the song. So that's how that happened.

LKB: I have noticed that you experiment a lot with different cultural forms in your own lyrics, like the song "Bissimilai," which I love.

Angélique: Yes. This is something I love to do. It's challenging, and it frees me. "Bissimilai" is composed in the Puerto Rican *plena* form, but I sing it in Fon and have backup by a chorus of

Muslim women who I recorded on a trip home to Benin. In the chorus you hear the similarity between traditional Zilin music and gospel music. By bringing all of these forms together, I want to make people feel united.

LKB: You have performed alongside and recorded a couple of songs with another singer-songwriter I'm fond of.

Angélique: It must be Cassandra Wilson you're speaking of. I love to work with Cassandra because she is very much in touch with her African roots, and of course I love the sound of her voice. She is a fantastic musician. I invited her to appear on my album *Oremi*. We sing together on the song "Never Know."

LKB: And you appear on her self-produced album, *Traveling Miles*. I especially like "Voodoo Reprise," sung by the two of you.

Angélique: It was important to Cassandra to have Yoruba chant on that song. So she invited me, and I was really honored not just to work with her but for her genuine spirit of camaraderie.

LKB: Several of your songs are titled after Yoruba orishas. Why do you feel it's important to write and perform songs like "Shango" off your *Fifa* album and "Yemanja" off the album *Ayé*?

Angélique: I believe in nature and culture. I believe these are the forces that sustain each and every one of us. Also, for me it is very, very important to acknowledge—not only acknowledge but to celebrate—my specific cultural spirituality, which connects me not only to my ancestors, but also to people living now in Brazil, Cuba, black America. It helps me to perform these songs. It sustains me by reminding me of where I come from and who I am.

LKB: Before you started to cowrite with your husband, Jean, were there or are there particular exercises that you feel foster the songwriting process?

Angélique: The thing is, if you force inspiration you won't come away with anything good at all. I like Phillip Glass's saying that inspiration is the domain of the unknown. And it's true. You don't know what inspires you. You don't know why at that time, at that moment something moves you to create. That's why inspired art touches so many people; it's beyond you. You're just the channel. Songs go through you because they have to. And a singer's rendition of the song is what gives the inspiration a life of its own. I've heard singers say that when they write a song the melody comes first or the lyric comes first. For me the song comes and brings everything at the same time. And I believe that if the inspiration is true, even if the song is badly sung, the listener will still feel the spirit of the inspiration, but that is not in your power to decide. I always say that when I write songs it is a painful process because some songs come like lightning and I'll wonder, is that right? Can that be right? Is it finished? Hell, yeah. It's really finished. But some of them torture you.

LKB: Because they take a long time to finish?

Angélique: Because even at the last minute you may not get it. For every album I write a minimum of twenty-five songs that I have to choose from. If I don't love them, they're not going to make it to the album.

LKB: You have to love them?

Angélique: Like is not good enough because I have to sing these songs over and over again.

LKB: It doesn't sound like you approach making an album by choosing a theme first, which is what some songwriters do.

Angélique: If you decide on a theme, what if the inspiration for that theme doesn't come? Then what? For me, inspiration is the key. The song might not be commercial, I don't care. You live your whole life with your songs; it's better to be absolutely in love with what you put out there. I love touring, I love being onstage much more than the studio, so it's important that I love the songs that I'm singing. I hate the studio. I only record because it's the way to get the music to the fans and because I have to for my career, but I hate the studio because it is not my culture. I come from a "live" culture. You wanna play music, just get the drum out. My mom used to tell me and other actors, "The day you don't feel like going onstage, don't go because if you're not true to yourself the public will feel it." No one wants you to bring your misery onstage, people have enough of their own misery. They come for joy and enlightenment. So I really believe in following what inspiration brings me—not deciding beforehand to write songs that are, for example, political, or songs that are sad. I won't compromise my music for commercial success. I do a lot of compromising in my life to be able to live with everybody, to do what I love to do the most, but the truth of my songs will never be called into question. I cherish so much what the elderly singers and musicians in my country think of my music and what they taught me. I wouldn't forfeit that for commercial success.

LKB: It sounds as though you feel a great deal of responsibility for the music you put out there. What do you think of some of the music made today?

Angélique: I know that hip-hop music catches a lot of flack. I like hip-hop when it's talking about a subject that we are all concerned about and want to change. Hip-hop musicians have the access to the young community, to the kids, so I am a fan of those artists who write informative lyrics, who educate us. I don't think that we benefit from degrading lyrics. Just look at the number of young blacks in jail in this country. What is wrong with that picture? And it's not ringing any bells for anybody? Many people are apathetic. They're like, "Well, he did something wrong so he deserves jail." But the system is wrong. When you live in a country where the only response to the troubles of the youth and to people's needs, people's lack of opportunity, people's ignorance, is jail, then something is definitely wrong. I believe that a lot of hip-hop is trying to address this wrongness. Hip-hop artists are ringing those bells. I don't always agree with the way they do it, but I realize that these young artists are speaking to us in the words that they know, the language they grew up with. It's up to us to listen to it and try to understand and to teach them other ways to say the same thing. I don't like the hip-hop where every woman is a bitch or a ho. And their mama is what, then? I'm nobody's bitch or ho, so I don't appreciate hearing that. If I'm a dirty bitch then he's dirty by extension, so what is the rapper saying? I don't like this especially because I have a thirteen-year-old daughter. I don't want her hearing this.

LKB: How do you account for your popularity in America? Here, I am thinking of the fact that you record and perform live singing in multiple languages, including French, Fon, Yoruba.

Angélique: Well, you know what they say. Music is the universal language. I think that Americans, or any audience I have whose language I'm not singing in, are relating to the sound, the emotion in my voice. I feel that is what people are connecting with.

Three

BRENDA RUSSELL

(APRIL 8, 1949)

Singer-songwriter Brenda Norman was born in Brooklyn, New York, where she grew up until the age of twelve. After her parents separated, she moved with her father to the Canadian town of Hamilton, Ontario. Despite having musician parents, as a youth Russell believed she would become a writer or journalist. It wasn't until she graduated high school and joined the Canadian company of the rock musical *Hair* that she began to experiment with songwriting. She recalls "picking out songs" for the first time on the piano in the lobby of the theater where the *Hair* cast rehearsed. Following *Hair*, Brenda was recruited to write songs for the CBC television variety show *Doctor Music*, where she met former husband and musical collaborator Brian Russell. The couple eventually moved to Los Angeles in 1973, where they both worked as session musicians. They recorded two albums together (under the name Brian and Brenda) on Rocket Records. Following the couple's divorce, Brenda embarked on a solo career. At A&M Records she formed a bond with label founder Herb Alpert and released two albums, *Brenda Russell* (1979) and *Love Life* (1981). In

1983, she put out the album *Two Eyes* with Warner Brothers. Returning to A&M, she released her most popular album, *Get Here* (1988), which featured the Top 10 single "Piano in the Dark" sung with Joe Esposito of Brooklyn Dreams. She received Grammy nominations in 1988 for Song of the Year and Best Pop Duo Performance (for "Piano in the Dark"), as well as Best Pop Female Vocal (for "Get Here"). After a final A&M album, 1990's *Kiss Me with the Wind*, Russell signed with EMI in 1991 and released one album with the label in 1993, entitled *Soul Talkin'*. For the next seven years, she went without a recording contract, reemerging in 2000 with *Paris Rain* on Hidden Beach. Her most recent album, *Between the Sun and the Moon* (2004), is on the UK label Dome Records. Russell has done session work for Barbra Streisand, Elton John, and Bette Midler, and her songs have been recorded by Joe Cocker ("So Good, So Right"), Oleta Adams, Randy Crawford, Barbara Mandrell, Patti LuPone ("Get Here"), Luther Vandross, Peabo Bryson and Roberta Flack ("If Only for One Night"), Donna Summer ("Dinner with Gershwin"), Rufus and Chaka Khan ("Please Pardon Me—You Remind Me of a Friend"), Ray Charles ("None of Us Are Free") and many others, including Mary J. Blige and Earth, Wind and Fire. Her songwriting talent has also been featured on television and in films such as *How Stella Got Her Groove Back* and Barry Levinson's *Liberty Heights*. In 2006, Russell received the American Theatre Wing's Tony nomination for cowriting with Allee Willis and Stephen Bray the lyrics and music for the musical *The Color Purple*, which was also nominated in the Best Musical Show Album category for the forty-ninth (2007) Annual Grammy Awards. Commenting on her songwriting, Brenda Russell, who makes her home in Los Angeles, says, "I never write songs that are without hope. People have to be inspired to another level, like: 'My heart can go on. I may feel like I'm going to die, but I won't because something good could be around the corner.' I take responsibility on myself to inspire people and even make them cry. Yes, I'll make you cry, but I won't leave you hopeless."

Selected Discography

Brenda Russell (A&M Records)
Get Here (A&M Records)
Kiss Me with the Wind (A&M Records)
Paris Rain (Hidden Beach Recordings)
Between the Sun and the Moon (Narada Jazz/Dome Records)

Brenda Russell

LKB: Can you talk about the kind of musical background you experienced growing up in Brooklyn?

Brenda: My parents were both in music. My mother was a singer and songwriter. She had a great ear for harmony. My father was a singer and a drummer. I always had music in my house. I thought everybody's parents wrote songs and sang.

LKB: Where in Brooklyn did you grow up?

Brenda: Different parts—Fulton Avenue, Atlantic Avenue—eventually Flatbush, which was a little more safe area Mom managed to get us into. The things that captivated me as a child were always musical. I used to love to listen to the black drum corps rehearsing in the park a few blocks away. [*mimicking a drum roll on the table*] *Da da da ti da da ti da da da—da da da ti da da ti da da da.* That music just killed me! It was so funky.

From that music to the doo-wop groups singing on the cor-
ners under the street lights to the music of the trains riding
overhead—all of it had an effect on me. It was a very musical
way to grow up.

LKB: Besides your parents, who were some of the singers or
musical groups that you grooved on as a youth?

Brenda: Whomever my folks were playing on their records. They
had very eclectic taste. My dad loved the big band stuff. He listened to Count Basie, Duke Ellington, artists like that. My
mom listened to the singers—Sarah Vaughan, Dinah Washington, all of these wonderful vocalists. We listened to
Broadway music. My dad used to have this songbook that
housed old Broadway tunes and I would go through it, point
to a song, and say, "Sing that one, Daddy." [*singing from* South
Pacific] "Happy, happy, happy talk . . ." I loved all of these
tunes. I didn't know they were show tunes at the time.

LKB: It's interesting that your parents' music became your music.
Sometimes children develop a musical taste that is very different from their parents—especially during a teen phase of
rebellion.

Brenda: You know, I hear you, but at that time, LaShonda, the music
was still loved by the parents and kids alike. There wasn't a big
separation in the musical taste. So the kids would be grooving
at the party with the parents playing the same music, which is
very rare now. It's not the same anymore. Back then there was
more family participation to be enjoyed while listening to the
music.

LKB: When did you begin to think that you could make a musical
career for yourself?

Brenda: Maybe when I was about five or six. I learned to read very early. My mom told me she was shocked that at maybe eighteen months I was drawing letters on my little chalkboard. I was making letters when no one had shown me how to do it. I remember her coming into the room and screaming. It's my first memory. I'll never forget that because I thought I'd done something wrong. She was freaked out because I was making all of these letters. I started memorizing music at four and five. I remember sitting in front of the speakers and singing James Moody's saxophone solo, note for note, from "Moody's Mood for Love." My mother says when she saw that she thought, *Oh, God, something's happening here.* She said to my dad, "She's going to private school." They didn't have any money, but they got me into private school during that time. They made it happen. So I had something going on very early with writing letters and music. I was also enamored of the newspaper. I remember thinking I wanted to write stories and have them appear in the newspaper. I thought I would become a journalist. As a kid I used to get beat up a lot in the school yard because I was skinny and black with short hair. Everybody wanted to beat me up. So the way I could get people to stop beating me up was to write little stories and read them to the kids in the school yard. I'd write these stories, and they'd listen instead of hitting me because I had managed to capture their imaginations. When my stories ended they'd yell, "Well, what happens next?" I'd have to write something more for the next day.

LKB: The Playground Griot.

Brenda: [*laughter*] Yes!

LKB: I read somewhere that you moved to Hamilton, Ontario, when you were twelve. What was that transition like culturally—specifically regarding your connection to black music?

Brenda: The move to Canada opened my mind to different cultures. Until then I had lived in a strictly black culture. Black and white people in Brooklyn did not really associate with each other. They went to school together and shopped at the same stores, but they did not socialize. So when I went to Canada I was the only black kid at my high school. My father is black, of course, but my stepmother was white Canadian. My dad and I were the only blacks for about four miles. Fortunately, Canadian people hadn't really grasped the racism thing. They didn't have enough black people to even deal with racism. I naturally had this musical ability, but all of the Canadian kids I encountered thought black people sang and danced; and it really irritated me that I sang and danced because that's what they expected. I knew that I did it from some soulful place, but not all black people sing and dance—I was always saying that. They were like, "Do you sing? Will you dance for us?" It used to drive me crazy. [*laughter*] But in Canada is where I started to listen to and learn about country music, and I realized that all people are the same. It was a huge lesson to get at a young age. To me that's the most important lesson that a child can learn.

LKB: Did you continue to write stories in Canada? And did this lead to the songwriting?

Brenda: I excelled in English and I was writing a little poetry as well as stories, but around this time music really started to creep in. I was listening to Motown songs. We couldn't afford a piano, but my dad bought me an accordion because the accordion man came by the house selling accordion lessons. That was as close as I was going to get to a piano, so I said "okay." I'd be in my room not practicing the accordion lessons, but making up my own songs on the accordion. My dad would knock on the door and shout, "Do your lesson, Brenda!" He didn't get that I was on to something far more special; I was creating. He was strictly, "Do your lesson, Brenda." That's how my involvement in music began.

LKB: What were your parents' aspirations for you?

Brenda: My dad was pretty open. He wanted me to be happy. He probably expected me to get married, settle down, and have children because that's what the women did of his generation. My mom, on the other hand, was very motivated. She wanted me to go to college. She wasn't thrilled about me doing the music, but told me if I did it, I should still get a degree, so I could teach or something. She knew how hard it was—my dad knew how hard it was, too, but they didn't discourage me from pursuing music because they knew I had the bug. And, too, they knew if you have that bug you have to do it. You have no choice.

LKB: After high school graduation, what happened?

Brenda: I had put together a band in high school. We were the Misfits. Then it became Brenda and the Misfits. I was the lead singer for the group. So, here we are two days after graduation trying to get in to see this group from Toronto called the Tiaras—this singing group. They were like the Supremes. My girlfriends and I had no money, so we were trying to get in for free through the back door. Here comes this guy who walks right up to me. He says, "Do you sing?" I said, "Yes." He said, "Well, I'm looking for someone to replace one of the girls who sings in the group. She's leaving. Maybe you'd be interested." I was like, "Yeah, of course." Meanwhile, I was like, "Yeah, right." For sure, my girlfriends and I thought the guy was just flirting—just trying to get close to these cute girls. But we went along with it because we wanted to get in to see the Tiaras. He gave me his card and told me to come to the studio on a certain date. So, here I come to Toronto with my little suitcase walking into the audition. They saw this suitcase and they were like, "Oh, this poor child. [*laughter*] She thinks she's got this job." You see, I didn't think it was an audition, I thought I already had the job. I had moved from Hamilton to the big city of Toronto. Well, they gave me the job. Thank God!

LKB: Were you at all nervous about the audition?

Brenda: No, because at that age I was fearless. I just thought, *This is my path.* You know, when you're young you don't understand that people can be cruel, that people can beat you down. You don't know that there will be many tests to go through. So I went in there and did my little thing. Later they said I was pretty bad, but they hired me anyway. And, within that group, to show you how daring youth is, I stepped in for our drummer during an important gig. We were opening for Sly Stone at some ski lodge up in northern Ontario. There was a big snowstorm and a couple of folks couldn't make it out, one of them was our drummer. Our manager was having heart failure because we had no drummer and we're opening for Sly Stone! So I said, "Well, I can play the drums." He was like, "What?" [*laughter*] He said, "Brenda, are you sure? Are you sure?" I said, "I'm so sure I can do this." I can't believe I had the guts. We were wearing long gowns and I sat behind those drums and played the whole set, singing right along with the girls. Sly came up to me afterwards and said, "How would you like to be in my band?" I was like, "Oh, no. No, thank you." I was terrified at the prospect of actually going out on the road with Sly Stone. But to this day, the girls who were in that group, the Tiaras—we remember that evening. We just had a reunion last year. LaShonda, it was amazing. That was a very special time for all of us.

LKB: At the time were you writing any of the songs that the Tiaras performed?

Brenda: No, I really didn't start to write songs for other people until I joined the *Hair* cast. I was about nineteen. They had a piano in the lobby of the theater. So I used to go up there and play before rehearsals. Doing *Hair* was amazing. I knew I was supposed to be in that show. I auditioned in three different cities because I was determined to be in that show.

LKB: What was it about *Hair* that spoke to you?

Brenda: It symbolized unity among people, which is something I have always believed in. It represented a new age, the ability to transcend racism and sexism. I wanted to be a part of that 'cause I knew that's where I lived. I lived in a world where those things were possible. So I got that job. Well, as I said, I used to play on this piano in the lobby. I would be so scared because I didn't really know how. I didn't know what I was doing. I'd just pick songs out on the piano. And one day I had this revelation that I was not really doing it; I had help. I realized I was a channel, the music was coming through me.

Once I realized that, wow. This huge weight lifted from my shoulders. I realized that there is this energy that is out there, that you can tap into and use. That changed everything because then I had confidence when I played. And then the owner of the theater had the piano locked because he heard people were playing it. [*laughter*] This was shocking to everyone. I mean, why would you lock a piano to prevent people from playing it?

LKB: Let me pause you here Brenda, just to clarify. You taught yourself the piano?

Brenda: Yes.

LKB: You have never had a formal lesson?

Brenda: No, I never had a lesson. That's why I always say faith is an amazing thing. And that's why that revelation was so important. This gets me very emotional. [*long pause*] People in the cast were always flaunting their musical theater training, and I found that incredibly intimidating because I had this passion to do this but I had no formal musical education. It was terribly intimidating, especially with the jazz guys. That revelation showed me: you don't have to take lessons to do this; God will show you how to do this. You will learn through me. That's how I did it. That's how I do it.

LKB: Let me take you back to discovering the locked piano in the theater. How did you compose after that?

Brenda: Well, for my twentieth birthday the musical director of *Hair* rented a piano and had it delivered to my apartment as a gift. Yes, a little upright piano. That changed my life. It was the most beautiful gift that I have ever received. I started picking songs out all of the time. I became a songwriter and started listening to people like Carole King and Nina Simone.

LKB: Because Carole had penned a lot of the Motown songs sung by the girl groups.

Brenda: Yes. In fact, growing up I thought Goffin and King was a brand name on a label. I had so many records with Goffin and King on it. So one day I said to one of my mom's friends, "What is Goffin and King?" And she said, "Oh, Gerry Goffin and Carole King are the songwriters." And then years later Carole King put out her own amazing album. I was inspired by that and thought, *Okay, I'm going to give myself a year to write and play my own song.* It didn't take me a year. Carole King really inspired me.

LKB: So when did you meet Brian Russell, because he is the first person you collaborated with musically?

Brenda: He's the first person I collaborated with on every level. He was the first major love of my life. I married him and yes, we wrote music and sang together. It's amazing to me how spirit works in your life. I was in the *Hair* cast and Bob Riley comes along, this big-time music producer in Toronto—he's putting a television music show together called *Doctor Music.* They needed eight singers to lead the show and I was one of the eight they picked out of the *Hair* cast. They picked Brian out of some other television production he was doing. Well, fast-forward to the first taping of the show. Somebody put us on the same microphone and we looked at each other and there was this glint of light. Bing! [*laughter*] Just like in the movies. I thought, *Oh, my God.* Next thing you know, we're in love, and we moved to California. We did have a good time working on *Doctor Music*. That was my true test in writing, LaShonda, because I had to write two gospel songs a week for this show on CBC. I really honed my craft.

LKB: Did you grow up in church? Were you attending church?

Brenda: No, I didn't grow up going to church, nor did I attend one. I have always been a spiritual person, but I am put off by religious dogma. My inspiration for writing the gospel songs came from my personal beliefs about spirituality. Those songs weren't reflections of any gospel music I'd grown up with. Those gospel songs came very easy because Jesus to me was a hippie. [*laughter*] He was a love child.

LKB: What was the impetus for your and Brian's move to L.A.?

Brenda: We'd sort of hit a ceiling in Toronto. The musicians that we knew who were older than we were at the time, who were middle aged, they were writing commercial jingles and waiting for the phone to ring. We thought, *We don't want to be forty waiting for the phone to ring.* Of course, my mother also encouraged me. She had moved out to California and she said I needed to be out there. She saw opportunities waiting there for me.

LKB: What was your first commercially released song as a duo?

Brenda: Well, prior to me and Brian's recordings of our music, other people recorded our songs. Rufus and Chaka Khan recorded our song "Please, Pardon Me." We also did a song called [*singing the title*] "That's Alright Too." We did an album for Elton John. Elton's producer saw us singing backup for Neil Sedaka. Neil Sedaka was making a comeback then. We were at the—this is a brilliant story. You'll love this story, LaShonda. We were at the Troubadour. Elton's comeback.

Neil's comeback. There are these stars in the audience. We had been trying to negotiate with John Leeds who owned Rocket Records for a long time, but he wasn't signing us. Well, the Troubadour has this real narrow passageway outside of the dressing room. We were on an intermission for the show, standing in the passageway. People were squeezing by us, making their way to say hi to Neil. One of those people was Clive Davis. He squeezes by us and says, "Excuse me." John Leeds comes running up to us: "What did he say? What did he say?" I said, "He said, 'Excuse me.'" John started in, "He wants to sign you, doesn't he? Doesn't he?" He took us next door to Dan Tana's and finalized the contract right there on the spot because he thought Clive Davis was trying to steal us!

LKB: That is a great story. You must've been thrilled.

Brenda: Are you kidding? We were dying. Elton was like the biggest thing on the planet, and his record company wanted to sign *us*.

LKB: How long were you with Rocket?

Brenda: For a couple of years. We made two albums for them. Elton played on one of the albums. It was an extraordinary experience.

LKB: When did you go solo?

Brenda: In 1978, I put out my first solo album, self-titled. And the song "So Good, So Right" is my first single. I was signed to A&M Records, which is where I wanted to be because at this point Brian and I had split up. And I had a new baby.

LKB: How many children do you have?

Brenda: One—a daughter, who's grown. She's a married lady now. Her name is Lindsay. Well, going solo was very scary for me. Until then I had been with Brian. Now here I was, another black woman out there singing . . . and there's not enough of us doing that, right? But I knew that writing my own music was going to distinguish me. So I made a list of record companies who I thought might want me. My best friend at the time, Brenda Dasher, who became my manager, corrected me right then and there. She said I should make a list of who *I* wanted, not a list of who I thought might want me.

LKB: I think that's a very important lesson for artists to get. You don't solicit any- and everybody for patronage. You don't get caught up in thinking, *Who will think I am good enough?* but rather, *Who is good enough for me?*

Brenda: Right. And, see, Brenda knew this. Thank God. So, at the top of my list was A&M because of Carole King. I knew that that record company stood behind their artists and really cultivated them, molded them. They didn't just make a record with them and throw them away because A&M was run by artists—Herb Alpert. So, long story short. It just so happens I had an "in" there. I called this girl and she told me they weren't signing any singers, but we went around her and found out about Horizon, which was an imprint of the label, and they're the ones who signed me. At Horizon I found a whole new family, including Tommy LiPuma, who is a brilliant producer. One day I was in his office where they were presenting me with the final contract, LiPuma was on his way to the Grammys. He came in, shook my hand, looked me in the eye—he hadn't heard a note—and welcomed me aboard.

LKB: When you are involved in the songwriting process, does the lyric come first or does the music come first?

Brenda: It depends on the song. It happens differently. A song like
"So Good, So Right," I wrote while I was washing dishes. I
had people over for a dinner party and had begun to clean up
and while I was standing there at the sink, the song just came
to me. So I went into the next room, sat down at the piano—
in front of my dinner guests, which is something I never do. I
never write in front of people, but I was afraid if I didn't do
that I would lose it, because I don't remember things if I don't
get them down right away.

LKB: You know what I especially love about that song? That little
harmonizing riff, which now I can hear as a bit of your past
with the Tiaras surfacing. That part that goes—*uh wee uh wee
uh wee uh ah*. It's a classic wordless hook.

Brenda: They used to call me the Uh-wee Uh-wee Girl. [*laughter*]
You know, I take my hints to write a song any way they come
to me. I really listen to people. Sometimes I hear titles in conversations and I write them down and the song starts from
there. I was talking to a girlfriend once and I said, "I wanna
have dinner with Gershwin, girl." And I liked the way that
sounded so I wrote it down.

LKB: Do you ever try to will a song to come to you? Have you
ever set out to write a song in a structured way?

Brenda: I do try to will songs to come, but you know what,
LaShonda? I find that very hard to do. My best songs don't
come that way. They come when they come. I am not one of
those writers who sits down and can just hammer out a tune.
Inspiration has to move me, and then I am subject to be buried
in song ideas for three months. But, I can also go months
without writing a note.

LKB: Where this might frustrate other artists, you don't seem intimidated by the off time.

Brenda: It doesn't frustrate me, but I'll tell you I used to think of myself as lazy because I'd look at my musician friends who were always writing and being very prolific and think, *Well what's wrong with me?*

LKB: I love the language, all of the metaphor for travel in the song "Get Here," which has been recorded by Oleta Adams, Randy Crawford, Barbara Mandrell, and Patti LuPone. Can you tell me how that song came to you?

Brenda: That song was such a gift to me. I was making a record on very little money. My manager and I went to Sweden—I had been invited there to do a show and fell in love with the place. When we finally had the record company on board, really interested in the project, there was all of this pressure to do an up-tempo number. They were like, "Brenda, you need a dance hit." As I'm trying to write something like that, out of nowhere here comes [*humming the first few chords of "Get Here"*] *da da da da da da da*. I thought, *Well that's not a dance hit, so let me move that to the side.* I go to bed; I wake up and [*humming the first few chords of "Get Here"*] *da da da da da da da*. There it is again! Well, this had never happened to me. Like I told you before, if I don't write it down it's gone. But, here this song was again. It would not go away. So I wrote it. This was during a very spiritual time in my life. We had no money and were really living on faith, so I saw this song as a spirit gift. I had rented this great room looking out over downtown Stockholm, and as I looked out of my window I started thinking of all of these ways to get to a person that you loved.

LKB: Were you thinking of someone in particular when you wrote that song? Because your performance of it, anyone who performs that song has to bare a lot of emotion and sentimentality.

Brenda: Yes. I was talking to the person that I had not met yet. I was singing to this dream lover. Yeah, I was thinking, *whoever and wherever you are, get here!*

LKB: I've always wanted to ask you what the impetus was for "Le Restaurant"—the song that got me in trouble when I was a young girl.

Brenda: [*laughing*] Oh yeah, how so?

LKB: I was thirteen years old, in the eighth grade, and there was this talent show at my school. I'd started playing "Le Restaurant" over and over and over and loudly in my bedroom because I was memorizing it to sing for the talent show. Finally, my mother had had it with me playing that song, and she stormed into my room and let me have it. I tried to explain to her that I was learning that song to sing at the talent show. She listened to a verse and said, "LaShonda, you are not singing that song." I said, "Why not?" And she said, "Because you just turned thirteen and that song is too mature for you. Why don't you sing something by New Edition?" We had the biggest fight! Well, to make a long story short, I ended up not being in the talent show because I didn't want to sing any other song.

Brenda: [*laughing*] That just touched me so. What a cute story. I love it! Well, that song, as soon as I wrote it, I fell in love with it. When I am writing a song, I'm trying to paint a picture with words. This is one of the songs where I feel I really was able to do that. After I wrote "Le Restaurant," I played it for my manager, and she said, "It's a nice tune, but it's not commercial." So

I put that song in a drawer for seven years. When I pulled it out later, a different friend loved the song and said to me, "Brenda, always get a second opinion." And I recorded it.

LKB: Talk about painting a picture. The scenes are so clear [*singing*]: "He teased François behind the bar. . . ."

Brenda and LKB: [*singing*] "And he left his tips in the candy jar / He carried on just like a song / And I always wondered where he'd gone / He never / Never knew / How I would dream about him / My rendez / Rendez vous / Down at Le Restaurant."

LKB: I can't believe I just sang part of that song with you.

Brenda and LKB: [*laughter*]

LKB: What inspired your song "Rainbow"?

Brenda: That song was built from an incident that happened to a girlfriend and me. It was a racial incident. This song is about people, and racism sparked it. When I sing, "You see color, and I see a rainbow," that's what I'm talking about. It's all about perspective. Some people really get hung up on race and ethnicity, and that's really too bad. That's why my early years in Canada were so critical. I never had a chance to develop those hangups, gratefully.

LKB: "If You Love the One You Lose."

Brenda: Love is eternal. This song reminds us of that.

LKB: And that memory is where love lingers and lives.

Brenda: Yes. This was a healing song for me. I was in love with someone and I couldn't have that person, so I had to deal with it. When I was younger and had a broken heart my mom would always say, "Write about it." So I did.

LKB: "Way Back When."

Brenda: When I was writing that, we didn't have drum machines or clicks. People were writing on the piano. So I hear this *dun dun dun . . . dun dun dun dun dun* and I had to keep that going while writing another harmonic line. Well, the first person I played the song for was Chaka. She came over and I was so excited and told her to listen to the drum part. I sang the song for her and she looked at me and said, "Brenda, you always like that complicated shit." [*laughter*] And to this day I say, "God, where was that place that I was when I wrote that? Where was that place in time and space?" I would like to visit that place again.

LKB: There is a lot of orchestration going on in that song. You have strings, percussion—

Brenda: And I heard everything. I just heard everything. That song wrote itself.

LKB: There's a similar magic happening in "No Time for Time."

Brenda: Thank you. I remember writing that song out of intense love feelings for someone. "No Time for Time," though, is another one of those songs that I'd put away. Herb Alpert made me bring that song out. I love to write songs when I'm in love.

LKB: That explains why they are so inspirational.

Brenda: Yes, I wear my heart on my sleeve. Like the song, "If Only for One Night." I could barely write that song I was crying so hard. I almost didn't write it because it was too painful.

LKB: Unrequited love seems to be a theme here, Brenda.

Brenda: [*laughter*] Yeah, right. It's like, "Will somebody, please, help the girl out?" Sometimes I think it is my path to experience these feelings, so I can write about them, so other people can feel this music deeply enough to find hope in it.

LKB: I'd like to talk to you about "Piano in the Dark." When it was released in 1988, there was no other song like it in adult contemporary music or R&B, receiving radio play.

Brenda: That song was another gift.

LKB: Were you surprised by its reception?

Brenda: I was amazed that people got a chance to hear it. Most of my problem has been that people don't get to hear my songs because they're "too different" to receive airplay. I had written the lyric for "Piano in the Dark," and my cowriters Jeff Huller and Scott Coulter sent me this music, which I thought was really beautiful. They kept pressuring me to come up with something for the music—they pushed me into it. So I told them I had this lyric, "Piano in the Dark." And they were like, "Well, what does *that* mean?" [*laughter*] When it came time to select a single, at the very last minute Herb Alpert picked "Piano in the Dark" to release because at first we were going to go with your typical dance song. I was so thankful.

LKB: From your most recent album, 2004's *Between the Sun and the Moon* on the UK label Narada Jazz, can you speak a little bit about "The Message"?

Brenda: I wrote that with my good friend Ron Spearman, who is such a genius. We were writing for a film. I believe that song was intended for the DreamWorks animated feature about Moses, *The Prince of Egypt*. They didn't pick up the song, but I loved writing a song about the spirit using you in a unique way. You know, there are so many ways to see God. That's basically what that song is about. There's an important line in that song that goes: "Even though we see the light through different eyes / There's only one creator giving sight." I'll tell you . . . you need to hear this; I think you'll be inspired about the power of dreams. I had this dream about George Harrison. In the dream I told him that I was going to England to make my next record, and he said to me, "That's really good, Brenda. I think you should do that." He had a cigarette in his hand and there was something surreal about the smoke coming from his cigarette. I kept hearing him repeat, "Good idea. Good idea." He died ten days later. First of all, I don't dream about George Harrison. Secondly, I got on the phone to my manager and moved on that dream so fast you would've thought somebody was ordering me to do so. That's how deeply I respect the dreamworld. You have to because that is the way the universe connects with us. I got that deal so fast. I've never had a record deal happen as fast as that deal.

LKB: I read somewhere, Brenda, where you referred to yourself as a closet rocker. It was a lightbulb moment for me because I thought, *Yes! That's what's so interesting about her sound and about her aesthetic.* You conceive these really beautiful harmonic and melodic lines and interpret them with a blues-rock vocal; or what I call the waily-waily tone. I mean, Brenda, you write gorgeous ballads and then what lends them such emotionality is this rock edge under the surface.

Brenda: The way you listen and talk about what you hear is so awesome, LaShonda. You're inspiring me so much because you get discouraged, you know. I saw an interview with Joni Mitchell recently where, when asked if she was songwriting these days, Joni said, "Well, I get ideas but I don't feel motivated to do the battle with record companies." Joni said, "I'm willing to go through the creative process, but it's such a battle with the companies and radio—the whole machine part."

LKB: Is Joni an inspiration?

Brenda: Absolutely.

LKB: What's your favorite album?

Brenda: Oh, my God. I like a lot of what she's done throughout her career. It took me like five years to get the *Mingus* album.

LKB: That's one of my favorites—especially songs like "God Must Be a Boogie Man" and "Goodbye Pork Pie Hat."

Brenda: Yes! Well, I started painting around this time. You know, it's really important to abandon the fear that you can't do something because you haven't been trained in it. It's all the same source—creative energy. So I put that *Mingus* album on later, after I'd taken up painting, and I was like, *Oh, my God*. I was listening to it with different ears and seeing different things, too.

LKB: I'm struck by the number of singer-songwriters who paint—Joni Mitchell, Abbey Lincoln, Cassandra Wilson, Tony Bennett . . . the list goes on and on. Who are some other songwriters that you admire?

Brenda: I love Stevie. Sting. Ivan Lins—he's from Brazil—maybe my favorite writer. He makes me cry. He's got an album that you should get. It's called *Um Novo Tempo*. You can get it off of iTunes. It's full of that Brazilian soul and love and pathos.

LKB: The Portuguese have a special word that encompasses all of those feelings and I find that it characterizes a lot of their music. They call it *saudade*. I was in Brazil last fall for the first time. When you land at the Antonio Carlos Jobim airport in Rio, you are greeted with the music. There are live bands set up right there before you can even get to your luggage. I love Brazilian music—it is my latest obsession.

Brenda: That music is life affirming. I put it on just to feel myself feeling.

LKB: Recently you were nominated for a Tony award for cowriting the lyrics and music for the musical *The Color Purple*. Can you tell me how the *Color Purple* project came to you?

Brenda: I'd read the novel back in the eighties. I had even auditioned for the movie, for the part of Shug Avery. I didn't consider myself an actress but the people in my community were encouraging me to audition, so I did. I got a few callbacks. Now, fast-forward twenty years. My friends Allee Willis and Stephen Bray and I were working together on another project Allee had going—some animated stuff, no money. And, here's another great lesson: don't always do things for money or for what you can get out of it. Oftentimes you don't know what you're going to get out of it, because look at what happened. We happened to be together writing music, having fun, and we realized we were writing some really soulful stuff and we needed a bigger project. So we just threw it out into the universe: we needed something bigger! The next thing you know, here comes this phone call from Allee's friend looking for writers to work on the musical *The Color Purple*. As soon as we heard it, we knew it was our job. We claimed it right then and there. We had to audition, so we were sent the working script and told to write two songs. We chose the hardest scenes, with lots of people coming and going. You know, the scenes involving a lot of the cast, and we scored two songs. It took us about two months to make them perfect. We made a record. Now, Broadway is usually just piano and vocal, but we're coming from the pop world, so we wanted to show this in our scoring. We Fed-Exed our record to the producer, Scott Sanders, and waited. And waited and waited. We thought that Scott didn't know how to finesse his call to us letting us know that we didn't have the job. As it turns out, he wanted us very much. He was just having so much fun and grooving so hard he forgot to call us.

LKB: Did you write all of the lyrics together? Because "What about Love?"—the song that made me bawl when I saw the show—sounds like classic Brenda balladry.

Brenda: It is because I am the only one in the trio who plays the piano so the melodies. . . . Ninety-nine percent of the chordal changes came from me. But everyone influenced the lyrics. We were all crying when we wrote that one—especially when we came up with that line: "What about tears when I'm happy? What about wings when I fall?"

LKB: I also loved the "Miss Celie's Pants" number. It reminded me of my grandmother and her cohorts from the chu'ch. When I watched the telecast of the Tonys I was hoping they would perform that one.

Brenda: I had to fight to keep that number in the show. I wrote that music and hook and brought it to the team and we all stretched out the lyric. It's one of those things that just came to me [singing]: "Who dat say? / Who dat say? / Who dat?" The producers did not want that number in the show. Well, it's not like they didn't want it, the show was already so long and we were trying to cut it.

LKB: Was it a challenge for your team to write the lyrics in black vernacular? The songs are uncannily close to the language in Walker's novel. It sounds like you studied her texts for years.

Brenda: Thank you. We tried so hard to do that because we love the novel and we love Alice Walker. Every scene we wrote, we would read those parts of the novel to each other. Early on we would watch the scenes in the movie also. But later we stuck very closely with her book. We would get to talk to her. That was one of the best parts of this whole project—to sit in a room with Alice and talk to her. She's unbelievable, such grace and fortitude.

LKB: When the news came about your nomination, what did you do?

Brenda: Laughed. Cried. I was with my daughter. On the day they posted the nominations, we went online together. We were shocked because things weren't looking so good. The critics weren't really loving us. People were saying we were not going to get nominated. The theater community was not totally embracing. They weren't exactly giving us love. So it was a very real possibility that they could freeze us out of the whole thing. But they didn't. LaChanze got hers!

Four
CHAKA KHAN
(MARCH 23, 1953)

Born and raised on Chicago's South Side, at the age of eleven Yvette
Marie Stevens formed her first group, the Crystalettes. While still in
high school, she joined the Afro-Arts Theater and toured with
Motown great Mary Wells. A few years later, Yvette adopted the
African name Chaka Khan while working as a volunteer on the
Black Panthers' Free Breakfast for Children program. After quitting
high school in 1969, Khan joined the group Lyfe, soon exiting to
join another dance band, the Babysitters. Although neither group
was fated to succeed, Khan's reversal in fortune came after teaming
up with ex–American Breed member Kevin Murphy and André
Fisher to form the group Rufus. Debuting in 1973 with a self-titled
effort on the ABC (purchased later by MCA Records) label, and
showcasing Khan's dynamic vocals, Rufus began their ascent as one
of the preeminent funk groups of the decade. They broke into both
pop and R&B music charts in 1974 with the hit "Tell Me Something Good," written by Stevie Wonder. Throughout the 1970s and
early 1980s, the band racked up a number of R&B hits, including
"Masterjam," "Sweet Thing," "Do You Love What You Feel?" and

"Once You Get Started." The group earned half a dozen gold or platinum albums and two gold singles, with "Tell Me Something Good" and "Sweet Thing," before Khan went solo in 1978, the same year she recorded the Arif Mardin–produced disco smash hit "I'm Every Woman" off the album *Chaka*. Khan's success, however, was somewhat tempered by the public rivalry with the Rufus band-mates, to whom she was contractually bound for two more albums. As a solo artist, Khan recorded backing vocals for Ry Cooder's 1979 effort "Bop Till You Drop," then cut her sophomore album, 1980's *Naughty*. Her next album, *What Cha' Gonna Do for Me*, was a mod-erate seller and included at least two hit singles on *Billboard*'s R&B singles chart, including the title song, which topped R&B and pop charts. In 1982, Khan recorded *Echoes of an Era*, a collection of jazz standards featuring performances by Chick Corea, Freddie Hub-bard, Joe Henderson, and Stanley Clarke. 1983 saw Chaka return to Rufus to record her last contractually obligated album, *Stompin' at the Savoy: Live*. The double album contained live versions of Rufus classics, Khan's solo hits, and a handful of additional newly recorded tracks. One of these tracks, "Ain't Nobody," returned Khan to the top of the urban and Top 40 charts. Khan's career was on shaky ground when she released 1984's *I Feel for You*, a platinum seller due to its title cut, a Grammy-winning hip-hop-based rendition of the Artist's (Prince) original song (with a cameo appearance by Stevie Wonder on harmonica and rap by Melle Mel), which launched her recording career back into full gear. Produced by David Foster, the popular ballad "Through the Fire" also reached the R&B Top 10, setting a record for spending the most consecu-tive weeks on the *Billboard* R&B chart. "Through the Fire" has since been sampled by Kanye West for his hit single "Through the Wire."

Despite the good reception of albums such as 1986's *Destiny* and 1988's *C.K.*, Khan took a brief sabbatical from music and relocated to Europe. In 1990 she won another Grammy for "I'll Be Good to You," a duet with Ray Charles and another R&B and Top 20 pop hit. The 1992 album *The Woman I Am*, for which Khan received a Grammy award for Best R&B Vocal Performance, contains the hit single "Love You All My Lifetime." Although she recorded a follow-up album, *Dare You to Love Me* (1995), Warner Brothers shelved the project. However, several of the album's tracks appear on the career retrospective recording *Epiphany: The Very Best of Chaka Khan*. Chaka Khan has made appearances on the soundtracks of *To Wong Foo, Thanks for Everything, Julie Newmar*, and *Waiting to Exhale*. Her album *Come 2 My House*, produced by the Artist, appeared in 1998, and a collection of pop and jazz standards, *ClassiKhan*, was released in 2004. Chaka Khan has received eighteen Grammy Award nominations and has won the award eight times. The recipient of an honorary doctorate degree from Berklee College of Music, her Earth Song Entertainment and Chaka Khan Foundation operate from Beverly Hills, where she makes her home.

Selected Discography

Chaka (Warner Bros.)

Naughty (Warner Bros.)

What Cha' Gonna Do for Me (Warner Bros.)

Chaka Khan (Warner Bros.)

I Feel for You (Warner Bros.)

C.K. (Warner Bros.)

I'm Every Woman (Warner Bros.)

ClassiKhan (Earth Song/Sanctuary)

Albums with Rufus

Rufus (MCA Records)

Rags to Rufus (MCA Records)

Rufusized (MCA Records)

Rufus featuring Chaka Khan (MCA Records)

Ask Rufus (MCA Records)

Chaka Khan

LKB: By age eleven you had already formed your first band with your sisters, the Crystalettes. What were some of the particular influences of your childhood home that inspired your musical creativity as a youth?

Chaka: At that point in time we were still in grammar school, so I figure probably Aretha, Gladys, and a lot of local groups like the Five Steps. And then, you know, some of the older acts like the Marvelettes, and Smokey.

LKB: In a 2004 interview you referred to jazz vocal music by artists such as Ella Fitzgerald, Sarah Vaughan, and Peggy Lee as your "first music." As a child growing up with this music, what ideas did you form about what it meant to be a singer? In other words, if you think of these singers as early teachers, what did you learn from them?

Chaka: Interesting question, but I have to tell you I have no idea what I learned from them. I mean I just loved the songs they did. People like Peggy Lee, Sarah Vaughan, Ella, Harry Belafonte, and Ray Charles, I adored them. I'll tell you though that as far as singing, I think that I learned about vocalizations from horn players. Charlie Parker and Miles Davis were my teachers. They taught me about the limitless ways to phrase.

LKB: What do you remember about your first attempts at songwriting?

Chaka: To me it was just poetry. I didn't really think that I was writing a song. I used to write a lot of poetry in school. And it's still the same way. My songs start out as poems. You know, I'm mindful of things like cadence and which rhyme scheme I'll use, like ABAB or ACAC. Content to me is very important—the relevance of the content and how eloquently I can say it.

LKB: When a song comes to you, does the music come first or the lyric?

Chaka: Actually, I've done it both ways. I still jot down my poetry and sometimes that's the song lyric. I have books and books of my poetry all around the place. I've gone into the studio recently. I've been collecting some of the stuff I've written down over the years. Sometimes the song comes in one fell swoop. It's truly an inspired thing and it comes very quickly.

LKB: It may come quickly for lots of folk, but you actually take the inspiration someplace and turn it into something special. To invoke some old-school lingo, you got it going on, Chaka.

Chaka: [laughter] Go on. No, really, go on . . . in what ways? [laughter]

LKB: You're an innovator. An intrepid innovator. When you came along, Chaka, it was a significant historical moment and you manifested all of these moments during your performances. We can especially look at your work with Rufus as embodiment of black pride, sexual liberation, and second-wave feminism. Tracing it all the way back to Ma Rainey singing the blues about everything from domestic violence to incarceration, black women have always used performance as a vehicle for activism, and you certainly continued this tradition. You flaunted multiple identities, reminding audiences that there's an inherent responsibility in fulfilling all aspects of yourself. And this during a time when *identity politics* and *multiculturalism* were not yet the buzz phrases they became a decade or more later. So, your iconoclastic stature is well deserved.

Chaka: Wow. You said that so eloquently. Can I use that for my professional bio? [*laughter*]

LKB: [*laughter*] You know, as a teacher of black history I often come across students who marvel at the complexities of the social movements of the sixties and seventies. They are always interested, as am I, about how a person negotiates what are seemingly conflicting identities. For example, your involvement with the Black Panther movement might have conflicted with your strong sense of gender equality. Yet you never seemed to compromise any aspect of yourself. You brought it all to your art and kept them all front and center.

Chaka: Thank you so much for that, sister. You know, I don't know how I did that. I'm not one who usually thinks about how I'm going to work this or that, or how it's going to be perceived. I've always been really concerned with being true to myself. When I was with Rufus, when I was wearing leather and feathers it was a conscious thing, but I wasn't necessarily attempting to send a message to my audience. I mean, if I was, the only message was—and continues to be—be proud of who you are. Be honest about who you are. I saw an Indian headdress somewhere and simply thought, *Oh, I want to wear that onstage.* Because at the time I was really tapping into my Indian heritage, learning about my Indian roots, and I wanted to identify with that. I mean, whatever I am is what I am. I am many things, seen and unseen.

LKB: So, would you say that your experience as a Black Panther, participating in that empowering activism and being inspired by people like the Last Poets, enabled you to make a conscious choice—

Chaka: I made a conscious choice not to carry a gun! [*laughter*] Okay? You know, at a point, I really did. I thought to myself, *I need to find another way of reaching people and making them aware of the plights of the black nation, the injustices of black life, but also the beauty of it.* I was inspired by how the Panther party had empowered me and I wanted to be able to do that—to empower people. I decided I would use music as a vehicle to get to people. And I wouldn't necessarily put the message in the music, you see what I'm saying?

LKB: Yes, as a singer you were afforded a platform.

Chaka: Yes, and combined with my circle of influence I could initiate some of the positive change I wanted to see in my communities. So what I'm saying is that my identity as a singer helped me to get an empowering message out there sometimes without even having to put it in my lyrics. But then too, of course, sometimes I used the lyrics for that.

LKB: By far one of the most popular R&B classics of the 1970s is your original "Sweet Thing," cowritten with Tony Maiden, which has been covered by numerous artists. Could you please talk about what inspired that song?

Chaka: Girl, I don't think anything inspired that song. [*laughter*] I told all of my boyfriends around that time that it was them that inspired that song. In fact, [*laughter*] I think Tony was my real boyfriend at the time. Yeah, Tony was my boyfriend then [*laughter*]. That song was just spontaneous. Tony and I were just sitting around and it happened—really. We had that kind of chemistry, and it was that kind of situation. We wrote the song in five minutes. It's all really chemistry when it boils down to it. Rufus and I had an amazing chemistry. That's what was underneath it all, you know. And the love we had for each other.

LKB: What do you think are the necessary ingredients a vocalist needs to get across, in memorable fashion, a ballad like "Through the Fire"? Or a two-stepping dance-groove classic like "Everlasting Love"?

Chaka: Honesty always. Honesty in everything, because believe me, people can see when you're faking the funk. The audience knows a fake when they see one.

LKB: Throughout your career you have had some of the most talented and musically gifted people compose songs which you have turned into major hits, like Stevie Wonder's "Tell Me Something Good," Ashford and Simpson's "I'm Every Woman," and, of course, Prince's "I Feel for You." As a vocalist interpreting other people's lyrics, what do you aim to bring to the song? Or, put another way, what do you feel you need to bring to a song in order to do a song justice?

Chaka: I have to feel like I wrote the song before I sing it. It has to already feel like it's mine way before I record it. Also, I've been careful to sing songs written by artists whom I have a deep respect and deep admiration for, so that when I come to their songs it falls together in the most natural way.

LKB: I'd like for you to talk a little bit about the process of your album *Come 2 My House*, which I think is one of your most significant projects because of your coauthorship on practically all of the album's tracks. Plus, your performances on songs like Larry Graham's "Hair," and the Artist's song "Don't Talk 2 Strangers" are riveting. Can you discuss the writing process you had working with the Artist and Larry Graham on this album?

Chaka: It was fantastic.

LKB: Of course. I knew you would say that.

Chaka: It was really unbelievable. We did that CD basically in two weeks. I'm telling you. When you put the work time down . . . and take away the fun time [*laughter*], we fundamentally did that CD in two weeks' time. It was like being with myself three times over! [*laughter*]

LKB: It seems to me that you have a gift for intuiting and choosing who you should work with. I mean, in terms of music, you're certainly not breaking bread with any- and everybody. Have you always possessed insight when it comes to working with musicians who really get you and vice versa?

Chaka: Yes, it's something I've always worked hard at. When doing your life's calling you have to take great care with it, because this is not a rehearsal.

LKB: Are there any artists whom you're just bursting at the seams to work with?

Chaka: Well, you know I would love to collaborate with Joni Mitchell. I'd love to do some writing with her. She's not singing anymore. She's devoting a lot to her painting. Stevie Wonder and I, I think we're rather overdue for something.

LKB: Yes, you are! I was thinking the same thing when I watched the BET awards show.

Chaka: When Stevie, Prince, and I were all jamming together?

LKB: Yes.

Chaka: Somebody ought to lock the three of us down. [*laughter*] Those two are so kind and so open. There's a lot of love between the three of us. It takes us twenty minutes just to say hello to each other. You know, in this business everyone's schedule is so hectic, so chaotic that it makes it really challenging to get together with each other. You just have to be ready to get up and jump to it at a moment's notice. Very rarely can you plan a project that requires multiple artists in advance. It was a miracle that Prince and I were able to get together and do what we did.

LKB: From the album *ClassiKhan* I am in love with a very moving ballad you wrote called "I Believe."

Chaka: Wow, a lot of people don't know about that album. Or about the album *Come 2 My House*. I so appreciate you shining a light on the music that I've created in every sense of the word.

LKB: What inspired "I Believe"?

Chaka: I was talking to myself, you know. I was in one of the moods . . . talking to the higher inner self, the God within.

LKB: What are some of the obstacles that impede your musical creativity, and how do you circumvent them? Or don't things get in the way of your music making?

Chaka: Hell yeah, all the time. Life. [*laughter*] Life gets in the way.

Often it's just tedious, humdrum stuff that needs to be done. And you just get them done. You learn to just do it so you can get back to the business of music. I have to say, I don't worry because I believe in a universal order. I believe that there is a greater spirit at work and that this spirit has my back—that it's handling it for me. All I have to do is be able to receive the blessings in a thankful mode. I walk in the fog in the name of God and I believe, I truly do. I do not worry. You know, LaShonda, you can't worry and have faith at the same time.

LKB: You're right, and yet I know many people who embrace that kind of contradictory faith. These are the ones who claim mixed blessings. I just claim blessings.

Chaka: See there? I know you're right.

LKB: Traversing much musical ground in your career, from funk and disco to jazz and hip-hop, you have not only maintained an incredible listening audience across generations, you have also left an imprint on each of these genres. Can you please speak to what you feel has enabled you to contribute to multiple musical genres?

Chaka: You know, I don't think I'm for everybody. Even though I have created music in lots of different genres and over many years, I still don't have this crazy huge following—not the kind of following somebody like, say, Michael Jackson has had. And I don't necessarily want that because I don't think I'm for everybody. I do think there are a great many people who get me, people who are able to hear my inner spirit in the voice. Not really the voice, but what's behind the voice. What I bring to the table, what I've brought to all of the musical tables that has made this career lasting, is me. Just me. Naked of spirit with no other intention but to be of service to the music and to tell the truth.

LKB: Let's say I turned back the hands of time and I was Indira, and I came to you and said, "Mommy, I'm going to sing." What advice would you give me? What advice *did* you give her?

Chaka: I would tell you not to sing, like I told her. [*laughter*] I told her to get a degree first, preferably one in entertainment law so she could handle her own business. But I also knew when I was saying that that ultimately I would have no say-so in what she chose to do with her life. So, she's doing her thing.

LKB: Speaking of which, what do you think of the Daughters of Soul project [www.daughtersofsoul.com]?

Chaka: I think it's a magnificent idea. I love Sara Hill and Sandra St. Victor, and I think they're all doing great work. Someone needs to really pick up on that. I think there's a lot of money to be made for those girls. It'll happen.

LKB: Chaka, how do want your musical legacy to be remembered?

Chaka: I just hope that it is remembered. I mean, I would hope to be one of those artists by which others set standards.

LKB: You're already that. You raised the bar to the stratosphere.

Chaka: Thank you, sister.

Five

DIANNE REEVES
(OCTOBER 23, 1956)

Born in Detroit, Michigan, and raised in Denver, Colorado, the singer-songwriter's current home, Dianne Reeves is considered one of the most important female jazz singers of our time. Descending from a very musical family (her father, who died when the singer was two years old, was also a singer; her mother, Vada Swanson, played trumpet; and her cousin, George Duke, is a well-known piano and keyboard player and producer), as a child Dianne took piano lessons and sang at every opportunity. At age eleven, an inspiring teacher piqued Dianne's interest in music by exposing the class to many different forms of music, and even encouraging them to write their own lyrics. At the age of sixteen Reeves was singing in her high school's big band. Fortuitously, that same year the band played at a music festival (Convention of the National Association of Jazz Educators) and won first place. It was there she met the trumpeter Clark Terry, who, after discovering her, became a mentor. A year later, Reeves embarked on music study at the University of Colorado, before she moved to Los Angeles in 1976. In L.A. her interest in Latin American music grew and she began experimenting with different kinds of vocal music. Reeves met Eduardo del Barrio, toured with his group Caldera, and sang in Billy Childs's jazz band Night Flights. She also toured with Sergio Mendes in 1981, and from 1983 until 1986 with Harry Belafonte as a lead singer. This period also witnessed Dianne's first experiences with world music. In 1987, Reeves became the first vocalist to sign with Blue Note Records. Writing in the *Best of Dianne Reeves* liner notes, A. Scott Galloway notes, "Reeves is jazz's replenishing empress. With her solar-powered contralto, expansive range, impeccable pitch, and evocative writings, she has returned jazz to mother nature, reconnecting it to its earthen roots. A woman of strength and grace, she is an artist unencumbered by the shackles of categorization." Since the 1977 album *Welcome to My Love*, Dianne Reeves has recorded eighteen albums. She has been awarded the Grammy four times in the category of Best Jazz Vocal Album for the albums *In The Moment* (2001), *The Calling* (2002), *A Little Moonlight* (2003), and the motion picture soundtrack *Good Night, and Good Luck* (2006). Rather than focus on all her plaudits, Reeves remarks, "I always have to remind myself of how far I've come in my career. . . . And how far there is to go. The most rewarding thing is to be able to continue to sing with my heart and soul." Dianne is currently at work on a new album, which will feature original compositions and is slated for release in the fall of 2007.

Selected Discography

Art and Survival (Palo Alto/Capitol)

Never Too Far (Palo Alto/Capitol)

Better Days also known as *Dianne Reeves* (Blue Note Records)

I Remember (Blue Note Records)
Quiet after the Storm (Blue Note Records)
The Grand Encounter (Blue Note Records)
Bridges (Blue Note Records)
In the Moment (Blue Note Records)
The Calling (Blue Note Records)
A Little Moonlight (Blue Note Records)

Diane Reeves

LKB: Dianne, who or what were your earliest influences in music?

Dianne: Interestingly enough, they were family. I have this wonderful great-aunt, the sister of my grandmother, who sang and played the piano. Her brother and her sister did, as well. She was married to my uncle Bill, who was a waiter on the railroad. They performed concerts all along that rail line—Chicago, Saint Louis, Kansas City, Denver, and Utah. That's actually how my great-aunt met my uncle Bill—on the railroad where she performed.

LKB: Did she perform secular music or—

Dianne: No, this was some low-down dirty blues, the club music and all of the music of the time. Early on she would teach me all of these songs.

LKB: How old were you?

Dianne: About five or six. Well, she would teach me all of these songs and I had no idea what they meant. I didn't know what I was singing. My grandmother would say, "Sing Grandmother a song." And I would shake and shimmy and sing the songs my great-aunt had taught me while she played the piano and my uncle played bass. I would sing Ma Rainey and Bessie Smith pieces, even a few pieces that my great-aunt had written herself. So that was the very beginning, though my mother says as soon as I could make a noise I was singing.

LKB: When did you decide that you wanted to pursue a career as a singer?

Dianne: In junior high school. You know, junior high school is a very difficult age. And I had this great teacher, Bennie Williams, who's still very much a part of my life. She had come from Texas, she'd taught at Bishop College and ended up coming to Denver. At the time, our class was the first class to be bused to this black teacher out someplace that we didn't even know existed. The way that Bennie thought she could bring the black and white students together was through her music class. It was through her class that we were introduced to all kinds of music and poetry. We came together and wrote our own shows. I remember walking down the hall thinking, "This is what I want to do." I'd heard people say, "Don't put all your eggs in one basket," and I thought to myself, "I'm putting all my eggs in one basket!"

LKB: As time went on, did you ever doubt that you would be able to make a life in music?

Dianne: Never. Not at all. Once I made up my mind, my uncle, who worked with the Denver Symphony for many, many years, found me an amazing music teacher and I also continued working with Ms. Williams. My family certainly put me on the road so I would get the proper training. I think that it was because of all of the encouragement and prayers and support from family and friends that I was able to pursue the music without any doubt. I mean, I had this gift, I knew it was big, but I didn't know what it was. I only knew that it made people look at me a different way, and I knew it made me feel powerful.

LKB: When did you begin formal vocal training?

Dianne: When I was eleven years old—with Ms. Williams first, and then I worked with another teacher. I ended up at the University of Colorado–Denver as a music composition major because they had a jazz program. At that time there weren't many jazz programs in the country, and I didn't know about Berklee in Boston. The gentleman who was the dean of the program at UCD, Dr. William Fowler, had sons who were out making music. So I thought I'd go there so I could go out into the world like Dr. Fowler's sons and make music.

LKB: Why did you choose to study composition?

Dianne: I had worked with a music teacher whose background and method was classical, but she understood that that wasn't the musical area that I was going to pursue.

LKB: You had never aspired to classical singing?

Dianne: No, I love it, but . . . now let me back up. When I first started singing, my uncle who worked with the Denver Symphony started surrounding me with the local musicians—really great musicians. So I started gaining experience in singing and communicating in music without words. I didn't understand it, but I liked how it felt because the musicians could play an idea and I could respond with words or I could change the time, or change the feel of a piece, but real subtle. And I thought, *I really like this*. So when I went to school I went to be a composition major because then I would be taught like the instrumentalists. That's the thing about singing; people often look at singers and singing like it's the shimmer in front of the real music—the musicians. This is especially the case in jazz music, unless the vocalist shows the musicians that she can compose, arrange, and use her voice just like he uses his instrument.

LKB: For some reason, though, often vocalists feel like they have to belong in one camp or the other. Either they place the emphasis on the lyric or they forsake articulating the lyric for phrasing and vocalizing. I read this article once, "Lady Day and Lady Time" by Will Friedwahl, where he cited a quote by Ella Fitzgerald, who said that for her the lyric was only something to hang the melody on. And then you have an opposite approach from someone like Abbey Lincoln, who will tell you in a minute that she is very clear about her role as singer. She says she "tells a story set to music." Abbey rejects scatting and says because the human voice is the carrier of words the singer's job is solely to do what the instrumentalist cannot—to tell the story. In your songs, however, your articulation is spot-on, the story of the lyric is emphasized, but you also play around with melody and harmony and do very improvisatory vocalizing—much to the delight of your audience. In other words, you have mastered both.

Dianne: I really understand Ella, because when she started singing she really viewed her voice as an instrument. She sang songs just like musicians play songs. Musicians are aware of the lyrics. Matter of fact, all of those musicians that Ella grew up in the music with never would've done a song unless they knew what the song was about. They all knew the lyrics. In Ella's case, the singing was very much about a variation on a theme, which made her so powerful. And I love that approach, too. When I first started out singing I wanted to be able to sing and feel the harmonies in a way that would allow me to access all of these different places. It really wasn't until I worked with Harry Belafonte in 1983 that I found the power of connecting all of these parts—the vocal instrument with all of its hues and colors and the emotion embedded in the content of a lyric.

LKB: What was it about your work with Harry Belafonte that helped you bring cohesion to all of the parts of your vocal approach?

Dianne: Harry had me singing all of these songs from all over the world that had a social or political message that was underneath. You really had to know what you were talking about to be able to transmit the code. So that's when I thought, *Wow, lyrics are really important.* I started going back and listening to Carmen McRae, Nina Simone, Billie Holiday, and Betty Carter. That whole experience of working with Harry changed everything.

LKB: Had you composed original songs prior to working with him, or did your songwriting also begin around this time?

Dianne: Actually, when I moved to Los Angeles I ended up working with a friend, who I just saw last night, Billy Childs, we've been working together for many years.

LKB: Let me back you up a second. This is after your one year at the University of Colorado? You left school and took off for L.A.?

Dianne: Yes. My cousin George Duke was doing all kinds of wonderful musical things and I had visited there before and really liked it. There were so many good teachers in L.A., and other things I felt I needed, so I left Denver. I ended up doing a lot of studio work because some of the guys from Earth, Wind, and Fire are from Denver and so they were producing, and one person in particular, Larry Dunn, always felt that I could sing anything. So he put me in all of these sessions with lots of different people. But anyway, getting back to Billy Childs. I met him during this whole process, because everybody kept saying he was a great pianist. So I called him for piano lessons. And he had already heard a recording I'd done with a group, so as it turns out he was looking for me. We were destined to meet. Once we met, we worked together and he taught me some things, but we really loved each other's musical spirit. We formed a group, Night Flight. The percussionist and the drummer, they were steeped in the Latin tradition. Billy was steeped in classical and jazz. Both Billy and the bassist were working with Freddie Hubbard. Then later on the bassist was with Carmen McRae. At the time, I was working a lot with Sergio Mendez, so I was learning a lot about Brazilian music. Everybody had something else that they did, so we experimented a lot. All of the songs Night Flight performed had to be unique; it was all about improvisation and taking the music as far as you could. I tell people how sometimes we took the music so far we didn't know how to get back, but it didn't matter. We worked in a club where the owner didn't pay us. The way we got paid was by passing a hat. We didn't owe anybody anything and that freedom really allowed us to be free on a musical plane. The whole concept of Night Flight was that all of the songs had to be songs that we wrote or arranged. I had to write because that was the only way my ideas were going to be heard. So, long before Harry I was writing. Matter of fact, "Better Days" was written in 1978.

LKB: Is "Better Days," then, one of your first originals?

Dianne: Yes, and it is the first one that I recorded.

LKB: When "Better Days" came out in 1988, I was an eighth grader. I was very, very close to my grandmother, so I fell in love with that song. I sang that song so much you would've thought I wrote it.

Dianne: [*laughter*]

LKB: Actually, I remember every black girl up and down our block and from around the way singing that song. When Big Mama passed away in 2001, one of the first things I did after I heard the news was find that song to play. Can you tell me who Denverada Burrell was?

Dianne: Denverada Burrell was my grandmother. I wrote "Better Days" with a friend of mine, Tony Lorrich. We wrote a lot of songs together. The song is about his mother and my grandmother, because both of them passed away around the same time. This was 1978, in the spring. When my grandmother passed, I remember not being able to sing or say anything. I had no voice. I couldn't tell anyone my feelings. It wasn't until much later—it seems the farther you get away from the passing the more things start to come out—that I was able to talk about who my grandmother was and what she meant to me. One day Tony and I just started talking about his mother and my grandmother, and that's how the song came about.

LKB: You were reared by your grandparents, right?

Dianne: No, people are always saying that. There are a lot of biographies out there about me that are wrong.

LKB: Well, let's set the record straight.

Dianne: I was raised by my amazing mother. My grandmother was very much a part of my life, but my mother and stepfather raised me.

LKB: What was your mother's profession?

Dianne: My mother was a pediatric nurse, an RN who really served her community. My mother was also an honorary doctor of medicine for the Black Panther party in Denver. People loved to bring their children anywhere she was. She worked in the community center and worked with many children from their birth until they turned eighteen. And to this day, those first patients of my mother are bringing their grandchildren to see her. Mama's eighty-two years old, but she still knows everybody. Has a mind like a steel trap, can remember everything. That's who I was raised by, my mother and my stepfather. My father died when I was two years old. I have no memory of him.

LKB: I want to backtrack a bit because you mentioned moving out to L.A., but I know that you didn't remain there. How long were you in L.A.?

Dianne: I lived in L.A. from . . . let's see, when did I move out there, '77? I was in L.A. from 1977 until 1983, when I moved to New York, which is where I started to work with Harry Belafonte. I lived in New York until '86, and then I moved back to L.A., where I stayed until 1991, when I moved back home to Denver.

LKB: And during all of these transitions you wrote some wonderful songs, several of them I'd like to talk to you about. Here is a portion from a very powerful lyric that you wrote: "They cut out my sex they bind my feet / Silence my reflex no tongue to speak / I work in the fields I work in the store / I type up the deals and I mop the floor." Can you tell me what inspired your song "Endangered Species"?

Dianne: I was reading *Finding the Secret of Joy*—

LKB: *Possessing the Secret of Joy*?

Dianne: Yes. First I read Walker's *The Temple of My Familiar*, then I read *Possessing the Secret of Joy*. Then I went on to read *Warrior Marks*.

LKB: The book about female genital mutilation cowritten by Alice Walker and Pratibha Parmar.

Dianne: Yes. And during my reading of these books for the first time I really understood just how connected the lives of all women are and my connection to every woman in the world. While I was sitting up here thinking that I was free to do all of these things, Walker's writing made me start to see things differently. And as I was traveling I began to look around and notice other women's situations. Out of this came the realization that I don't really have the freedom that I thought I had here. "Endangered Species" grew out of this awareness. Matter of fact, a lot of the music from that album I wrote during this time. That album was cathartic. It really changed my life in many ways.

LKB: *Art and Survival* is probably my absolute favorite album of yours.

Dianne: I'm glad, because it almost killed me. [*laughter*]

LKB: Your song "Josa Lee" is also from that album. You give such a poignant description, I'm wondering what she represents for you.

Dianne: Everybody asks me, "Is that you?" I tell them no, it really isn't. She's a preacher's daughter who's been reared in a situation where she definitely knows right from wrong. She's been taught the right things, but she goes out into a very cold and seductive world. With that song I was exploring how even when you know certain things, sometimes you still get pulled in, and women are especially vulnerable in this sense because often we don't have the resources to get ourselves straightened out. Even though I told the story with a preacher's daughter I think it applies to many people who get caught up out there in the streets and feel like there is no way to get back. It's funny, after I recorded "Josa Lee," much later, I read Sister Souljah's *The Coldest Winter Ever* and, while the characters are different, they fall prey to the same seduction. And, at the same time, there's a little bit of me in the song. When I first moved out to California I was trying to be about my business and I found that there was a lot of lure—a lot of that, "Well, if you come over here I'll give you this." Some of this made me begin to doubt some of my self-worth, and it's ironic that this should start to happen when I really had some sense of who I was as a woman and as a musician. I finally realized that this could destroy me—even fighting it could destroy me. The album *Art and Survival* was the beginning of that end. By the time the album was completed, I had already moved back home to Denver. For the first time in my life I had gotten to a place where I really didn't know where I was going or what I was supposed to do next because I had ended up in a record company where I really didn't want to be, where my creativity was really threatened. So I was like, *How do I get through this? Do a record that I know they're not going to want but that is my heart and my soul.* And it worked. [*laughter*]

That's a whole other story, one of these days I'm going to write about it. But that record literally saved my life. And the song that was so threatening to people was "Endangered Species." Folks would say to me, "Why would you want to record a song like that?" During interviews I would have people say to me, "But look at you, you don't look like an endangered species." And I got it. I realized, *Okay, now that I am standing in my own light—*

LKB: And signifying on all that is wrong—

Dianne: *People are bothered by it.*

LKB: Yes, it's true that when you stand in your own light you stand alone, but I've found that that kind of solitude is holy.

Dianne: Yes, it is. Holy and healing.

LKB: Dianne, does songwriting come easy for you?

Dianne: No. It is often very, very difficult for me. The hardest thing for me to do is to silence my inner critic. That really takes a lot out of me. Also, the conditions for me to write a song have to be just so. For instance, some musicians can write music while they are on the road. I can't write anything while I am traveling. I have to be at home and very grounded.

LKB: Talk to me about your song "Old Souls."

Dianne: Well, when I lived in New York and was working with Harry Belafonte, I found myself in the presence of a lot of amazing musicians who were really steeped in African spiritual traditions. One of them, Harry's percussionist at the time, introduced me to the Yoruba tradition. One day I stopped by his place—we were all on our way out to eat and he invited me in. And he did it on purpose because he knew I was this curious person; I am always searching for answers. He had this whole setup on the floor, and he's moving things around and saying things I don't understand, and I thought to myself, *What is this man doing?* Well, turns out he was communing with his Elegba, his warrior. After that, I started asking all kinds of questions and we would get into these really deep conversations. I would share with him my philosophies on the spirit world, things I'd always felt deeply. He told me I needed to speak with his godmother, so I went to her and I found a whole spiritual philosophy that mirrored what I had always felt and believed in. When I first started out pursuing a singing career, while my mother and all of them were very, very supportive, they couldn't tell me who to talk to—how to choose the right manager or lawyer. I was out there on my own. So when I had certain things that I needed answers to I would really pray, but I always believed in being conscious because all my life this is what has saved me—prayer and awareness. So finally here I was in this place learning about ancestry and how just like you can look like those who came before you, you can also hold the knowledge they held—you can know things and not even understand how you know them. Your ancestors are definitely a part of your being, your soul.

LKB: There is a beautiful bridge in "Old Souls" that goes, "I am a curious spirit child / Who fell to earth through a crack of lightning / But God so kind and merciful sent old souls to guide."

Dianne: When I wrote the line about "the crack of lightning" I was referring to my rebirth after becoming aware of this African spiritual tradition and the understanding that I come from something much bigger. It changed my whole outlook. From that point on I went into the world knowing that whoever dealt with me also had to deal with my army. And as a young person aspiring in the music business, trying to understand how these businesspeople think—'cause there is nothing spiritual about the music industry—embracing Yoruba spirituality helped me tremendously. You see, in the Yoruba religion through the orishas you learn that there are truly two sides to every coin—that this energy goes with that energy. This is what I have used to navigate my way through the business.

LKB: Your song "Olokun" from the *Bridges* album is relevant here. When you speak of feeling connected to ancestors and having an unseen army, "Olokun" has greater significance.

Dianne: Olokun is an orisha that represents the deep part of the ocean, but this orisha is also closely connected to the dead. Olokun gives stability, both spiritually and materially.

LKB: [*singing*] "Runnin' and jumpin' and skippin' and laughin' / Rollin' and shakin' and jokin' and hidin' / Mother may I / Simon says / You're it / You spit / Hide-n-seek / You peeked / No I didn't / Yes you did / You're unfair / I don't care / I saw Sammy's underwear . . ."

LKB and Dianne: [*laughter*]

LKB: What was the genesis for your wonderfully whimsical song "Nine"? And, why not "Eight"? Or "Eleven," Dianne? I have to tell you, this song has special meaning for me because third grade was my absolute favorite grade in elementary school. I am still very close to my third-grade teacher, Blanche White. You put me in touch with so many wonderful memories whenever I listen to that song.

Dianne: "Nine" because it's the last time you're a single-digit age. Like you mentioned third grade, I remember my third-grade teacher, Ms. LaGuardia, so fondly. And I can recall all the excitement that came with being nine because I just could not wait to be ten! *Ten!* [*laughter*] Sometimes that's how love is. You know that whole thing that happens when you're swept up— all of that joy. For me, nine was very important because I was on the edge where there was so much joy. So, for these reasons I wrote "Nine," which is also written in an odd meter— seven—and that was because children are all over the place. There is an innocence in that. I remember my godchild said, "Aunt Dianne, this song is a triangle and a square." When he listened to the music that was the pattern he made with his feet. I told him yes, three and four. He got it. Also, the time signature of the song represents how crazy the world is and how innocence and imagination let you just soar over the top of it all.

LKB: One of my favorite verses in the song is when you paint a picture of the neighborhood where elders looked out for the young people: "Everybody's child belonged to the neighborhood / So you could tell your troubles to old Aunt Savannah 'cause she always understood."

Dianne: Well, I had an Aunt Savannah. You see, I also really wanted to capture community in this song. I remember growing up—we were talking about this not too long ago— and the music that I was listening to my mother was also listening to. The generations weren't so separate. She loved the Temptations and Aretha Franklin and all of that, and I did, too. Even though we sometimes had different music we could all gather in one place and enjoy the music together— James Brown and Sly and the Family Stone. Sam Cooke. I loved Sam Cooke even though he was the generation before me. When I was in junior high and high school the majority of the music that was out there was embraced by all of us, all of the generations, because it talked about what we were going through at the time. It was talking about the war and the need for black consciousness.

LKB: What inspired your song "Testify"?

Dianne: My little cousin was getting ready to go off to college, and she was asking me a lot of questions about being on her own. She's a generation younger than me. And it's changed, now many young people are afraid to leave their families. When I was nineteen I was *gone*. Now they are afraid, and they stay home for a long time. So she was asking me about things, and I was telling her as much as I knew and things that my mom and my grandmother had told me. I started thinking about my own life. We had gone into the studio and my percussionist put down this whole track of percussion. I told George Duke—'cause he was producing *Bridges*—to give me that track so I could see what I could do with it. One day I was listening to one of my favorite records of all times, *What's Going On*. I just love how that album is such a commentary on what everybody was going through—being hooked on drugs, struggling to pay high taxes, finding Jesus, all of these things. One song in particular really moved me that day, the song when he sings, "Little children of today, are really gonna suffer tomorrow."

LKB: "Save the Children."

Dianne: Yes. You know in that song Marvin Gaye is speaking and singing and I always loved that so I just started to write a song about my life. In my head, while I was writing it, I heard certain parts that would be spoken and certain parts that I would sing.

LKB: "Eyes on the Prize," an original from the 1990 LP *Never Too Far*, has a similar advice-giving sentiment like your song "Testify." One verse reads: "Go ahead little brother / There's a place just for you / Go ahead little sister but whatever you do / Keep your eyes on the prize and your back to the wind / You're the generation with the world in your hands / But life won't get better without taking a stand / Keep your eyes on the prize / Let your heart be your guide / And keep your back to the wind."

Dianne: Do you know I had forgotten about that song? I wrote that for another family member. I am very inspired by my family, especially since they have been such a tremendous support for me. I wrote that for a young cousin just before he left home for college. He is the apple of many people's eye. He is just golden. I wanted to uplift him with this song.

LKB: Your song "1863" is very interesting to me.

Dianne: When I read Toni Morrison's *Beloved*, I was very, very moved by the character Denver. There are parts of "1863" that are written from what I think would be Denver's perspective— the new generation after slavery has ended. I also wanted to get at the point that knowing your history is very, very important.

LKB: It sounds as though you are very inspired by black women's fiction.

Dianne: Yes, I'm hearing that, too. I am a voracious reader, and of course I love books written by black women. Out of curiosity, LaShonda, who is your next interview?

LKB: Dionne Warwick. She is the only person I am including in the book who is not really a songwriter and the reason is—

Dianne: She made music that affected every generation and every race.

LKB: I was born in 1974, and I remember my mother playing lots of Dionne Warwick around the house. Some of the records she played were from the sixties, but you would not have been able to tell. Her songs—and even though she didn't write them, I still refer to them as *her* songs—had this timeless quality. In the late seventies I was a little girl singing around the house [*singing*] "Do you—"

LKB and Dianne: "—know the way to San Jose? I'm going back to find some peace of mind in San Jose." [*laughter*]

Dianne: Her voice was and is the kind of voice that children, teens, and adults are attracted to. I wanted to sing the theme song from *Valley of the Dolls* and I didn't even know what that movie was about. I was always singing, "Walk on By," "Promises, Promises," all of those wonderful songs which will always be with us because of her masterful interpretations. Had it not been for her, he would not be Burt Bacharach, I really feel that way.

LKB: So do I, which is why I want to interview her. Dianne, in a June 1994 interview with *Essence* magazine you said that if you weren't a musician you'd probably be doing social work. Do you still feel that way?

Dianne: Yes. I'd work with young people—from junior high schoolers to young adults, because when I look back on my life it's so clear to me that what got me through was all of the adult guidance. It's so important for young people to have adults that really care enough to help them know themselves, to help them find out what they are good at and then to help them make some of those things happen.

Six

DIONNE WARWICK
(DECEMBER 12, 1940)

Dionne Warwick began singing in church during her childhood years in East Orange, New Jersey. Occasionally she sang as a soloist and fill-in voice for the renowned Drinkard Singers, a group that included her mother, Lee, and her aunts and uncles. During her teens, Dionne and sister Dee Dee started their own gospel group, the Gospelaires. While attending the Hartt College of Music in Hartford, Connecticut, Dionne began making trips to do regular session work in New York. She sang behind many of the biggest stars of the 1960s, including Dinah Washington, Brook Benton, Chuck Jackson, and Solomon Burke, to name a few. After logging session work with the Drifters, Warwick teamed up with song-writing team Burt Bacharach and Hal David. In 1962, Bacharach and David presented a demo featuring Dionne to Scepter Records. Florence Greenberg, label president, expressed no interest in the song; however, she did want the voice, and Dionne began a twelve-year association with the New York label. At Scepter, the Warwick/Bacharach/David trio racked up thirty hit singles, including "Do You Know the Way to San Jose," for which Dionne received her first Grammy Award in 1968, "Message to Michael," "Walk On By," "Anyone Who Had a Heart," and "I'll Never Fall in Love Again," for which she received her second Grammy in 1970. In 1976, after earning a master's degree in music from her alma mater (the Hartt College of Music), Dionne signed with Arista Records, where she embarked on a third decade of hit making. Labelmate Barry Manilow produced her first platinum-selling album, *Dionne*. The album included back-to-back hits like "I'll Never Love This Way Again" and "Déjà Vu." Both recordings earned Grammy Awards, making Dionne the first female artist to win the Best Female Pop and Best Female R&B Performance awards. On the heels of this success, Dionne began her first stint as host for the highly successful television show *Solid Gold*. Dionne's 1982 album *Heartbreaker*, coproduced by Barry Gibb and the Bee Gees, became an international chart topper. In 1985, Dionne reunited with producer Burt Bacharach and longtime friends Gladys Knight, Stevie Wonder, and Elton John, to record the classic "That's What Friends Are For." Profits from the sale of that song were donated to the American Foundation for AIDS Research. In 1990, Dionne joined forces with a number of Arista labelmates to raise over $2.5 million for various AIDS organizations during the star-studded That's What Friends Are For benefit at New York's Radio City Music Hall. In addition to cohosting and helping to launch the Soul Train Music Awards, Warwick also starred in her own show, *Dionne and Friends*. She was co–executive producer of "Celebrate the Soul of American Music," which honored and rec-ognized many of her fellow musical pioneers. Throughout the 1980s and 1990s, Dionne toured extensively with Burt Bacharach. The show won rave reviews from fans and press alike for reinforcing the timeless musical legacy of the Bacharach, David, and Warwick team. Dionne's status as a musical icon and humanitarian is legendary. With her own star on the Hollywood Walk of Fame, she continues to work tirelessly with various organizations dedicated to empowering and inspiring others. In 1997 she was awarded the Luminary Award by the American Society of Young Musicians. That same year she joined General Colin Powell in celebrating the tenth anniversary of the Best Friends program, an abstinence and character-building program for young women. Dionne's East Orange, New Jersey, elementary school, Lincoln Elementary, honored her by renaming itself the Dionne Warwick Institute of Economics and Entrepreneurship. Displaying her own business skills, Dionne plans to reactivate her skin-care regimen and fragrance. In 2006, Warwick celebrated her fortieth year in the recording industry with a new release, *My Friends and Me*. The album is a series of duets featuring well-known performers Gladys Knight, Cliff Richard, Whitney Houston, Angie Stone, and Olivia Newton-John.

Selected Discography

Here Where There Is Love (Collector's Choice)
The Magic of Believing (Collector's Choice)
Soulful (Collector's Choice)
On Stage and in the Movies (Scepter Records)
The Windows of the World (Scepter Records)
Promises, Promises (Scepter Records)
Just Being Myself (Warner Brothers)
Track of the Cat (Warner Brothers)
Dionne (Arista)

No Night So Long (Arista)
Heartbreaker (Arista)
Reservations for Two (Arista)
Aquarela Do Brazil (Arista)

Dionne Warwick

LKB: You come from a highly musical family, but I'm wondering if there were other career paths you might've chosen besides that of a musician.

Dionne: Oh, I was going to do a thousand things, of course. I still have aspirations of teaching eventually—not in a traditional classroom setting but special seminars, weekend workshops, that kind of thing. I could never sit in a classroom five days a week.

LKB: And you would teach music education?

Dionne: But of course.

LKB: Which was your major when you attended the Hartt School of Music at the University of Connecticut as an undergraduate, and also where you later returned to earn a master's degree.

Dionne: Right on.

LKB: Do you recall the moment when you knew that music was going to be your life?

Dionne: Yes, it was when I graduated from high school. I had a hit record as my graduation present. [*laughter*] So I knew I was gon' be—in show business.

LKB: Have you ever composed any songs?

Dionne: Not really. I have written a couple of songs, but nothing of any consequence.

LKB: You have recorded over fifty albums—

Dionne: Sixty to be exact—that includes live albums and everything.

LKB: One album that really stands out for me is *Aquarela Do Brazil*. I love that album.

Dionne: I do, too. Well, Brazil is where I live. I happen to have a great affinity for the people and the country and the music. Their musical heritage is really rich, so that choosing music for the album was a real joy. I went with some old favorites, like some of the Jobim pieces, but I also included music by lesser-known Brazilian composers.

LKB: When writing about you, critics and music writers have often referred to you as a "songwriter's singer." What qualities do you think they are attributing to that appellation?

Dionne: Well, I believe more than anything else they are referring to the respect that I have for what the songwriter has written. You know, when a songwriter writes a melody, they want to hear the notes that they wrote, not an improvisation on what they wrote. And they want to hear the words that they wrote. I am also a musician, so I work hard to give life to all of the musicality in a composer's song.

LKB: In your own words, how would you describe your instrument?

Dionne: That's the one thing I've never been able to do.

LKB: What are some of the key elements that you strive to bring to each performance? What are you consciously trying to give your audience?

Dionne: Well, a smile for one thing. Warm memories. In a nutshell, me. Literally me—what they see is what they get. I am always striving to be myself.

LKB: On the subject of the highly praised—with good reason—

Dionne Warwick, Burt Bacharach, and Hal David collaborations, were you ever invited to contribute to the music or the
lyrics in any way?

Dionne: The only thing that did occur—seldom, but every now
and then a word would not suit a note and I would change
the word, but aside from that I didn't have a hand in creating
those songs. I've always been very clear that my job is to
interpret the songwriter's songs.

LKB: Many people feel, and I am one of them, that you performed
those songs in a way that no other singer could have. So, when
you say you didn't create them, in a way that's true, but in a way
it's not. Those songs live because of your lasting interpretations.

Dionne: Thank you.

LKB: Who were some of your musical influences while growing
up, Dionne?

Dionne: My family. You know, I didn't have to go far. Listening to
music in my home, I heard everybody—Nat King Cole, Dinah
Washington, Ella Fitzgerald, Lena Horne, Sarah Vaughan, and
lots of gospel. The only music that I didn't listen to was
country-and-western music.

LKB: What do you think of the whole concept of placing artists
within a genre? I mean, here you are the headliner at the
Litchfield Jazz Festival, but many people would associate you
with adult contemporary music.

Dionne: I hate it. I hate the whole labeling thing. I've always
thought that who the singer is is whatever the listening ear
decides. But I am fortunate enough to be able to say that
despite what I have been labeled in the press when it has come
to my career, when it has come down to the actual opportu-

nities to perform the music I like, I have never been pigeon-holed. For a long time the music industry couldn't decide if I was R&B or what. The only reason they would even put that label on me is because I am a black woman.

LKB: Nina Simone said the same thing in numerous interviews and in her autobiography, *I Put a Spell on You*. She said she hated being labeled a jazz artist, and that the only reason she was labeled that was because she was a black woman. She considered herself first and foremost a classically trained pianist who performed black classical music.

Dionne: You see. It doesn't help the artists to be labeled. I remember it was like the biggest surprise in the world when I won in the best contemporary female artist category at the Grammys. People were like, "She's not a white girl." You're right. [*laughter*] I'm glad you're able to see that. I really find it offensive to pigeonhole anybody who is bringing music to people's ears.

LKB: Is there anything musically that you'd like to do that you haven't done?

Dionne: No, there really isn't. I've even done an opera. I thought I was gon' die—[*laughter*] but I did it.

LKB: Where did you perform the opera?

Dionne: In Japan.

LKB: Will you talk a little bit about that experience? What was the name of it?

Dionne: Ah, don't ask me that, girl. Don't you dare ask me that. [*laughter*] I couldn't tell you now. But I performed it in Tokyo about eight or nine years ago. It was fun; it was different.

LKB: How long was the run?

Dionne: It was only for two nights. They were raising funds for
some reason, but I can't remember what it was.

LKB: This year marks your forty-fifth anniversary in music. How
do you practice voice care?

Dionne: You know, everybody's needs are different. People have lots
of different remedies to take care of their vocal cords. Stevie
eats cayenne pepper. Some people have to have honey. I can't
have honey because it produces phlegm. I believe there's
nothing I can do for my voice other than rest. This is a muscle,
so it requires rest.

LKB: What words of wisdom would you pass on to someone who
is interested in pursuing a musical calling? I think whatever
you have to say on this is significant because you have managed to stay true to yourself over the years.

Dionne: I would say exactly those words: stay true to yourself. And,
understand that it is not given to you—you earn it. It is a job.
You're doing something you love to do and you're getting paid
for it, too, which is an unbelievable situation. However, you
also have to know that in this work your best foot forward is
really the only foot you can put forward.

LKB: Why do you believe you have had such staying power in this
business?

Dionne: Well, it's a lot of parts and parcels to why I'm still here. I
have always valued the kinds of music that I sing and the company that I keep. I attribute the longevity of my career to the
music I have chosen to sing. People expect that I will sing
good music. That's the way I entered this business and that's the
way I'm going to go out of it.

LKB: You select songs that you can interpret in such a personal and

original way, but that also have universal appeal—songs that
your audience can really connect with. What is your song
selection process like?

Dionne: I look at the lyric first. I pay close attention to what I'm
saying based on the fact that if it is not something I would nor-
mally say or have not heard said, then I think it's not going to
be of any interest to anyone since it isn't of any interest to me.
It has to be something that *you* would say or that *you* would
feel. Something that, as you just said, the listening audience can
connect with. Of course, I'm also hooked by a memorable
melody. I've been very fortunate. I've had some of our most
talented and prolific composers compose for me.

LKB: What do you think of black music today? And do you think
that the music will have staying power?

Dionne: It's different. [*laughter*] It's music for today's youngsters,
but I'm going to be truly honest here and I may get some
backlash from my babies, but that's okay, I've gotten that before.
No, I don't think that the music of today is going to be
around forty or fifty years from now. It is for the time
and as I have said to all of them—their ears are going to
grow up and there's going to be a shift in what they want
to listen to. And I believe a little of that is beginning to
happen now. It seems that the music is now coming back
to melodies and things of a real musical nature. As I said to
them, when their ears grow up, then that's when they're
going to understand that it ain't about cussing at me, and it
ain't about calling me out of my name, and it's not about
degrading people. It's about, can you get your story across
without doing those things.

LKB: I asked a young person once, "How does a line like, 'It's getting hot in here, so take off all your clothes' help you to live?" How does it inspire you? Which is what art does.

Dionne: What it's supposed to do. The important thing there is that you gave him something to think about—when the party is over. It's your generation that is making this music, what do you feel about it?

LKB: I am worried that so much of today's black music isn't giving the people anything useful. Historically, we have been a people, and we still are a people, that have always valued social awareness and have had social ideas reflected in our art forms—in music, literature, drama, visual art. And, I might add, that often there wasn't only a problem presented but also a solution. Now, I am very aware that there is some hip-hop music out there that really is quite progressive, but that's not receiving airplay and that's not being played by most club DJs. If you want that music you have to really hunt for it because it's not widely accessible, and since record companies don't think it'll make money it's not widely available, either. I guess at the end of the day, it's lost on me how you can feel good even partying to music that degrades you and your people. Perhaps I would be able to if I could turn my mind off and just go with the flow, but I've never been able to do that.

Dionne: You are right about everything you said. I have a feeling, though, that as some of these young artists grow up and are exposed to greater issues, this will be reflected in what they produce. And then, we also have youngsters, at least I call them youngsters because I'm a bit older than these folks, who are committed to making serious music. Like Babyface, he writes beautifully, and Mariah Carey, who really writes beautifully. I don't know why she's jumping into an area she doesn't really belong in for the sake of a hit record. I mean, how long does a hit record last? She'll be in the studio next week trying to make another one. I love "Hero." It's one of the finest songs I've heard in a long, long time. And those are the songs that she excels in—not only in writing but also vocally.

LKB: Many of today's musicians are seduced by the dollar—

Dionne: Well, hey, if somebody throws a couple million dollars at you, what you gon' do?

LKB: Certainly not cuss my mama. What happened to integrity?

Dionne: Well, now, that's the way *you've* been brought up. Most of the youngsters having this kind of dollar thrown at them have not been brought up the way you have. There's that element missing: values. The element of: you will not do it and it's not because it's the wrong thing, it's because I just said you won't. Okay? And that used to be enough back when. It doesn't work that way today. It appalls me to think about some of the conversations that I've had with some parents, people actually terrified of their children. I mean absolutely terrified. I look at them like they're completely insane. Terrified? You terrified of what? Did you not bring that baby in here? Now come on, gimme a break. The elements of respect and caring and loving are so far removed from a lot of the music we are surrounded with today it's frightening. It really is frightening. People always ask me, "Why did you choose to live in Brazil?" Because of those very elements I just spoke of. They are still in practice there—the respect for their elders. They love their children. They love God and are not afraid to let you know it.

LKB: While visiting Rio de Janeiro last October, a carioca talked to me about the New Year's Eve celebration that occurs on Copacabana beach.

Dionne: Everybody dresses in white on New Year's Eve. It is not a raucous, drunken affair or whatever this has become here in the United States. It is about prayer. It is about spirituality, getting rid of the old and welcoming the new. And the people sit on the beach, and they wait for an answer. Now come on, how could you not love something like that?

Seven

JOAN ARMATRADING
(DECEMBER 9, 1950)

Born in Basseterre, Saint Kitts, and spending her formative years in her mother's native Antigua, Joan Armatrading moved with her family to Birmingham, England, at age seven. Her first guitar, a gift from her mother that was the result of a pawn shop exchange for two old baby carriages, would eventually result in Joan being one of Britain's most important female artists to emerge in the twentieth century. By the early 1970s, Armatrading had moved to London and released her debut, *Whatever's for Us.* The career that followed has seen the birth of classics like "Love and Affection," "Willow," "Drop the Pilot," "Down to Zero," and "Lovers Speak." Effortlessly eclectic, Joan's sound has ranged from true soul to sophisticated pop driven by her passionate guitar. Though she counts working with some of the finest musicians around and the ability to devote time writing her own songs among her greatest treasures, Joan Armatrading has achieved numerous musical accolades and awards. She has received countless gold, platinum, and silver discs, been nominated twice for the Brit and Grammy Award in the category of

Best Female Vocalist, and is the recipient of the Ivor Novello Award for Outstanding Contemporary Song Collection. Additionally, she figured large in VH1's Top 100 voted poll of the Most Influential Woman in Rock and has been honored by the queen of England. In 2001, after five years of studying, Joan received her BA in history from the Open University. She has been awarded an honorary degree from Birmingham University. She was made an honorary fellow of the John Moores University of Liverpool and of Northampton University. In 2003 Joan was invited to become one of the trustees of the Open University. Joan was elected president of Women of the Year in the United Kingdom in 2005 for a term of five years. For thirty-three years, she has stood the test of time. Known as a true craftswoman, her distinctive vocals and consummate musicianship (she arranged as well as played nearly every instrument on her 2007 album, *Into the Blues*) have led to unanimous, widespread, and, perhaps most importantly, consistent critical acclaim.

Selected Discography

Whatever's for Us (A&M Records)
Back to the Night (A&M Records)
Joan Armatrading (A&M Records)
Show Some Emotion (A&M Records)
To the Limit (A&M Records)
Me Myself I (A&M Records)
Walk under Ladders (A&M Records)
The Key (A&M Records)
Secret Secrets (A&M Records)
Sleight of Hand (A&M Records)

The Shouting Stage (A&M Records)

Hearts and Flowers (A&M Records)

Square the Circle (A&M Records)

What's Inside (RCA)

Lullabies with a Difference (RCA)

Lovers Speak (Denon)

Into the Blues (Hypertension)

Joan Armatrading

LKB: When you were younger, which singers or musicians were you fond of?

Joan: I didn't buy records or listen to the radio when I was a child. I wrote a lot. I started writing very early. I used to write a little limerick. Do you know limerick?

LKB: Yes.

Joan: And then my mother bought a piano, put it in the front room, and that was when I really started to make up and write songs. It wasn't because of hearing anybody else particularly. I think I was just born to it. Yes. When the piano arrived, that was it.

LKB: How old were you when the piano arrived?

Joan: The piano would have arrived probably when I was twelve or thirteen. I always say I started writing when I was fourteen, because that's when I was playing with a band, but really it was before that. I don't remember exactly, but it was around twelve or thirteen.

LKB: From your earlier comment about writing limericks it sounds like you might have been fond of literature classes as a youngster.

Joan: I believe I was. I'm not such a great reader now, but when I
was younger you could always find me in a library. I'd be
reading Shakespeare, Dickens, Jane Austen, or one of those
classic writers. These days I don't read as much as I used to. I'm
too busy writing. I just recorded my eighteenth or nineteenth
album.

LKB: Yes, I know. *Into the Blues* is released next month in the
States. And this is a perfect segue into that part of the dis-
cussion. I wonder if you'd talk about what inspired this
collection.

Joan: Well, anybody who knows me knows I'm an eclectic writer.

LKB: Yes, you are, and I love that about your music. Recently I was
listening to your [1990] album, *Hearts and Flowers*. It's a staple,
I think, for any solid music collection because the range of
material is so vast—from the beautiful ballads "Always" and
"The Power of Dreams" to the funky, rollicking "Something in
the Air Tonight."

Joan: Yes. So you know that I write a bit of blues and a bit of jazz,
or pop, reggae, all kinds of things are apt to appear on my
records. I like the blues a lot, and if you go back to my cata-
logue of albums I think you'll find that there's a blues on all of
them somewhere.

LKB: I'm thinking now about one of your earlier recordings, the
self-titled one. My favorite song on that album is a blues. I'm
referring to "Like Fire." I love it so much that I recorded it
myself on my second indie CD.

Joan: That's so cool to hear, LaShonda. You should get your version to me. You know, I had always promised myself at some
point that I would write just a blues CD. And whatever

made me decide that this was the moment to do it, I will never know. Inspiration is such a strange thing. There's no knowing when, where, why, and how it is going to strike. For instance, there's a song on the CD called "Something's Gotta Blow," and it's about a tube journey I took. On that particular day it was frustrating for everybody because the escalators weren't working. We were really hot and bothered waiting for the tube to arrive because it was going to be a delay and everything. Now, I had been in that situation before, why didn't I write that song before? When I was on the last tour I decided—and I can tell you exactly where: Wales—that I was going to write the song "Play the Blues," which is ironic because we were staying in this really posh hotel in the middle of I-don't-know where, a place where you'd think, why would they build a hotel here? Who's going to come stay? Anyway, I don't know what about that hotel or being in that place made me feel like "playing the blues," but I started to write the lyric there. I didn't finish there, and I didn't write anything else on that tour. I waited until I got home. Then I spent quite a lot of time just thinking about the beginning lyric and what else I'd like to say.

LKB: Is that your process when you're writing an album, Joan? Do you generally sit with an idea or a germ of an idea for a while and let the idea gestate before you write the lyric?

Joan: I do that quite often.

LKB: So the lyric always precedes the music.

Joan: No, it doesn't always, but I do quite often think about what it is I want to write before I even try. And I spend quite a lot of time just walking around, sitting around, watching the television, but often I'm thinking about the song I'm going to create. The process is ongoing internally with me for a while because I've found that it is best to sit with it instead of blurting it all down on paper. At least for me anyway. I must think about it. I'll tell you, I'm really glad I gave this album a lot of process time. As you know, we're on tour now, and when I started the tour in the UK, on February the thirteenth the CD hadn't come out. It came out April the ninth. So the audience didn't know the songs at all, but the reception has been incredible.

LKB: It's so interesting, Joan, everyone knows that you're a virtuoso; you're phenomenal on the guitar; but what really strikes me about this album is, I really feel that there are two very prominent voices on each track. It's almost as if your solos punctuate the story that you're singing or else the solos have a different device; there's a bit of call and response going on, and the solo is a different voice altogether but still commenting on the main story. It's almost as if there's a story and subplot on every single on this album. It's relentless and makes for a rigorous and really enjoyable listening experience. It makes me want to go back and listen to all the other eighteen albums. I mean, maybe it's where I am in my own life that I'm able to hear this now; I'm certainly really struck by it on *Into the Blues*.

Joan: That's really nice of you to say. And I think you're right as well, because when I play and when I write and arrange, to me it is often multiple voices and they have to all fit. That's why I write and arrange myself, because it's not just the melody and the lyric, it's the whole thing, and although when I write I write on the guitar or the piano, I have to make sure that the song stands up just on that solo instrument, too. But when I do the arrangement it needs to complete the song. And when I play the solos, they are an important part of the song. It's not just a matter of playing to show off during the solos. It has to complement the song and, as you say, it should relate to the story being told.

LKB: One of the things that strikes me about your songs, particularly your love songs, Joan, is that they always sound new. When I hear something like the rhythmic, very sexy "A Woman in Love" or "Into the Blues," I'm struck by how fresh your approach is, and I wonder if you could share with me a little bit of your secret. How do you craft so many love songs and yet sidestep the trappings of clichéd and trite lines and images?

Joan: Well, love is a very dominant thing, so it's important to write about to me—all forms of it, whether we're talking about the love of food, our favorite meal, our favorite clothes, our favorite person, as a friend, as a lover, as a partner, whatever. And, you know, love is a really important factor in a career choice because in order to make something really work you have to have a love and a passion for it. It's really, seriously important. So let me first say that that's why I think lots of people end up writing about love. People, I think, wrongly decide that we write about love because it's simple. But it isn't simple. It's probably one of the most complicated emotions we have. It's the thing that connects us to somebody else, yet we complicate how we process it. I know so many people and yet there are certain people as friends that I would place way above the others. Why is that? What is that process? What is that thing that singles that person out as somebody really special? These questions are part of the secret, LaShonda. You go through all the things that you feel make that person really special to you, and that's the beginning of your love song.

LKB: That's interesting, because what I think I hear you saying is that by acknowledging the complexity and the uniqueness of individual loves, you are able to sidestep the clichéd trappings so many love songs fall prey to. You're tuned in, and you're able to hone in on that complexity rather than giving us the tried and not-so-true. In the numerous biographies written about you, you're quoted as saying, "I write because I love it." I'd like for you to expand on that comment. What are some of the things that occur for you during writing that are especially cathartic or joy bringing? What is it for you that makes you love it?

Joan: It's a combination of things. I think the most important thing for me is that I think I'm born to it. I always say I had no choice in writing. I didn't choose to write. I didn't wake up one day and say, "I wonder if I can write"; I woke up one day and wrote. So that's the very first thing. It's a God-given thing. This is what I think, though sometimes I would also say that I can't even take credit for my talent because I had nothing to do with it. I didn't seek it out; I didn't ask for it; I just was given it. That's the most important thing. And because I have it, it's a choice to use it. I see people with certain talent and they don't use it and in a relatively short span of time they lose the ability completely. Whatever it is, somewhere along the line it just disappears. I'm really grateful to be given this talent. I don't want to let myself, or the energy that gave it to me, down. So I really get involved in it, and I do love it.

LKB: When did you start to play the guitar?

Joan: Again, around about the same time as I started the piano and writing. The two happened very quickly. My mother bought the piano. My father had a guitar, but he used to hide it so I couldn't play it. Then shortly after my mother got the piano for us, I saw a guitar at a pawn shop and my mother traded in two prams—baby buggies I believe you call them—and that's how I got my first guitar. So they both came pretty close together. And I think the reason I wanted to play the guitar was because my father wouldn't let me play his. Because of that as well, I think, that's why it became my lead instrument. [*laughter*] I also find it challenging. Whenever I learn something new on the guitar, it makes me realize how much I don't know, and it inspires me to keep trying and discovering new things.

LKB: What kinds of guitars do you play, Joan?

Joan: When I play electric, it's a Tom Anderson; I like it with the whammy. When I use the whammy bar, I tend to move it forward all the time. Of course, I'm aware of who Jimi Hendrix is. I'd heard his music, but not in great quantity, so I didn't really, really know what Jimi Hendrix was about apart from knowing he was very respected, and that he's worshipped by guitarists. I mean, I appreciated him and all that, but I didn't really *know* him. Well, about a week ago we were in Vienna and there, for the first time, I saw that Woodstock movie and I thought, *My goodness, now I know what all the fuss is about.* I know it's a bit late for me to come to this, but I am just amazed. I noticed when he did the whammy bar that he not only went forward, but he very often pulled backward, and my guitar is only set up to go forward. After seeing that, I want to go backward as well so I'm inspired to practice something new. I knew the whammy bar could do that, but I never thought to really use it because I set my guitar to just go forward all the time. So now I'll make it go backwards and forwards as well.

LKB: Is the Anderson similar to a Fender?

Joan: It's made in the style of a Fender. The difference between that and a Fender is that Tom Anderson makes it so when you're onstage and there's lights and those earpieces that people wear, and all those kinds of things that cause hums and buzzes don't affect your playing. That's one of the main reasons I got this instrument. I love playing it anyway, but it is very quiet onstage.

LKB: Do you have a guitar preference? Acoustic or electric?

Joan: I like both. I play a lot of both. I think people for some reason don't notice that I play electric. But I play a lot of electric on the new CD. The record company did a focus-group thing where they played snippets of my guitar solos to a group of people and asked, "Who's the guitarist on it?" Everybody said other people; not one person said me.

LKB: Okay, this is my last question. It's sort of a whopper actually. This is the question in which I get to throw out all of my favorites and a lot of other people's, many, many other people's favorites. In the interest of time, I won't ask you for the story behind the songs in every case, but I'd just like to throw out some, and if you could recall for me the impetus behind a few of them, I would really love that.

Joan: Let's see what you have on your list. Ask me one.

LKB: "Tall in the Saddle."

Joan: "Tall in the Saddle" was actually a funny one. I was watching a John Wayne film. In fact, I'm not sure, but maybe the movie was even called *Tall in the Saddle*. If it wasn't titled that it should have been, because in this movie John Wayne is always sitting up on this horse and he looks huge. I'm telling you, when he jumped on that horse he looked like a giant to me. He looked as if no other man would ever be as tall as him, as big as him, as charismatic as he was, all of those things. And when he dismounted the horse, too, although he's tall, in some scenes he's not even as tall as the horse because of the angle of the camera.

LKB: The first time I heard that song that line really struck me because I didn't have any kind of Western imagery in my head. When I heard that line I thought, *Oh wow, what an amazing metaphor.* "One of these days you'll have to dismount for humility," you know, one of these days you'll be brought down to size. An appropriate warning to give to a haughty person.

Joan: The great thing about songwriting is that you are free to choose from all of the images, all of the metaphor that surrounds you and not just the ones in your own culture—John Wayne is not a prominent figure in the UK, of course, but he certainly stands for something in America. In a song, if you

want to reach people, to have impact it's best not to be too lit-
eral. It is something about songs that demand that the lyric be
as poetic as the notes you've strung together.

LKB: "I'm Lucky."

Joan: That's true about me. I just feel very lucky. Any song that says
I'm lucky or blessed, or anything that has anything like that,
that will always be me writing about me. I feel very looked
after. I just really have a very nice life.

LKB: "Drop the Pilot."

Joan: "Drop the Pilot" is a song I learned to write in order to have
a hit single. I wanted to just write things that were catchy, and
that's when "Drop the Pilot" came about. I just wanted things
that would catch people's attention. It's the only time I ever sat
down to do that really. To say, "I'm sitting down to write a
single." And it worked. It was very successful, a very popular
song. Who knows why I wrote it, but it worked.

LKB: "Show Some Emotion."

Joan: I was watching a group of men talking to each other, they
were always laughing and jolly enough, grabbing at each
other's shoulders and all that. All except for one guy among
them. The one guy, when I looked in his eyes he was somewhere else. Something wasn't right. You know sometimes
you can look at people, strangers, and get a strong sense that
something isn't right. That's why I wrote "Show Some Emotion." I wanted to know what that was about, that deadness
in his eyes. I wanted to know why he wasn't sharing that
with his friends. And I wanted to send this message out
there, too. Our emotions are our greatest gifts, why don't we
show them?

LKB: "I Love It When My Baby Calls Me Names."

Joan: That's another strange song. It was written because of two members of my band, one tall and one short, and they were always getting into fights. Not physical, but it was getting there. I happen to think that they kind of loved it. One of them certainly did.

LKB: People will send angry e-mails to me if I don't ask about two of your most well-known songs, "Willow" and "Love and Affection," which of course are among my personal favorites as well.

Joan: "Love and Affection," that's one of the ones I think I mentioned to you earlier about not being able to discuss with you. It's just deeply, deeply personal, and I can't talk about it without talking about the person I wrote it for, which I never, ever do. But "Willow" I wrote in West Palm Beach. At that point, I was somewhere in my life, both literally and metaphorically—geographically and emotionally—that I didn't particularly want to be. I was in my hotel room one afternoon and outside my window there was this willow tree. At the time it seemed to be the one constant thing in my life, the willow tree. So, it's sort of a love song for the tree.

LKB: Joan, I'd like to end our conversation on the subject of the kernels of wisdom that you've gathered over the course of your long career. What would you pass on to other singer-songwriters who solicited advice from you? What would you have them know, whether they're in the very beginning stages of their career or the midpoint?

Joan: The main thing that I would say is to be true to yourself. You've got to find an authentic path to this thing—music—

that you love. Make sure that you're not doing it for fame. I don't write songs because I want to be rich and famous, I write songs because I absolutely love the process of doing it. You see people on *American Idol,* and you have the feeling that they're there purely for the fame and the money. If you're true to yourself that will help your creative process, I think. That's the main thing. So that's what I would tend to say, LaShonda. If you want to be a singer, just make sure that you really want to be a singer for the right reasons, and it will come through. You see it with people who are successful. You know Fantasia, who won on *American Idol?* Well, she definitely sings because she wants to sing. There's no question that she sings because she loves to sing. You can feel it, and you can see it, her emotion comes through the voice and everything.

LKB: In 2001 you completed your BA honors degree in history from the Open University. What was the impetus behind your decision to return to school?

Joan: I always wanted to do the higher-education thing, even long after I was out of school. When I'd come off a gig very often it would be the only thing on the television, the Open University program. At the end of the program they would say, "Get up with the pack." One day I decided to get up with the pack. And that was it, really. I mean it's something I've always wanted, I've always wanted a degree.

LKB: Why history?

Joan: Well, no one would appreciate this answer more than you, LaShonda, I took a degree in history because we *are* history.

Eight

MIRIAM MAKEBA
(MARCH 4, 1932)

Known around the world as Mama Africa, Miriam Zenzile Makeba was born to a Swazi *sangoma*, a traditional healer, and a Xhosa coalminer father in the segregated township of Prospect on the outskirts of Johannesburg, South Africa. Educated at Kimerton Training Institute in Pretoria, Makeba began singing in a church choir in her youth. She gained national attention as a backup vocalist for the Manhattan Brothers, a popular South African group in the 1950s. Her debut single, "Lakutshona Llange," appeared in 1953. In 1959, Makeba left the group to join the all-female group the Skylarks. Her tenure with the Skylarks garnered her considerable local and regional success, and she subsequently landed the lead role in the show *King Kong*, a South African musical publicized as a jazz opera. With the aid of friend and mentor Harry Belafonte, Makeba first traveled to the United States in 1959, where she performed at the Village Vanguard, then one of New York's most celebrated jazz listening rooms. That year she also earned a Grammy for the recording *An Evening with Belafonte and Makeba*. Attracting Miles Davis, Sidney Poitier, Elizabeth Taylor, and Bing Crosby to her shows, Makeba introduced African music to American listeners through notable songs such as the original "Click Song," "Pata Pata," and the Tanzanian "Malaika." However, she also utilized the stage to educate audiences on the plight of her countrymen ensnared in the vicious sociopolitical system known as apartheid. Makeba drew the ire of the apartheid government for her participation in *Come Back Africa*, a documentary critical of the system. When she attended the documentary's opening at the Venice Film Festival in 1962, the South African government denied her reentry to the country.

The following year Makeba testified about South African apartheid before the United Nations Commission on Decolonization and its Commission on Apartheid. Pursuant to her testimony, Makeba's music was banned in her native land and her citizenship revoked. In 1968, after two previous marriages (one to trumpet legend Hugh Masekela), she married the controversial Black Panther leader Stokely Carmichael. Soon after, the singer-songwriter's U.S. career declined. Encouraged by fellow artist-activists Nina Simone and Abbey Lincoln, Makeba continued to voice the strife in South Africa, drawing parallels between it and black American life. The cancellation of tour dates and the intimidation tactics employed by the U.S. government eventually impelled Makeba and Carmicheal into exile in Guinea, West Africa, where the couple was well received by the country's nationalist leader, Ahmed Sékou Touré. In what would be her home for the next thirty years, until the end of the apartheid era, Makeba collaborated with Guinea's national orchestra on compositions tinged with the elements of Manding praise songs. *The Guinea Years*, a collection of recordings made during her years of exile, contains some of her best work.

Poor management at the height of her career left her dependent on performances for her income, and during the 1970s, Makeba toured Europe, South America, and Africa. In 1975 she addressed the General Assembly of the United Nations on the horrors of apartheid and recorded the album *A Promise* with Joe Sample. During the late 1980s, she toured with Paul Simon and Ladysmith Black Mambazo on the Graceland project. After Nelson Mandela was released from prison and the system of apartheid collapsed, Makeba returned to her homeland in 1991. Makeba starred in the 1992 film *Sarafina!*, about the Soweto youth uprisings (1976), as the title character's mother, Angelina. She also participated in 2002's *Amandla!: A Revolution in Four-Part Harmony*, the acclaimed documentary where she and others recalled the days of apartheid. At age seventy-three, "Mama Africa," who receives little money from her recordings, and none, she contends, from the hits she made in the 1960s, announced her retirement before embarking on a fourteen-month-long world tour. Released on the tenth anniversary of South Africa's independence, her most recent album, *Reflections*, finds Makeba singing songs from Brazil, France, England, and all over Africa. In addition to French pop, bossa nova, and jazz, she sings traditional South African music in Xhosa (her native tongue). The record includes the requisite "Pata Pata" and "The Click Song," along with a cover of Van Morrison's "I Shall Sing." With over forty-five albums to her credit, Makeba's music awards (from multiple countries) are staggering. However, she is very proud of the honors bestowed upon her for humanitarian acts. President Thabo Mbeki named her South Africa's FAO (Food and Agriculture Organization of the United Nations) goodwill ambassador. In that capacity, some of her actions have included arranging an exchange between West African and South African women and bringing relief, in the form of fishing boats and nets, to Mozambican fisher communities. Makeba was also awarded the Otto Hahn Peace Medal in Gold (2001) for "outstanding service to peace and international understanding" by the United Nations Association of Germany. In 2003, the Makeba Rehabilitation Centre for Girls opened in Midrand, South Africa. For the girls, who are orphans or come from dysfunctional families and range in age from eleven to seventeen years old, the center is their home and enables them to attend nearby local schools. Miriam Makeba lives in Johannesburg, South Africa.

Selected Discography

The Best of Miriam Makeba with The Skylarks (BMG International)

The Guinea Years (Stern's Africa)

An Evening with Belafonte and Makeba (RCA)

The World of Miriam Makeba (Collectables)

The Empress of African Song (Manteca)

Africa (RCA)

Miriam Makeba Sings (RCA)

The World of Miriam Makeba (RCA)

Back of the Moon (Kapp)

Pata Pata (Rhino)

Sangoma (Warner Bros.)

Welela (Verve)

Eyes on Tomorrow (Polygram Records)

Sing Me a Song (DRG Records)

A Promise (Goya)

Live from Paris & Conakry (DRG Records)
Sounds of South Africa (Arc Music)
Homeland (Putumayo World Music)
Keep Me in Mind (DRG Records)
Reflections (Heads Up International)

Miriam Makeba

LKB: Ms. Makeba, you have the distinction of being the first vocalist to popularize African music on an international scale during the 1960s. In fact, some music historians cite your performances as the beginning of the world music movement.

Miriam: Tell me why you think it is that our music is called "world" music?

LKB: I think in an effort to be politically correct, though it really isn't correct at all to divorce people from their cultures, from their countries, and lump them under the umbrella term *world*; this label has been applied to music that isn't American or European.

Miriam: I think people are being polite. I think it is shorthand of a sort, because what they really want to label African music is third world music, and I have a problem with that. We all live in the world. We all come from the world. Do you know of music from other planets? [*laughter*] So what is it to say that African singers or Indian singers are performing world music?

LKB: I think also that the term *world music* is a marketing strategy.

Miriam: You're probably right about that.

LKB: And, also, this is particularly true of radio in America, we are exposed to such a very, very small spectrum of music. People are not quite sure what to make of music produced in other cultures because of the very unfortunate truth that unless you seek it out, you really won't ever experience it on American radio.

Miriam: Yes, and you know here, we listen to American music constantly. So why is it that in America so little airtime is given to other cultures' music? People need to see and hear different cultures' art. This is how we learn about each other, and this is how we defeat prejudice and racism.

LKB: When I read your autobiography, *Makeba: My Story*, I learned that you were very much inspired by many black American jazz vocalists, such as Billie Holiday, Ella Fitzgerald, and Carmen McRae.

Miriam: Yes. And, don't forget Sarah Vaughan and Dinah Washington. Yes, I liked them all very much. I still listen to their albums. Their records were my mentors. I learned a lot from them.

LKB: What are some of the things you learned?

Miriam: For instance, you do not have to listen twice to understand what Dinah Washington is saying. She had perfect diction. So did Carmen McRae and Ella Fitzgerald. When I first arrived in America, Sarah Vaughan was singing at the Waldorf Astoria. Even though there was some trouble about letting me in, Sarah Vaughan insisted they let me in. After I told her I was from South Africa, she received me and she was quite gracious and friendly.

LKB: I know that you forged connections, friendships, with Abbey Lincoln and Nina Simone. In fact, you were instrumental in both artists traveling to Africa. You invited Nina to Liberia in 1974 and Abbey to your home in Guinea in 1975.

Miriam: Yes, and they came. I have always felt it very important to be a cultural ambassador—especially to my black sisters in music. We have a lot of work to do to right the wrongs inflicted on our people in the past, and we can only do this work by sharing and teaching one another. The sharing is the spiritual aspect; the teaching is the practical aspect.

LKB: These aspects, community and spiritual connection, run through your repertoire like a golden thread, and I do mean golden.

Miriam: Thank you for saying that. I have always liked to create songs and to sing songs about love. Not romantic love for a man, but love for people period, and love of life.

LKB: Like Simone and Lincoln, in America you have been known as a political singer. I wonder—

Miriam: That has always been curious to me about the West. I know I am thought of as the one who sings politics, but I don't sing politics, I sing about my life and the observations of others' lives around me. In the West, I think there is a perception that if you come to enjoy yourself at a concert, musical event, that you should not also be told a message. I am aware of this, but I have always given messages.

LKB: Along the way, did you meet any other black American female vocalists who had inspired and encouraged you?

Miriam: I met Ella and I met Carmen McRae, who invited me to her home when she lived in Greenwich Village. They were both very, very gracious to me. And when you are received in kindness, sincere kindness, it emboldens you. How could it not? What I regret is that I did not meet Billie. Billie Holiday died the year before I made it to America.

LKB: Fans of your music know you devote equal energy to

humanitarian projects. I am particularly interested in the
Makeba Rehabilitation Centre for Girls in Midrand.

Miriam: It is difficult to live in a society that disregards its children.
Many children are lost, and some children are not so much lost
as they need help. Our help. There are a lot of facilities for boys
but very few for girls. I established this center to get some of
South Africa's beautiful girls and young women off of the
streets. We have fourteen now, but the house can take up to
eighteen. Some of the girls have no parents, or very troubled
parents. All of the girls have been put back into school. Coun-
selors work with them and guests come and talk to them about
different aspects of life, art, careers. We cannot throw away the
mothers and the leaders of tomorrow. If we do, tomorrow will
never come.

LKB: Your latest album, *Reflections*, contains such Makeba classics as
"The Click Song" and "Pata Pata." What inspired you to revisit
these songs while making this album?

Miriam: When I was in exile—physical exile because emotionally
I was always at home—as painful as that sometimes was, I
wanted people here at home to hear some of the songs that I
was singing during my absence from home, and the absence of
my recordings, which were banned. That is why I titled the
album *Reflections*.

LKB: When you reflect on your career, Ms. Makeba, what do you
remember the most?

Miriam: My music. My music gave me the world. It literally
afforded me the opportunity to visit so many different places,
to meet and know so many different cultures. At the same
time, this voice of mine, because it won't quiet if the topic is

injustice, has brought me sorrow. In other words, speaking against apartheid, singing about life in Africa, gave me legions of fans but also some enemies. I was not able to come home when my mother died, you know? I was not even permitted reentry into my country to bury my mother.

LKB: Ms. Makeba, you have enjoyed a five-decade-long singing career, and I am curious about some of the things you do to care for your instrument?

Miriam: Do you mean what do I do if I lose my voice?

LKB: Well, yes. That's part of it.

Miriam: There is something here called Jamaica ginger. If my voice is not totally gone I add some of that to warm water, gargle with it, and that seems to help any problem with my throat. Are you a singer also?

LKB: I love singing, but I do not do it professionally. I don't aspire to do it professionally, but I really enjoy it. I've even made a few records—for fun.

Miriam: Then you are a singer!

LKB: I guess you're right. Who are some of the musicians you enjoy?

Miriam: Well, Brenda Fassie and Busi Mhlongo, of course. Dorothy Masuka, Abdullah Ibrahim, and young South African artists Thandiswa and Judith Sephuma.

LKB: What are some of the tenets of music making that you feel younger artists should be mindful of?

Miriam: I think musicians need to be more accountable for the music they are making. With this work comes great responsibility, and the stories we tell as singers have tremendous impact on those who hear them. Also, artists have to be strong enough to demand fair and good treatment. Often we are treated poorly and led into poor business deals. I have always wanted to change this about the business, but I realize now that instead of trying to change the business I should instead try to educate more artists in ways to protect themselves. There is honor and glory in being chosen to be an artist, but it doesn't mean you shouldn't be organized and protective of your career.

Nine

NARISSA BOND

(MAY 14, 1960)

Narissa Bond was born to playwright/college professor/jazz guitarist Horace Bond and administrator-turned-college-president
Zelema Harris in Beaumont, Texas. As a youth Bond was inspired
by discussions on black art and civil rights buzzing through her
home, often the hub where her parents' friends and colleagues from
Prairie View A&M University gathered. The soundtrack of Bond's
youth included folk and jazz artists Odetta; Nina Simone; Peter,
Paul, and Mary; the Jazz Crusaders; Wes Montgomery; Ella
Fitzgerald; and Dinah Washington. In 1966 the Bond family moved
to Lawrence, Kansas, where both parents worked at the University
of Kansas. The following year, when she was seven years old,
Narissa's parents bought her first three-quarter-size steel-string
guitar, and she began to study folk guitar. Later she studied cello and
played with the school orchestra. When her parents divorced in
1972, Narissa and her sister, actress/writer Cynthia Bond, moved
with their mother to Las Cruces, New Mexico. Though they
resided there a short time, Narissa, whose music education now
included classical guitar, connected to the indigenous people there

and she continues to look upon New Mexico as a place of sanctuary. The fortuitous move to Kansas City, an area long noted for nurturing some of the nation's finest blues and jazz musicians, saw Narissa studying jazz guitar at the Charlie Parker Foundation with Sonny Kenner. She also played jazz guitar for the summer jazz program sponsored by the Charlie Parker Foundation. Playing guitar and bass with a Top 40 band in high school, she also performed at school dances and clubs. Additionally, on Sunday mornings she played bass guitar with a gospel band. Following her high school graduation, Narissa attended the University of Kansas.

While living in the fine-arts dormitory, she began writing her own songs. Following receipt of the BFA degree in graphic design, Narissa supported herself working in various sectors, including Macy's department store and Johnson County Community College. Narissa devoted her evenings to writing original songs, often among her cohorts of the Songwriters' Circle. Performing in local listening rooms, clubs, and coffeehouses like the Point, Fedora's, the Supreme Bean, Toto's, and American Bandstand allowed her to attract a large following in the Kansas City area throughout the '90s. The 1993 dissolution of her marriage to a prominent city attorney and her decision to come out represent a crucial juncture in the singer-songwriter's life. Long influenced by the music of Joan Armatrading, Joni Mitchell, Janis Ian, and Tracy Chapman, Narissa moved away from the pop feel that characterized her earlier songs, like "One Step Ahead," "I'm a Loser," and "Private" and started developing songs with a strong narrative core. Story songs wherein she celebrates a new lifestyle ("Partners in Crime" and "Forever Is in Your Eyes") and questions societal values ("What Does Love

Mean?") are found on her first recording, *A Free Spirit (Can't Run Fast in High Heels)*. In 1999 Narissa released her second independent recording, the CD *Knocking at the Doorway to My Soul*. Writing for the *Kansas City Star* newspaper, Danny Alexander wrote of her performance on this album, "She crafts beautiful, reassuring songs out of life's most daunting pains. The key to the music's transcendence lies with her lithe vocals, which handle tough subjects with uncommon delicacy." Proving that talent only deepens with time, the songs that make up the 2002 release, *Between Two Rivers*, mark the passing away of some of life's most significant elements, chief among them Narissa's father, a romance, and old fears. Deeply personal, these songs give a glimpse of a person searching for spiritual truth, a person whose goals are not material but rather to gain an unshakeable faith. The result? Ethereal songs like "Church of Souls" (a song about the spiritual nature of music, inspired by the Folk Music Festival in Kerrville, Texas), for which Narissa credits arrangement ideas to Dr. Ysaye Barnwell of the famed group Sweet Honey in the Rock, and the prayer-songs "Will You Catch Me if I Fall" and "Save Me." Narissa has played numerous national folk festivals and college campuses, and she is the recipient of a fellowship from the Kansas Commission of the Arts and songwriting awards such as first place at the Winfield Oak Valley Music Festival for her song based on the true life of a slave, "Celia." Narissa makes her home in Norfolk, Virginia, where she enjoys performing for her Tidewater fan base. She also tours and performs in the Midwest and on the West Coast. Her recordings, on the independent label House On A Hill, are available through CD Baby, iTunes, and Rhapsody Music.

Selected Discography

A Free Spirit (Can't Run Fast in High Heels) (self-released)

Knocking at the Doorway to My Soul (House on a Hill Records)

Between Two Rivers (House on a Hill Records)

Three Words (House on a Hill Records)

Narissa Bond

LKB: Take me all the way back to Beaumont, Texas, Narissa, and tell me the ways your childhood home inspired you musically.

Narissa: My father played jazz guitar with a quartet or trio on the weekends when he was not teaching. For as long as I can remember, I have always wanted to play the guitar. I used to sneak and play my dad's guitar when he wasn't around.

LKB: When you were deciding what to study at college, why didn't you pursue music?

Narissa: Growing up, I was a visual artist and a musician. As a teenager I was more developed as a visual artist than I was as a musical artist, so I thought it would be easier to make a living as a commercial artist than as a musician. Also, my father discouraged me from pursuing music as a career. He thought the lifestyle was not appropriate for a young lady. Of course, as I came into my own, I rebelled against these ideas.

LKB: Do you recall the moment when you decided to devote your life, or at least a significant part of it, to performing your own music?

Narissa: I'm not sure. For me, it has been a continuous process.

LKB: I know from previous conversations with you that your

decision to come out as lesbian affected your music in some significant ways. Could you talk a little about that?

Narissa: After my divorce and during my coming-out process, I started to visit and perform at women's and folk music festivals, where I discovered a new niche for singer-songwriters outside the pop music world. I heard all kinds of musical genres within these venues. Most of the music I heard had a grassroots feel, which I naturally fell into. I took workshops for songwriting, guitar, and vocal performance. I decided to get back to the basics, sold my electric guitars, and started working extensively on acoustic guitar.

LKB: What do you remember the most about your first attempts at songwriting?

Narissa: My songs were painfully raw, emotionally speaking. In my songwriting I bared my soul and left myself very vulnerable.

LKB: What are some of obstacles that get in the way of your creativity?

Narissa: Noise is the greatest obstacle in writing for me. Whether it is internal negative talk or the noise of television, radio, or industrial sounds. Many times I have to find a nice quiet place to connect to the music in my soul or to the music that exists in nature.

LKB: Do you have specific tools, exercises, or rituals that foster your songwriting process?

Narissa: I usually write early in the morning with a tea ritual and Japanese incense burning.

LKB: What would you say are some of the predominant themes that unite many of your lyrics?

Narissa: I would say that most of my music is about love and the spirit of hope.

LKB: When you compose a song do you usually create the music first or write the lyric first?

Narissa: The two usually come to me at the same time.

LKB: When planning an album, do you begin by conceiving a plan or aesthetic structure for the album?

Narissa: Yes, I usually do have a theme in planning an album. My next CD is mostly a collection of love songs. It will be titled *Three Words*.

LKB: When I attended your shows years ago, Narissa, I was always struck by your decision to stick strictly to performing your own music. Even though covering other people's music, or music that audiences are familiar with, seems to bring some independent artists a larger following, you have remained committed to performing your music, and only your music. Talk to me about this conscious decision—what it means for you on a creative level.

Narissa: It has not been challenging for me to abstain from singing songs that have been performed over and over again by other performers, it's not something I'm good at. I have to feel really close to a song emotionally to be able to perform the song. For me, the whole point of performing is to share something new and to create as much as I can.

LKB: What are some of the things that you are striving to give to your audience during live performance?

Narissa: I want the audience to feel a sense of peace, love, and hope. And sometimes I want to share a new perspective with my audiences.

LKB: I've been listening to your music since the midnineties, when you worked a nine-to-five job and played Kansas City

coffeehouses and listening rooms in the evenings and on weekends. Since you have fully devoted yourself to performing and
songwriting, I wonder if you would speak about some of the
forces that influenced you to make the brave transition from
full-time employee to singer-songwriter.

Narissa: I was unhappy as a graphic designer. The transition to
journey toward the thing I loved the most, which has always
been my music, was natural. Certain situations presented themselves that allowed me to move forward with my plans. Like, I
developed carpel tunnel syndrome after working on the
computer long hours, every day for many years, as a graphic
designer. It was easy deciding to give up the career as a
graphic designer. I settled with my employer's insurance company, collected my settlement, and quit my full-time job.
Then I moved to the East Coast to write and work on my
second CD.

LKB: From songs like "Higher Ground" to the more recent "Ask,"
spirituality is an overarching theme in much of your music.
Nowhere is this more striking than on your most recent
recording, *Between Two Rivers*, where songs like "Conversation," "Save Me," and "Will You Catch Me if I Fall" sound and
read like prayers. In a culture where a great portion of the popular music forsakes what is substantive, let alone spiritual, could
you share how some of the listeners have responded to this
spiritual music?

Narissa: Many times people will speak to me about a personal
obstacle that one of my songs has shed some light upon. Since
my songs are about working through pain and moving to a
higher place of healing and wholeness, audiences sometimes

feel consoled in some way after listening to one of my songs. On one occasion a woman came to the stage and hugged me after a Mother's Day performance at the Norfolk Unitarian Church. She had just lost her mother and she told me my songs made her feel a sense of peace. The overwhelming response to my music is that it is calming and relaxing. I would say there are many songwriters who are writing songs about hope and personal growth outside of the pop idiom.

LKB: Many artists struggle with wanting to achieve mass popularity with their music. Was there ever a time in your career when you were among these artists? If so, how did you make the transition to where you are now?

Narissa: When I was younger I wrote from my heart and personal experiences. I listened to a lot of pop music, so I was influenced by the music I listened to. Later I started to work from a spiritual place. I found that when I was quiet enough, like early in the morning or late at night, melodies would come to me. Lyrics started to come to me in the same way. I started to view these songs as gifts given to me from a higher power. This is mostly how I write, or, should I say, channel this universal power. I believe artists are the chosen ones sensitive enough to see and feel the messages that are always there.

LKB: The last time I saw you perform you sang the song "I Live Here Too." What was the impetus for this song?

Narissa: "I Live Here Too" is a political song. I have been banned from playing it at certain venues in Virginia. I wrote this song several years after coming out. Fred Phelps, a minister well-known for his hate messages against gays and lesbians, protested at the college in Kansas where I once worked. I was furious after I witnessed his group distributing hate literature there. I decided to channel my anger in creating this song.

LKB: I've always thought that you compose music and write songs like the best authors write, with an eye that sees all, even the seemingly banal, and describes what it sees with subtle yet evocative language. For me, also, there is a strong visual, almost painterly element in your music, too, almost as if you see the picture and then create a song for it. Do you think your background in art history and your professional experience as a graphic designer somehow translates sonically? Does there exist for you a relationship between the visual art world and your music? And, if so, how?

Narissa: I find that my studies in visual arts have enhanced my music and continue to do so, but I don't really have a process in using the two elements. The two just feed off of each other.

LKB: Before I get to my next question, I want to recite some verses from two of your songs that I am especially fond of. First, from "Woman in the Moon": "The sculptor casted in her plaster / Delicate, strong, and smooth / Then he placed her in the shop window / Like he was hanging the moon / She wasn't expensive / Not a one of a kind / But she is a masterpiece in my eyes." And from "Waitress": "I walk the steps to the non-smoking section / While our song plays on the radio / I see the chair where you sat the other day / I can still feel your presence / Well I don't have my mind on this / I've got my mind on you / Someone says, 'Waitress, take an order here.'" These are two of my favorite songs from your repertoire because the stories are so vivid, so accessible. In part this stems from your melodies, which reach out, gently take the listener by the hand, and lead them into the narrative tapestry you're weaving. The lyrics themselves are clear stories with a beginning, what writers refer to as "the arc" or denouement, and an end. Will you take me through your process for writing these songs, or, broadly speaking, a story song in general?

Narissa: I don't really have a process per se. These songs are pages from my life experiences. The experiences and the songs have a life of their own. "Woman in the Moon" is about a small piece of sculpture I bought in Eureka Springs, Arkansas. The artist was a man who sculpted such beautiful work. All of his subjects were women. I remember thinking after looking at the small piece I purchased that he was a man who truly loved and respected women. He was a very kind man and had a wonderful vibe. "Waitress" is a love song about a long-distance relationship.

LKB: I don't want to give the impression that you don't also get down and jam. Songs like "Knocking at the Doorway to My Soul" and "Rhythm" show the fullness of your spectrum. For you, does the songwriting process differ—do you feel you're writing from another place, a different place, when you pen a sexy groove as opposed to a ballad?

Narissa: Not really. After an idea comes to me, the song itself dictates what the tempo or groove will be. I have a song that will appear on my upcoming CD called "Play." It's an upbeat, jazzy song centering on overcoming past obstacles and moving forward.

LKB: I wonder if you would discuss the challenges you encounter working with two instruments simultaneously—your voice and the guitar.

Narissa: I think the only challenge has been time. I have worked
    with guitar and vocal coaches from time to time to learn new
    techniques and enhance my skills.

LKB: When you look back over the songs you have written over
    the last twenty years, how would you describe the evolution of
    your compositional style?

Narissa: I believe my songwriting is becoming more simplified and
    refined in its style.

LKB: What music are you listening to these days? Who are some of
    the artists who are inspiring you?

Narissa: I'm listening to Cassandra Wilson, Dianne Reeves, Janis
    Ian, Tracy Chapman, and singer-songwriters like Vance Gilbert,
    Erika Luckett, Brian Joseph, Susan Greenbaum, and many,
    many others that are just under the radar. There is an incred-
    ible husband and wife duo I met in Seattle named Hand to
    Mouth. Listen to them if you get the chance.

Ten

NINA SIMONE
(FEBRUARY 21, 1933–APRIL 21, 2003)

Classically trained pianist, singer, and songwriter Eunice Kathleen Waymon was born in Tryon, North Carolina, on February 21, 1933. The sixth of eight children and a child prodigy at the piano by the age of four, Simone's musical talent blossomed at the AME church where her mother was a minister and where Simone played piano and sang in the choir. With the help of her music teacher and local supporters who set up the Eunice Waymon Fund, Simone continued her musical education and studied classical piano at the Juilliard School of Music in New York, where she prepared for entrance into the Curtis Institute of Music in Philadelphia. When she was not accepted, Simone attributed her rejection to racism. By this time her family had moved from Tryon to Philadelphia, and to support them as well as to finance private music lessons, Simone worked as an accompanist. In the summer of 1954, Simone took a job at the Midtown Bar and Grill in Atlantic City, where she cultivated a fan base. By 1957 she had an agent, and in 1958 Simone's first album, *Jazz as Played in an Exclusive Side Street Club* (later known as *Little Girl Blue*) was issued on the independent label Bethlehem Records. The single "I Loves You Porgy," from *Porgy and Bess*, her only Top 20 hit, sold over a million copies. From the outset, however, it should be noted that charting Simone's recording career is a dubious undertaking, for while an "official" discography exists that credits the artist with thirty-five albums, numerous unauthorized or bootlegged recordings exist. Still, we can trace Simone's lawful recordings and group them into four periods according to record labels: Bethlehem (1957–1959), Colpix (1959–1964), Philips (1964–1967), and RCA (1967–1974). Following Simone's second album on Bethlehem, *Nina Simone and Her Friends* (1959), she signed with the national label Colpix (Columbia Pictures Records), who released nine albums, among them several important live ones, including *Nina Simone at Town Hall* (1959), *Nina Simone at the Village Gate* (1962) and *Nina Simone at Carnegie Hall* (1963). Simone briefly married Don Ross in 1958, and divorced him the next year. A second marriage to Andy Stroud, a former police detective who became her recording agent and with whom she had a daughter, Lisa Celeste, lasted from 1960 to 1970. In 1964 Simone left Colpix for the international Philips label, for whom she recorded seven albums, which included her well-known protest songs. Like Abbey Lincoln, who often traveled in Simone's circle of artist friends, including James Baldwin, Langston Hughes, and Lorraine Hansberry—significantly, all writers—Simone's musical repertoire shifted away from show tunes and ballads to original songs about America's racial problems. Often cited as the voice of the civil rights movement, Simone's album *Nina Simone in Concert* (1964) featured "Mississippi Goddam," written after the assassination of Medgar Evers in Mississippi (June 1963) and the bombing of a

Baptist church in Alabama that killed four black girls (September 1963). Although "Mississippi Goddam" was banned from radio, the artist continued to compose songs that expressed her feelings about racism and black pride; they include "Old Jim Crow" and "To Be Young, Gifted, and Black." The latter, composed with the keyboardist Weldon Irvine Jr., honored playwright Lorraine Hansberry (who was writing a play with the same title at the time of her death) and became an anthem for the growing Black Power movement. As a welcome departure from the frustration, tragedy, and injustice of the civil rights era, Simone also performed a plethora of songs that explicitly named sexual desire, such as "I Want a Little Sugar in My Bowl," "Gimme Some," "Chauffeur," "Take Care of Business," and "Don't Take All Night." Simone's recordings of sexual blues bear significance in that they draw on and expand upon the musical tradition of the early blues of the Jim Crow and great migration era. By revising old blues imagery and combining it with the social themes of her time, Simone represented a different kind of black female symbol—sexual, nurturant, authoritative, and committed to racial uplift. The era of the sixties also witnessed a physical transformation in Simone. One of the first artists to wear her hair natural, Simone rejected beehives and supper-club gowns, wearing instead short, natural hair, often cornrowed or braided, and African clothes—what she considered a symbolic representation of her racial pride. Her song "Four Women," in which she creates stark representations of black womanhood throughout American history by describing each woman's skin tone and hairstyle in relation to her objectification, reflected the exclusion of black women from dominant Eurocentric representations of beauty. Considered a jazz singer by many, Nina

Simone recorded in the blues, folk, soul, pop, and even spiritual idioms, often over the course of the same album. Describing her voice, music critic Adam Shatz wrote in the *Nation* (May 2003), "Simone had one of the most astonishing voices in postwar American music—impossibly deep yet unmistakably feminine, lacerating in its intensity yet also capable of disarming tenderness. To listen to her voice was to feel almost hijacked by its power." Simone's piano playing often revealed her talent for signifying upon the compositions of others. Nowhere is this more evident than in "Little Girl Blue," where Simone appropriates Broadway composers Rodgers and Hart's song, enhancing the piece by playing Bachlike riffs between her richly emotive phrasing. Nonvocal piano recordings such as "African Mailman," "Central Park Blues," "Good Bait," and "You'll Never Walk Alone" affirm Simone's astonishing virtuosity. In 1967 Simone was awarded the Female Jazz Singer of the Year award by the National Association of Television and Radio and became the first woman to win the Jazz Cultural Award. However, embittered by racism, Simone renounced the United States as her homeland in 1969 and would live, over the next two decades, in several countries including Barbados, Liberia, the United Kingdom, Switzerland, and the Netherlands. Embroiled in legal battles over music royalties and U.S. taxation laws during the seventies and early eighties, Simone's musical outpouring waned significantly. As a result, her discography of this time reflects scant recordings spread out across multiple labels, including CTI, Carrere, Hendring-Wadham, and Elektra. By the mideighties it seemed that Simone had drifted into obscurity. Her reputation as a difficult and tempestuous performer garnered her few invitations for performance. It wasn't until the fashion conglomerate Chanel adopted the single "My Baby Just Cares for Me" for a British commercial in 1987 that Simone regained her audience. A sold-out live performance at Ronnie Scott's in London in 1988, alongside many European dance-club disc jockeys' adoption of Simone's music, put the artist back in the spotlight. Joining a tradition of African-American artists such as Josephine Baker, Sidney Bechet, James Baldwin, Chester Himes, and Richard Wright, Simone adopted France as her home in 1991. That same year she published her autobiography *I Put a Spell on You*, and her music was featured in the film *Point of No Return*. Removed from the racial oppression and the struggle to forge her image on the cultural scene in the United States, Simone, like the black artists before her, experienced the freedom to explore new aesthetic and social perspectives in her music. In 1992 Verve Records released *Let It Be Me! Nina Simone at the Vine Street Bar and Grill in Hollywood*. On April 21, 2003, ten years after Elektra released her last album, *A Single Woman*, Nina Simone, recipient of honorary doctorates in music and humanities and composer of over five hundred songs, died at Carry-le-Rouet, France.

Selected Discography

The Amazing Nina Simone (Colpix)
Nina Simone with Strings (Colpix)
Folksy Nina/Nina with Strings (Colpix)
Nina Simone in Concert (Philips)
I Put a Spell on You (Philips)
Wild Is the Wind (Philips)
High Priestess of Soul (Philips)
Baltimore (CTI)

Fodder on My Wings (Carrere)

'Nuff Said (RCA Victor)

Nina Simone and Piano (RCA Victor)

Black Gold (RCA Victor)

It Is Finished (RCA Victor)

Nina Simone Sings Nina (Verve)

Let It Be Me (Verve)

A Single Woman (Elektra)

Nina Simone

LKB: In your autobiography, *I Put a Spell on You* (1991), you voice discomfort in being labeled a jazz singer.

Nina: That is because to most people *jazz* means "black," and jazz is uneducated, uninformed. There are those who think jazz is intuitive and simply improvisatory—as if improvisation could ever be simple. To improvise one must have a great understanding, a deep knowledge of the original form, you see? But there are those who think jazz is scatting and nonsense. Jazz is associated with drugs, alcohol, and degradation. I have always resented the label because jazz is not what I play or how I live. Duke Ellington resented the label also. So did Bessie Smith. I play black classical music, which I feel includes all of the forms I experiment with—the classical tradition, gospel, rhythm and blues, popular music.

LKB: In many music reviews written during the late 1950s, and after your single "I Loves You, Porgy" became a hit, you were often compared to Billie Holiday.

Nina: Yes! And I deeply resented it because the comparison had nothing to do with our musicianship and everything to do with the fact that we were both black. I have never been a drug addict. I am a classically trained pianist who was a prodigy on the piano at age four. I studied at Juilliard and would've gone on to the Curtis Institute, but racism barred me from there. I recall reading the comparisons of myself to Holiday and thinking a comparison to Maria Callas was more apt, but in American society a black woman's talents are never truly seen for what they are.

LKB: Why Maria Callas, Dr. Simone?

Nina: Because she studied her music more than anyone else in her generation. She was tempestuous and defied a lot of performance rules, and yet the world would listen simply because she was Maria Callas.

LKB: You speak of Callas's defiance; here I think you are addressing that, like you, she didn't suffer rude audience behavior.

Nina: It is true that I'm known for berating audiences. You have to understand, my original plan was to be the first black concert pianist—not a singer. I never thought that I would play to audiences that were talking and drinking and carrying on. There is a standard for those who attend art music concerts, you see? Even though I was never given the opportunity to play only classical music, I am determined that those who come to hear my music will listen. I demand perfection from myself and the audience. I practice very hard before I give a concert, often three to six hours. It you don't want to listen, stay the hell home. I've been saying this for years.

LKB: During your early performances you developed a unique approach by building a multigenre repertoire and bringing classical music to folk and popular music. How much of this approach was planned innovation?

Nina: I played a lot of Bach, Stravinsky, and gospel because that is
what I knew best. My mother was a Methodist minister, so I
simultaneously received gospel music training and private tute-
lage in classical music as a young girl. Some people in the town
where I grew up in North Carolina raised money so that I
could receive training from a superb Russian classical pianist.
To the classical and gospel that I played, I brought in folk, popular music, and what they call jazz standards. You see, I didn't
know a lot of popular music so I sang what I knew to fill up
the set lists. When I first started to perform in nightclubs, often
I had to play five or six hourlong sets. I'd play for forty-five
minutes and break for fifteen. Playing for that many hours
requires that you know a lot of music. Even if I had known a
great deal of popular music, I doubt that I would've played it
all night long. That's not who I am.

LKB: In the midsixties your repertoire began to reflect songs that
you had written. What inspired you to write music?

Nina: I have composed over five hundred songs, most of them
without words. I think you are speaking of the lyrics I wrote?

LKB: Yes.

Nina: Well, you know your history, so you know I had to write
because of what was happening here. I had to tell America
about herself. I still have to tell America about herself, which
is why when you come to one of my concerts I am still singing
"Mississippi Goddam," "Four Women," "Backlash Blues," and
"Old Jim Crow."

LKB: What is your message to America?

Nina: I don't like this country; I never did. America will sell her
soul for money. You see this everywhere, people selling

themselves, their mothers, brothers, and sisters for money. Black people don't get their due here. They kill all of the black leaders. How can anyone expect me to live in a country where, bang-bang, our leaders are shot dead. Black people won't ever get their due because they kill anyone who stands up for the rights of their people. I couldn't live here if I wanted to, because I have to stand up for my rights and those rights of black people everywhere. I'm sure they would find a way to silence me.

LKB: Can you talk to me a little about the songwriting process of some of the earlier songs you recorded, songs you mentioned earlier such as "Mississippi Goddam," "Four Women," and "Old Jim Crow."

Nina: When I heard about the bombing of the church in which the four little black girls were killed in Alabama, I shut myself up in a room and that song happened. Medgar Evers had been recently slain in Mississippi. At first I tried to make myself a gun.

LKB: Really?

Nina: Yes! I gathered some materials. I was going to take one of them out, and I didn't care who it was. Then Andy, my husband at that time, said to me—he said to me, "Nina, you can't kill anyone. You are a musician. Do what you do." When I sat down the whole sang happened. I never stopped writing until the thing was finished. What were the others you asked about?

LKB: "Four Women" and "Old Jim Crow."

Nina: Really, these songs are all saying the same thing. I am emphatically against the injustices of black people, of third world people. "Four Women" came to me after conversations

I had with black women. It seemed we were all suffering from self-hatred. We hated our complexions, our hair, our bodies. I realized we had been brainwashed into feeling this way about ourselves by some black men and many white people. I tried to speak to this in the song. And do you know, some black radio stations wouldn't play it? It is true what they say: the truth hurts.

LKB: Are there certain practices that you've employed over the years to care for your voice?

Nina: I never set out to become a singer, so I don't think much about singing. I am concerned—I am always concerned—with the message I am singing. If I am singing a protest song, it is crucial that the audience feel the way I feel. They have to understand the injustice that I am trying to name, you see. If I am singing something intimate, I want utter silence and I want an audience that I can see, so I know whom I'm singing to. I am very concerned with the perfection of my piano playing and articulating the song's message, but I don't worry about my voice.

LKB: You've lived in Barbados, Liberia, and several European countries, most notably France, where you currently make your home. How have these experiences informed your approach to the music?

Nina: In Barbados, I collaborated with a man, [Tony] McKay. I learned a lot about the musical culture from him. I also learned about African Caribbean spirituality. You see, I am a deeply spiritual person. This is reflected in my songs "Obeah Woman" and "Dambalah." When I got to Africa, I was so happy to be home I didn't perform live for some time—except for private play. I am always practicing for myself.

LKB: What made you happy about being in Africa, Dr. Simone?

Nina: I felt embraced by the people. Nobody demanded that I
performed. They didn't want me to play a concert so they
could make money off of me. I was just accepted for who I
am. I took my shoes off and walked in the dirt streets. I danced
with the new friends all around me. I was just happy. I wrote
about this in my song "Liberian Calypso," because my time in
Liberia was one of the few happy times I have known. But I
love my home in the south of France. It is very beautiful
there. I have a huge garden for bearing fruit in the winter:
strawberries, peaches, grapes, and things. The French people
have been good to me, so I sing and have recorded many
songs in French. I sing "Ne Me Quitte Pas" for them. Jacques
Brel is a master. It does me good to re-create the music of
masters. I only study the best.

LKB: I'm very familiar with "Ne Me Quitte Pas," it is one of my
favorites. You've also recorded African and Israeli folk tunes.

Nina: Yes, they all reflect who I am. I don't claim America as my
home. I am a citizen of the world—it's all my music. No other
black woman singer is doing that, that I know. No other popular black woman singer is addressing songs from other parts
of the world.

LKB: Actually, Dee Dee Bridgewater springs to mind.

Nina: And do they call her a jazz singer?

LKB: Many consider her a jazz singer. I think if you went into a
record store to look for her albums, you'd find them housed in
the jazz section, though she is much more of a cabaret artist, if
you ask me. And Abbey Lincoln, as you probably know, has also
recorded in French and Spanish.

Nina: Well, more musicians should do this—should experiment in
many forms.

LKB: Dr. Simone, what do you think of rap music?

Nina: It is another way that America has learned to sell us. Slavery
has never been abolished from this country's way of thinking.

LKB: It's interesting that you make an analogy between slavery and
the rap music industry.

Nina: Well, how the hell could I not?! I have been robbed by record
companies all of my life, so it is upsetting to hear about how
these youngsters are being paid to cuss us all! To cuss their
mothers, sisters, and lovers. It's damned pathetic.

LKB: But a lot of rap music is about protest. Many rap artists are
protesting the same things you protested in your music.

Nina: What they are doing is not musical. Yes, they are protesting
against racism in this country, but it's just a beat and some talk.
During the sixties, I was told that every SNCC group played
Nina Simone recordings. They played my music because they
knew where I was coming from, my message was the same as
theirs. They were inspired by it. Who is getting the message
from protest rap? Hardly anyone, it's just something to shake
your ass to. If the message of the music was taken seriously,
there would be more noticeable black political leaders. And
there would be a movement! Rappers have ruined music, as far
as I'm concerned.

LKB: Are you aware that several artists from the hip-hop gener-
ation revere you as a musical icon? Lauryn Hill, on the
Fugees' album *The Score*, likens herself to you in the song
"Ready or Not."

Nina: I've heard of her. If they are going to call my name and emulate me, they should acknowledge that I am a perfectionist. I work very hard to create music.

LKB: Are you inspired by any contemporary music?

Nina: No.

LKB: Where do you glean inspiration?

Nina: Nothing made in America inspires me now. I wish that a young black American leader would come along and lead his people out of darkness. That would inspire me.

LKB: Do you think there is a likelihood of that happening?

Nina: No, because black people don't know their history. Black parents don't tell their children who Dr. Martin Luther King Jr. really was. Who Malcolm X was. Who Lorraine Hansberry was—the author of the first black play to appear on Broadway, *A Raisin in the Sun.* Who Nelson Mandela is. Who I am. I don't know if you know this, but my song "To Be Young, Gifted, and Black" has been translated and performed in Chinese. I am known all over Asia, the Middle East, not to mention South Africa. If you have knowledge of what came before you, who walked before you, then you know who you are and what you can achieve. If you stand on the shoulders of giants, doesn't that make you a giant, too? You see, Hansberry, Langston Hughes, James Baldwin, they were my friends. They were my inspiration. They taught me about the black history I didn't know.

LKB: How do you feel knowing that much of your legacy includes the "angry" performer image?

Nina: Listen, I once believed that it was possible to change the race problem in the United States. I believed that it was possible for Jesse Jackson to become president. I don't believe that anymore. Many of the songs that I wrote in the sixties and seventies reflect those earlier beliefs. Now that I am older I realize I can't change the world, but I still believe that if anybody can, it is the artist. It is always through art that society changes—not politics or even education. Art, and music especially, speaks to people more than government and education. Why do you think great nations have patronage for their artists? It doesn't bother me that people call me angry. I have a right to be angry. If you're a black person and you're not angry, you're damned mad. Damned mad.

Eleven

NONA HENDRYX

(OCTOBER 9, 1944)

Nona Hendryx's fans know her as a third of the groundbreaking trio Labelle, a funk star, rhythm and blues solo artist, and a hard art-rock diva. The Trenton, New Jersey, homegirl rose to prominence while singing with Patti LaBelle and the Bluebelles, later the glam-funk band Labelle (with Patti LaBelle and Sarah Dash), where, beginning with the group's first album, *Moonshadow*, Hendryx was the primary songwriter. Nona's provocative, often political and empowering messages enabled Labelle to break the traditional girl-group mold. However, success did not come overnight. Although Labelle opened for the Who in 1971 and also collaborated with Laura Nyro on the album *Gonna Take a Miracle* in the same year, they were signed to many record labels, including Atlantic, Warner Brothers, and RCA, before her Epic Records 1974 critical success, *Nightbirds*. A year earlier, they played the Bottom Line in New York and foreshadowed their new image: they wore glittered outfits and gold and silver lamé space-suit costumes. Under the direction of Vicki Wickham, Labelle cultivated epic stage shows. Labelle was the only contemporary

black group to take their Wear Something Silver show to New
York's prestigious Metropolitan Opera House and to major the-
aters and opera houses across the world. Labelle racked up three
gold albums and a number-one worldwide hit with "Lady Marmalade (Voulez-Vous Coucher Avec Moi Ce Soir?)." In 1977
they broke up and each member went their solo way. Nona
Hendryx has always been on the cutting edge of music, proven
by the diverse and unconventional themes that abound in the
songs she has written and performed as a solo artist. From the
heavy metal *Nona* (1977) to the funk-based *Female Trouble* to the
New Age *SkinDiver*, she has made a career out of musical exper-
imentation. She has enjoyed several Top 10 hits, such as "Bustin'
Out," "Keep It Confidential," "Transformation," "Why Sould I
Cry?," "I Sweat (Goin' thru the Motions)," "Winds of Change,"
and several fruitful collaborations with the Artist (Prince), Material, Arthur Baker, Peter Gabriel, Dan Hartman, and Talking
Heads. Like several other artists featured in this collection, Nona
flexes her songwriting muscles in broader ways. She wrote the
music and lyrics for Charles Randolph-Wright's off-Broadway
musical play *Blue*. Beginning at the Arena Stage in Washington,
D.C., *Blue*, which starred Phylicia Rashad and Michael McElroy,
transferred to New York City's Roundabout Theatre, where it
sold out every night of its three-month run, breaking box office
records. The Randolph-Wright and Hendryx team are working
on a multimedia cyber-rock theatrical musical based on Nona's
SkinDiver CD. Nona has also been performing at summer festivals across Europe with the Daughters of Soul, a music project
featuring Lalah Hathaway, Indira Khan, Simone, Joyce Kennedy,
Caron Wheeler, and Sandra St. Victor. Hendryx is a Grammy

nominee for "Rock This House" (featuring Keith Richards of the Rolling Stones on guitar) and an Emmy nominee for her collaboration with Jason Miles on the composition "Children of the World," recorded by Sounds of Blackness for *People*, a Disney animated children's special. In 2004 Hendryx cofounded Rhythmbank Entertainment, a record label and multimedia company. Inducted into the Rhythm and Blues Foundation's Hall of Fame in 1999, the singer-songwriter and author of the children's book *Brownies* is based in New York City.

Selected Discography

Nona Hendryx (Epic)
Nona (RCA)
The Art of Defense (RCA)
The Heat (RCA)
Female Trouble (EMI)
Skindiver (Private Music)
You Have to Cry Sometime (with Billy Vera) (Shanachie)
Transformation: The Best of Nona Hendryx (Razor & Tie)
Rough and Tough (EMI)

Albums with Labelle

Labelle (Warner Bros.)
Moonshadow (Warner Bros.)
Pressure Cookin' (RCA)
Nightbirds (Epic)
Phoenix (Epic)
Chameleon (Epic)

Nona Hendryx

LKB: What is your earliest memory of music?

Nona: I have to think about that. I would imagine it is of my mother singing around the house, because she was always cooking and cleaning. And she was no stranger to her own voice. She had been raised in the church, my grandfather's church, and sang in the choir. My father actually sang in the AME church we attended when I was a child.

LKB: What was your mother's profession?

Nona: She was a full-time mother and later a domestic. You know, she comes from the South; she was of the generation that worked the fields. She and my father are both southerners, but she came from a sharecropping, a farming life, and my father was from a family of educators. His mother was a principal of a school and their family included many schoolteachers. My father, though, worked for the electric company, and he worked for the railroad. He didn't follow the path of the rest of his family to become an educator. He decided he didn't want to do that and his mother pampered him, which I think in retrospect might not have been a good thing to do. [*laughter*] He chose to become somewhat of a scoundrel and a scalawag. [*laughter*]

LKB: Those are strong words.

Nona: But he did. You know, he just sort of used people and shirked responsibility; and you know it's not like he was this awful person. He was absolutely loveable—great personality and all of that.

LKB: Um-hum. I know exactly what you're talking about. I have a father like that.

Nona: Yes, he used his charisma to just sort of float along. But he was from the white-collar side of the family—the generation of real evolution in terms of people of color coming into their own in this society.

LKB: With the emphasis on education on your father's side of the family, I'm wondering if this encouraged you to be a strong student.

Nona: Well, you know, I dropped out of high school. I was sixteen and it was during my senior year—just six months shy of graduation. You know, what happened was that Sarah Dash was aspiring to sing, and she was a part of a local group. Through a set of different circumstances, because Sarah went to a different high school in Trenton, she asked me if I wanted to sing with the group. I thought it sounded like fun, so I did.

LKB: Was there a moment of epiphany when you started to sing with the Del Capris that you had stumbled upon your calling?

Nona: No. It was just something fun to do. I thought of it like I thought of sports night at school. I was very athletic as a youth and used to play tennis, archery, all kinds of sports. Even though I had left high school my plan was still to attend college. We were a small local group—I think we played four clubs in New Jersey; one was where my brother bartended. So, no, I didn't think it would really go anywhere. It was just a fun thing to do, but Saundra Mingo, she really wanted to do this. So her mother found a manager in Philadelphia, the big city, and he showed an interest in us coming there so he could hear us. He was managing another group called the Odettes, which is the group Patti was in and Cyndi had also been a part of. It was a series of synchronicities, or fate, that we would wind up singing in a group together. Mr. Montague, our manager, knew Bobby Martin, who eventually became sort of the Philly international sound. He was the creator and the director of the band who played the music for this guy named Holly Robinson who had this huge car dealership, and he had a recording studio in the same building where the car dealership was. They had started a label called New Town Records and had signed a group from Chicago and recorded them, but that didn't work out. So they were looking for other girls to record. So Mr. Montague picked Sarah and me from our group—I guess he had also talked to Saundra who decided not to get involved—and Patti and Cyndi to form a new group. We met and liked each other and started recording for New Town Records.

LKB: At this point are you still thinking college?

Nona: Yes, I'm still on track for my plan to go to college and become a schoolteacher. It never entered my mind that this could lead to a career.

LKB: What was the response from your family around this time?

Nona: My mother was concerned. She was like, "What are you doing? You need to finish school. You need to go on with your education"—and stuff like that. My father didn't really talk about it. He really had his own issues. [laughter] He had seven kids to deal with and my mother as a wife. He had enough! It was mainly my mother who was the voice of reason and the voice of wisdom in my life. She was truly a matriarch who took care of her family.

LKB: And how was the first record received?

Nona: The record was successful. I don't know if anyone thought

it was going to be, but it was. Now, just months after I decided
to do this, my mother had to sign these papers, we had to have
a chaperone, and the next thing I knew we were performing
on all of these local television shows, and then we landed the
national show, *Bandstand*. Still, it was not in my head that
singing was a way to earn a living for myself. I decided to finish
my high school education so I signed up with something
called the American School, I don't know if it still exists, but it
was a way to get your education away from school—a corre-
spondence program. I had this mentor from my junior high
school period, Mrs. Dinkins, who was our former mayor's
mother, and when I went to high school she transferred to the
same high school to teach English. In her classes I fell in love
with poetry, which was a real passion of mine that sort of
evolved into an unspoken dream to become a poet-writer.
Mrs. Dinkins saw a writing talent in me and nurtured it. She
got me involved in public speaking and the theater. I didn't
realize all of this, but my sister recently gave me a copy of
my picture from the yearbook—because I had taken the senior
picture and everything before dropping out—and it listed all
of the activities I was a part of—the debate team, theater,
which I had totally forgotten. Mrs. Dinkins helped me a lot
and used to talk to me about college possibilities. She was
involved in organizations like Jack and Jill—

LKB: The Links.

Nona: Yes, exactly right. You know what I'm talking about. She was
that *kind* of woman. I would talk to her about my music stuff
and she encouraged me to explore it, but education for her was
of the utmost importance. It didn't really hit me that singing

was something I could do for a career for several years and I think that's because I wasn't the lead singer. And I had never really dreamed that I could be this singer up onstage. My desire was to teach history. Music was not a real passion for me until I discovered songwriting.

LKB: When did you write your first song?

Nona: I wrote my first song about six years after first performing with the Bluebelles. So, that was 1966, '67.

LKB: Weren't you the only one writing songs in the Bluebelles?

Nona: Yes. And we only recorded one song that I wrote. I don't know whether I would've carried on if it hadn't been for something that happened one night while we were playing the Howard Theater. Curtis Mayfield and the Impressions were on the show and Curtis's younger brother—I can't remember his name—looked at some lyrics that I had written. Curtis was writing, too, at that time. I don't know where I got the nerve to show Curtis my song, because I didn't have any musical theory background or any training—I could only compose in terms of melody and ear, but I did get up the courage. Curtis liked what I had written and said, "That's a good song," and helped me to develop the song. I needed that experience to turn the key to the fact that melody and lyric could be wed together in a way that it could become a voice for me.

LKB: When you were performing with Labelle did it occur to you all that you were beating new paths, that you were making history? Certainly you helped pave the way for groups like En Vogue, SWV, Destiny's Child.

Nona: When we were Labelle it was all about exploration. It wasn't really about creating something that would break a mold or reset a mold. I think some of the inklings of that were there, but I think that was more from Vicki's visions in terms of directing us. The idea that we were creating something new was not what we were about. The music we were making we identified with because it was about the times, what we were living in, and that's what was important to us. We weren't trying to set ourselves apart. Having traveled through the South and experienced discrimination, having lived during the time of active civil rights struggle, knowing Black Panthers, all of that stuff brought an organic influence to the music we were making. And because we were able to sing about all of these things in a way that belied a confluence of gospel, R&B, rock, blues, you know, all of those things, well, it was just natural for us to do that. I'm sure to the outside world it looked like, What is that?! [*laughter*] What is that?! What are they doing? And I know because my mother said to me—we had done a television show and at that time I had basically shaved my head— my mother, she was gentle with her statement, but she said, 'Baby, next time you go on television will you *please* put on some hair?' [*laughter*]

LKB: I want to fast-forward now to your solo career. Was the main attraction in performing as a solo artist the fact that you could write more songs and record them?

Nona: Music has always been sort of leading me. That's my feeling about it. I bring no set expectations or demands to music; I make myself available for what's in the air.

LKB: May I stop you there, because this interests me. I want to press you further on the comment you just made because many artists have expressed a similar sentiment. The idea that you see yourself as a vessel or as a a conduit of the music is a thread that connects many of these interviews, no matter what genre the artist is working in. For someone who has aspirations on becoming a singer-songwriter, what does it entail to make oneself "available for what's in the air"?

Nona: Well, my immediate response to that is either you are a singer-songwriter and it is the intention for your life, or you aren't. Just having the desire to do so does not mean that that is the intention for your life, so therefore, what that means to me is that you learn to avail yourself in order to be used once you have accepted the calling—either consciously or unconsciously. In other words, I believe I was meant to listen and hear the music. I'm a transcriber, basically, of musical information. And I had really no other choice but to do this, because this is what was given to me when I was created. So to say to someone who has a desire to do this—and I speak to many aspiring artists—the work you do in a sense is not a chosen work but a vocation. You come to it because you're prepared for it in some way. When I say I make myself available to what is in the air, I mean that is my sensitivity; I'm a sensitive observer. That's why some people are nurses and doctors; they have that sensitivity to healing and caregiving. Why would I stop in the middle of something and write a song—like "Winds of Change," which I wrote while reading Winnie Mandela's book. My immediate response to that which moves me is to write a song, or a poem that will often become a song.

LKB: When writing a song, Nona, what generally comes first, the poem or lyric or the music?

Nona: Both come together. Rarely do they come apart. When a song comes, I try to write it down immediately, but it's the nature of my life that sometimes I'm somewhere—like walking down the street—and I can't write it down immediately. I believe, though, that if a song is meant to have a life then it will come back again. It may come back in another way, or there will be this memory and not like a memory in a conscious way but a familiarity is present, so that when I'm in a space where I can listen, the song just comes.

LKB: Does your process ever include the sit-down-and-write without particular inspiration?

Nona: I've tried that but it's really not my way. I can develop some things that way but I think the things that stay are usually come fully born, fully formed in terms of topic or theme.

LKB: So a song like "Winds of Change" didn't come one verse at a time, over time, it was all there?

Nona: Specifically "Winds of Change." I wrote that song in thirty minutes. After reading the book it was just there. I was home with my piano so I could just sit down and write what that book did to me. I started it and couldn't stop. I would say that the majority of what I have written on my own has come that way.

LKB: Besides talking to wonderfully talented and brilliant people, the major boon of this work is that I have the chance to inquire about the inspiration behind my personal favorite songs. When I was growing my ears up as a child—

Nona: Growing your ears up? [*laughter*] I like that.

LKB: Well, that's what it was all about for me. Listening to as much music and as varied as possible in order to develop my own musical taste. Anyway, around this time your song "Why Should I Cry?" was floating on all the airwaves in Chicago, but I'd like to talk to you about some other, perhaps lesser-known, songs you wrote, such as "Women Who Fly," "Nightbirds," "You Turn Me On," and "Leaving Here Today," for all of which you wrote both the music and the lyrics, correct?

Nona: Yes. And I would say that all of the songs that you listed were given to me like "Winds of Change." They all sort of had a magical spontaneity.

LKB: What inspired "Leaving Here Today"?

Nona: Well, that's sort of a mourning prayer. I'm a huge fan of science fiction and I drew from that when writing that song. In the song, I'm looking for someplace in the future where a lot of the things that plague us as a people won't be an issue anymore. I'm searching for a time when we can reach a different place as a people. When I wrote that song I was at a point in my life where I really needed to go forward, because you know it's very easy to get mired in what has been created by people who may not be thinking or living on a higher vibration. We get caught up in the sort of day-to-day treadmill and the things that are posited as important, which really aren't at all, and before you know it you've forgotten where you were headed. So that's what that song is about.

LKB: "Women Who Fly."

Nona: Again, that song touches on not getting stuck in other people's ideologies. Not believing you are limited or bound to what others say is "female."

LKB: "Women who fly have wings of their own. . . ."

Nona: Yes, no one's giving them wings.

LKB: So wings are a metaphor for beliefs, thoughts, opinions, self-perception?

Nona: Yes. You don't have to settle. Here I'm warning against limiting yourself.

LKB: Who are you talking to in the song?

Nona: I was talking to myself. You know *SkinDiver*, that album is a topographic musical of my insides. Because I believe we live these dual lives. There's who I am and who I *am*. And, who I *am* was pretty much in "SkinDiver." "Women Who Fly" is an internal struggle with myself.

LKB: "Nightbirds."

Nona: That's really about being an artist. You know, we live in the night. For many, many years I didn't leave my apartment before 4:00 P.M. I had no idea what people were doing during the morning hours. This was a life during that whole disco club period. I was a club bunny—I just discovered a picture yesterday of me, Grace Jones, and Divine and some other people at Studio 54 for Grace Jones's birthday party. And I'm looking at the picture and I said to Vicki, "Is *that* me?" I mean, I was a nightbird. I lived in the night. I still am very much a nightbird. It's very difficult for me to go to sleep before 2:00 A.M. It's something about the night—maybe it's because the world is quieter. And there are no nightbirds—birds don't fly at night, but you do if you're an artist, metaphorically speaking.

LKB: How do you care for your voice, Nona?

Nona: I avoid dairy. Rest. I never eat quite a few hours before singing. I find a full stomach not conducive to singing. I'm careful about what I eat and what I drink. The other things, complications like a sore throat or losing your voice, well, for that I've tried every remedy known to mankind, but other than voice lessons, strengthening, and me being conscious of where in my body I'm singing from, there's nothing else I focus on in terms of voice care.

LKB: Recently, I interviewed Phylicia Rashad, who had very nice things to say about the music you wrote for Charles Randolph-Wright's musical play *Blue*. I wonder if you would talk about the process of composing for a play, because I assume it was very different from your usual way of coming to a song and developing it.

Nona: Well, Charles is like my little brother, and part of his mission has been to get me to write music for the theater. Writing this music was really difficult for me because I don't like musical theater. I mean, there are great musicals like *South Pacific*, but vicissitude singing drives me absolutely bananas! The whole idea of people breaking into song and dance after talking, I just can't take it. Then, too, since the early days when I studied with Mrs. Dinkins I've been much more interested in dramatic theater. The structure of *Blue*, though, resonated with my background, my preference for dramatic theater because it isn't a musical in the sense of a traditional musical. It's a play with music in it—more in the vein of something like *Tommy* the rock opera as opposed to *Oklahoma!* Charles gave me a lot of freedom. He'd hand me the script and say, "Okay, now, what do you see? What do you hear?" And actually I was able to write the whole song in one sitting, as I have with the songs we've talked about today. It happened with the song "No Matter," from *Blue*, for instance. In some cases, Charles said to me, "I need a song like this or that," and then I'd see what I could come up with in that direction. But even then I didn't sit down and just try to write the song. I let the idea germinate, and then when inspiration came I wrote the song.

LKB: So my assumption was wrong, then, because it sounds as though your process is the same even though there's some collaboration on the song's theme.

Nona: Yes, because writing any other way just isn't natural for me. Sometimes people will send me a track to write lyrics and melody to, and that I can do because the melody and lyric are all one cloth.

LKB: Are there any artists whom you would like to write for or collaborate with?

Nona: There are people I'd like to write with because their track record, their musical legacies are inspirational or meaningful to me. Like, a while back I was going to do some writing with Dylan and that was exciting for me because I really love his writing. But what excites me about a possibility like that is not so much the writing together. I look at it as getting in the ring with another artist, but not competitively speaking.

LKB: I get that. You're talking about creative sparring. The act of throwing ideas at each other where each time the idea gets stronger and better.

Nona: Yes. It's like cross-pollinating. However, I don't sit around and think things like, "I want to write a song for Mary J. Blige." When I signed the publishing contract at one point, however, there was that element present. I can't approach writing that way. I just can't do it.

LKB: Nona, if I looked in your CD changer right now, who would I find?

Nona: Tupac. I listen to Tupac often.

LKB: You enjoy hip-hop music?

Nona: I love the way Tupac and Snoop deliver. With Snoop, it's not
so much the content of the music but his phrasing. I did like
quite a bit of what Tupac had to say, but again it was his
delivery that hooked me. With hip-hop music in general I try
not to get hung up on the sometimes degrading or derogatory
aspects of the lyrics because that's where they come from in
their lives. Until they reach a certain point and become more
conscious, that's just the truth about what they're dealing with
and the level they're dealing on. So, you'll find Tupac, Hendrix,
Ella Fitzgerald, Shirley Horn. Oh, I just love Shirley Horn's
style of singing. For me, she epitomizes "less is more." You'll
also find Duke Ellington, the master of orchestration and composition, and Holst's *Planets*. I love classical music.

LKB: What was the impetus for the 2004 launch of your own label,
Rhythmbank Entertainment?

Nona: I wanted to create a label that nurtured artists the way labels
once nurtured artists, labels like A&M and Atlantic, where
artists really had the support and environment to grow into
their own. My partner, who was financing the label, didn't
really understand the kind of vision I had for the label.

LKB: That's because nurturing an artist is unheard-of today. It's all
about making "the hit," and if you can't or won't then they'll
put you out to pasture.

Nona: Yes, you got it, but in the tradition of John Hammond, I'm
interested in finding *real* artists—people for whom music is a
vocation, music is all that they were put here to do. I'm not
interested in the person who's in it just to get paid or for the

perceived glamour of show business. And I think we've been successful at acquiring real artists. David Ryan Harris is extremely talented. Najiyah, who's an eleven-year-old gospel singer, is gifted. I don't know how anyone at that age would have that kind of ability if they weren't gifted. I listen to her and I hear Mahalia Jackson and Ella. Our young band Some Velvet Morning—they're real music aficionados. Dez, who is the group's main songwriter, is a very talented writer and that is what struck me the most about them. And I'm continuing on my mission in terms of supporting real new artists on my own terms.

Twelve
ODETTA
(DECEMBER 31, 1930)

Odetta Holmes Felious Gordon was born in Birmingham, Alabama, and grew up in Los Angeles. Though her singing voice was discovered at church and school around the age of ten, Odetta first began classical training at Los Angeles City College when she was thirteen. A remarkable talent was noted by vocal coaches early on, but Odetta's training was interrupted when her mother could no longer pay for lessons. When she was nineteen, Odetta performed in a summer production of *Finian's Rainbow* at the Greek Theatre in Los Angeles. The following summer she again performed in summerstock in California. Aound this time, the singer "fell in with an enthusiastic group of young balladeers" and became aware of a growing local folk music scene. With Baby (the singer's nickname for her first wood-bodied guitar) in tow, Odetta made her solo debut in San Francisco in 1949. Working as a live-in housekeeper, Odetta found her way into the folk music scene in the early 1950s, winning audiences at the famed Hungry I and the Tin Angel in San Francisco, and at the Blue Angel in New York City, where her appearances caused Pete Seeger and Harry Belafonte to become champions of her remarkable talent. Odetta recorded her first album, appropriately titled *Tin Angel*, in 1954, and subsequently cut many albums, including two vastly influential live LPs in the 1960s, *Odetta at Carnegie Hall* and *Odetta at Town Hall*, followed by the studio album *Odetta Sings Dylan*—the first completely dedicated to his songs. By the late 1950s, she had starred at Carnegie Hall and appeared in film and national television. Dubbed the Queen of American Folk Music by Martin Luther King Jr. in 1961 and the "Mother Goddess of Folk/Blues" by the *New York Times* in 1999, Odetta is undoubtedly one of the most influential artists of the twentieth century, with countless artists indebted to her pioneering ways. Before Odetta, no solo woman performer singing blues, folk, and work and protest songs had recorded or toured. A staunch human rights activist, she sang for the masses at the 1963 march on Washington; took part in the march on Selma, and performed for President Kennedy and his cabinet on the nationally televised civil rights special "Dinner with the President." She also participated in the 1983 march on Washington. In 1994, she was appointed an "elder" to the International Women's Conference in Beijing. In 1999, President Clinton presented her with the National Medal of Arts and Humanities. In addition to acting in films and theater, Odetta has sung with symphony orchestras and in operas; hosted the Montreux Jazz Festival; and starred in countless TV specials. Her 2000 album, *Blues Everywhere I Go*, earned a Grammy nomination, and the subsequent album, *Looking for a Home*, was nominated for two 2002 W. C. Handy Awards. 2004 saw Odetta nominated for another W. C. Handy Award, as Best

Traditional Female Blues Artist of the Year. She's a recipient of both the International Folk Alliance and World Folk Music Association's Lifetime Achievement awards and a holder of honorary doctorates from Bennett College, Johnson C. Smith University, and Colby College. In a stunning fifty-eight-year career, Odetta has recorded twenty-seven albums. The 2007 Grammy nominee for the album *Gonna Let It Shine* (M.C. Records) lives in New York City.

Selected Discography
Odetta at the Gate of Horn (Empire Musicwerks)
Ballad for Americans and Other American Ballads (Universe)
Odetta at Town Hall (Vanguard Records)
Sometimes I Feel Like Cryin' (RCA)
Odetta Sings Folk Songs (RCA)
It's a Mighty World (RCA)
Odetta Sings of Many Things (RCA)
Odetta Sings Dylan (RCA)
The Essential Odetta (Vanguard Records)
One Grain of Sand (Vanguard Records)
Living with the Blues (Vanguard Records)
Odetta (Verve)
Odetta at the Best of Harlem (Four Leaf Clover)
Movin' It On (M.C. Records)
Blues Everywhere I Go (M.C. Records)
Looking for a Home (M.C. Records)
Women in (E)motion (Tradition & Moderne)
Odetta (Silverwolf)
Gonna Let It Shine (M.C. Records)

Odetta

LKB: What is your first memory of music?

Odetta: I must've been around five, because this memory is while we lived in Alabama, and we moved to Los Angeles when I was six. I had gone to some blues show with my aunt, and when I returned to the house, I remember my grandmother, whom I was very close to, asking me to sing a song. There were several adults sitting around the kitchen table and they put me on top of the table, where I belted out one of the blues numbers I'd heard with my aunt.

LKB: I've read in numerous bios that as a youth you were trained and being groomed for an operatic career. How, then, did you become interested in the folk music world?

Odetta: Well, you know, through my life I have noticed that when you start getting interested in something, guides come to you who, as it turns out, are interested in those same things and who will give you directions to this song or that book. So when I returned to Los Angeles after having performed in *Finian's Rainbow* in San Francisco—I was around nineteen then—I borrowed a guitar and starting hanging out with people around this music. A lady who was going to play the guitar had a child and a husband whom she found required all of her time, so she loaned me her guitar that was strung with really heavy wire for these tender little fingers of mine, and she showed me the chords C, G, and F. Other people would show me chords and the rest of it was self-defense, because my guitar ended up being a very interesting rhythm guitar, but I knew I was not a guitarist. I mean, I heard some *real* guitar playing so I didn't delude myself into thinking I was a real guitarist.

During this time I was a live-in housekeeper in Los Angeles. After I finished my work I would be in my room practicing the guitar and I would call a friend of mine, Jane, who was studying dance at Horton Studio. Do you know about Lester Horton?

LKB: No.

Odetta: He was a man who taught us blacks and Hispanics ballet. We knew that we could not study or perform with the Ballets Russes or whatever, but he was committed to teaching those who loved dance. Every older black dancer/choreographer that we now know came through Lester Horton's school. I'm talking about people like Carmen DeLavallade and Geoffrey Holder. Anyway, so Jane would be in from her class and I would call her and play my chords for her and sing a song. Now, in folk music, with three chords you could sing at least a hundred songs. [*laughter*]

LKB: [*laughter*] Right.

Odetta: Then you take the little capo and put it on a bar, change the key . . . another hundred songs, honey.

LKB and Odetta: [*laughter*]

Odetta: Speaking of guides and angels, that was around the time that I was meeting more and more people in the folk community who were taking around petitions to save Ethel and Julius Rosenberg. So my interest in folk music has always been around my interest in—

LKB: Social justice.

Odetta: Yes. Social problems and fixing stuff. Recently, one of the things that I've started sharing with audiences is that I'm a retarded person. That's what I figure, because after a while

you're supposed to get the picture. When you're a kid, you
look for what's fair, right?

LKB: Yes.

Odetta: All right, then. But after a while . . . well . . .

LKB: You become jaded. You lower your expectations.

Odetta: You're supposed to get the point that change comes slow
or not at all, right? And you're to know better than to
whine: "That's not fair. That's not fair." Well, here I still am
saying "That's not fair" and working on making it fair and
right through my music. So I say I'm just a retarded child,
that's all there is to it.

LKB: Or you're the eternal optimist. You maintain hope.

Odetta: That has a better sound to it. [*laughter*]

LKB: Odetta, your first album, the 1954 *Tin Angel*, and several subsequent albums coincided with key events in the struggle for
civil rights such as the Supreme Court decision on Brown vs.
the Board of Ed., the murder of Emmett Till, the Montgomery
Bus Boycott, and the "Little Rock Nine." I'm wondering if
you could speak more about the influence the civil rights
movement had on you as you were forging a career in the
music business?

Odetta: It's a wondrous thing, this time period that you speak of.
In the country, things were really coming to a boil. Those who
were interested in the injustices and getting things fixed
became aware of Odetta and her folk songs. So they would
invite her to perform for them whether it was a demonstration
or amassing monies for—you're not old enough to know
about mimeographing, but there was a need to raise money for
mimeographing to get materials out there. Those who were

putting things together were aware of my work. And I talked a lot—that's no surprise to you—between songs because I was so absolutely fascinated by the things that I was learning and I felt more people needed to know about the things of pertinent value to American life—all American lives. There was a period in my early career when I needed to learn what to say and what to leave out, but I felt I had to say a lot because our schools certainly weren't teaching us anything about ourselves. We didn't know the stock or the people we descended from and nothing of the cleverness, the vision, the will it took for our ancestors to get over, under, through, or around. Well, as momentum really started lighting up, that's when folks started hearing about me. I certainly wasn't on the radio. My feeling has been, and I've said this for years, that if I was white, looked like a dog, and had only a fraction of what I have going on I would've been out there! Really out there! I believe, though, that the civil rights movement gave me my career, it certainly made it viable for folks to see me. There was no other way a black girl singing folk songs about injustice during that time period was ever going to gain an audience.

LKB: Every singer wants to make an album like *Live at the Gate of Horn*, which spans time and any fad our society has been taken with. What is the secret, Odetta? How do you cull from the many, many songs available to you to put together an album as magical, as uplifting and thoughtful as *Gate of Horn*?

Odetta: Well, actually I was inspired by grief and loss. Around that time there was a deep sadness there—everywhere in the nation, but because music was being done it wasn't all doom and gloom. The very possibility that something that beautiful could come out of the misery we were living taught me something very fundamental about music and art in general—it is insistent on living and life!

LKB: Writing in the liner notes for your album *My Eyes Have Seen* [1959], Harry Belafonte opined: "Few possess that fine understanding of a song's meaning, which transforms it from a melody into a dramatic experience. Odetta, who has influenced me greatly in this area of dramatic interpretation, is just such an artist." Why is dramatic interpretation something you have strived to achieve during song performance?

Odetta: I'll start out by saying that I hid in my music. Nobody knew me 'cause I didn't know myself. I'm still trying to meet up with me. I got into dramatic interpretation because I was a young person who hated the situation that was mine. I hated myself. I was fat and I was black and I hated everybody else. There was such resentment in my life. During performance I always wore something long to make myself gender-neutral. When I sang the "Prison Song," I became the prisoner. When I went into that state, I got my rocks off and dealt with my anger. After a while, that particular area of music finally healed me.

LKB: So it really wasn't a matter of you reaching for dramatic—

Odetta: I wasn't reaching for nothing. It just *was*. I don't even know if I had sense enough to know that I could do it. Those prison work songs were the first things—"John Henry," matter of fact—they were the songs that got me to get up and walk out of my door. I hadn't sung for a while. Somebody requested it and I sang it and was very unhappy with it. I felt I couldn't act it. I had tried my best to act out the emotions of that song, but felt I couldn't.

LKB: That reminds me of an interview I heard between you and
  Steve Inskeep on NPR in 2005. In the interview, you said that
  you learned about phrasing listening to Alberta Hunter.

Odetta: What I learned from Alberta Hunter was how to leave a
  song alone. When my generation really started to listen to the
  women blues singers of the twenties, thirties, and forties, we
  heard and felt energy. So, in response to that energy, the way
  we approached those songs was to holler!

LKB and Odetta: [*laughter*]

Odetta: We thought that energy came from hollering. Ms. Hunter
  would just lean back and throw it out at you. She left you
  alone to take it wherever you felt you were big enough and
  bad enough to take it.

LKB: As you know, many singer-songwriters cite you as the primary influence on their careers; I'm speaking of people like
  Joan Armatrading, Joan Baez, Pete Seeger, Bob Dylan, but with
  the exception of someone like Elizabeth Cotten, who is little-
  known to nonmusicians, no woman of color had ever cultivated a national following singing folk music. When you began
  recording in the folk tradition, who did you look to?

Odetta: Well, first let me say that I loved Libba Cotten—just
  absolutely adored her. I'm so glad that someone from your
  generation knows about her. And in terms of who I learned
  from . . . well now, I listened to a lot of recordings from Folkways records and the Library of Congress. I had and still have
  many of those records. I listened to men and women. It was
  what I received from those singers that informed for me where
  it was possible to go. It wasn't like listening to somebody and
  trying to phrase like them. My ego was much too big for

that. Matter of fact, I had a voice teacher who looked at her student—me—who was this young big black girl and decided she was going to create another Marian Anderson, who is a hero of mine. Well, even in my dumb days I knew that I didn't want to be another Somebody. So, I was listening to those Folkways records for textures. If we consider a song a recipe, let's call what the singer brings to the song the spices they use. When I went to that bowl to make the recipe I pulled a little of that spice from here and a little of that spice from there. So it was a matter of choosing what affected me, allowing that to inform me and reaching as far as I could go with it.

LKB: I like your metaphor, Odetta. A good cook's recipe can't be duplicated just the same as an extraordinary vocalist's sound can't be replicated.

Odetta: That's right.

LKB: I'm very intrigued by your admiration for and connection to Leadbelly. You've recorded an entire album of his music, *I'm Looking for a Home*, as well as the singles "Take This Hammer" and "Midnight Special." Plus which, many music critics and writers have given you the appellation "the female Leadbelly." What speaks to you about Leadbelly's work?

Odetta: I wish I knew. I was in Los Angeles while he was here in New York and he died before I got here. So I never witnessed the man. That's something I really would've loved to have experienced—to hear that magnificent twelve-string guitar and his singing. Well, there are some people you meet and with no prior history you just click. There is some quality in Lead-belly that just goes to the soul of me. I can't really say what it is. I suppose if we could put words to those areas of response, those areas that hold for us such significant feeling, we would say the words, then dissect them, and then we'd mess that up, too. So I can appreciate the fact that there is no way for me to really describe everything that I feel when I listen to Leadbelly.

LKB: I know exactly what you mean. There is a way in which music is a fugitive spirit, it's very hard to capture in words, to fully articulate what it is about an artist or artist's work that draws us so intimately near. One of the reasons that I wanted to do this book is because while working on my music dissertation I became fascinated with the artist's process but the scholarly writing, as fulfilling as it can be, didn't satisfy my desire to learn more from the artists themselves. I struggled with balancing the artist's commentary on her own work and the scholar's theoretical claims to that work.

Odetta: Well, I think both sides are important. The response to the music and then finding out what the artist was thinking and feeling and also what inspired the song in the first place, these are all important vantage points. I wonder, LaShonda, with the interviews you've collected so far if there have been similarities between the artists.

LKB: So far I have interviewed over twenty artists and I am struck by the fact that everybody received her calling to the music at a young age—I'm talking younger than ten years old. In some cases, the artist pursued other careers as a matter of course, but even in these cases those careers didn't work out in a short amount of time and she ended up making music. It is a striking similarity.

Odetta: It's like we came to the planet with an assignment, huh?

LKB: Yes! And I am inspired and awed by the courage and conviction of all artists, but especially those who pursue their creative impulses when the stakes are particularly high. It's more than a notion to commit oneself to creative endeavors when you're not wealthy and bills have to be paid and health insurance secured.

Odetta: You're right and you know, it's getting harder and harder. When we were coming along, we didn't have to display our belly buttons. [*laughter*]

LKB: [*laughter*] Right.

Odetta: When we were coming along there was still a work ethic. They've changed the language on us! The government has put foxes in place to guard the henhouses. Henhouses being us—the public—and foxes being oil companies or record companies, if you know what I mean. The whole country has gotten rather loose, a lot of integrity has been lost and so the youngsters coming along today have to meet that. And how do you successfully battle that with dignity? I just know there are some really gracious and glorious ones out there trying to get somebody to listen to them, but who are aren't getting the attention they deserve because they won't play by today's music industry rules. We could all be missing out on the best voice ever. I would say that the ones you've been talking to, we are the very lucky ones. We've been blessed—even if some of us only touched success for a minute.

LKB: Odetta, I know you have recorded a few of the songs you've written. When did you first begin to write songs? And could you share with me a little about your process?

Odetta: As a matter of fact, I'm very shy about writing songs. There have been songs that have insisted on coming through me. I adore the honesty that I've heard in some of Joni Mitchell's early songs, where it's clear she had some kind of a worry or a problem and wrote it in a poem or song and got rid of it. Now, I mentioned before that I hide in my music, so I'm afraid if I write somebody will see and discover something about me that I don't know about me. And I, of course, want to be in control. As a result, I haven't written many songs. I had a book of songs in my guitar case that was stolen at LaGuardia airport many years ago. I never did go back to those songs. I remember a few of them, though. I'd written a song about Winnie the Pooh—I just adore Winnie the Pooh—a song called "Hit or Miss," and a Christmas song called "Beautiful Star."

LKB: I really like your song "Keep on Movin' It On." What inspired that one?

Odetta: That song grew out of the conversational greeting we extend to each other in the black community. I just wanted to celebrate that—celebrate the ways that blacks so often embrace each other and how even a stranger can build you up when they give you the kind of greeting that tells you to keep on keepin' on or keep on movin' it on. I guess that's all. I don't know, girl, don't you be asking me no hard questions. [laughter]

LKB: Odetta, I've read in a few places that you don't listen to your recordings. Is this true?

Odetta: Yes. My ex-husband once said to me, "Odetta, maybe you should listen to some of the things that you've done. You may have stopped performing songs that you'd now like to put back into your repertoire." I said, "Oh, that's a great idea." I listened to one-half of one record and that was enough for me. I don't even remember most of the albums I've made.

LKB: I wonder if you would discuss the challenges you encounter working with two instruments simultaneously—your voice and the guitar.

Odetta: With the voice and the guitar going simultaneously, you set up your own pace, your own pulse, and I find that it makes all the difference. You can really make a song your own when you accompany yourself on an instrument. If you have the time, I'd like to tell you a story about Richie Havens.

LKB: Of course.

Odetta: I went to the Village many years ago and I went to a coffeehouse where Richie Havens was playing. After seeing Richie I went to Albert Guzman, my manager at that point—a man who built his business on my back and I never benefited from it, but anyway I told Guzman he should go listen to Richie. Albert did go listen to him but then turned Richie over to his partner, John Cort. Well, John Cort was interested in jazz. They signed Richie, went into the recording studio, and Richie sang with a jazz band. When I heard the record, I went storming into Albert's office and said to him, "You didn't get that his *specialness* is that his voice and that guitar are one? That together his voice and guitar set up that special pulse? And even if you didn't get that, why not let Richie set up that pulse so that the jazz musicians would know where to go?" They just didn't get it.

LKB: You no longer accompany yourself in live performance, so I'm wondering if your approach to a song has changed somewhat.

Odetta: Since I am working with a pianist now, I find that I can concentrate more fully on the lyric. I am able to better portray who that person is in the song and what they're going through, and I'm loving it!

Thirteen
OLETA ADAMS
(UNDISCLOSED)

Born the daughter of a preacher and homemaker in Seattle, Washington, where she was the youngest of three girls and two boys, Oleta Adams first demonstrated her vocal gifts in the church where her father served as minister. When Adams was eleven, her family moved to Yakima, Washington, an idyllic Pacific Northwest town of sixty thousand. An accomplished pianist at age eleven, Oleta directed and accompanied four church choirs. However, the church was not the only musical outlet for young Adams. She credits her further musical development in junior high school to Lee Farrell, "the brilliant Juilliard-trained teacher and voice coach who changed my life." In her senior year Oleta broke barriers and traditions as the star of *Hello Dolly!* Declining a scholarship to Pacific Lutheran University, and along with it the chance to pursue an operatic career as a lyric soprano, Oleta instead spent a summer in Europe before heading south to Los Angeles in the early 1970s. Five thousand dollars and a demo tape later, she discovered "that the disco movement had deafened music executives." With the help of coach Lee Farrell, she wound up in Kansas City, where she launched her career playing piano bars, hotel lounges, and show-rooms. Oleta quickly became a local institution, with her own bill-board and a regular gig at the Hyatt Regency Hotel. Oleta's recording career began in the early 1980s with two self-financed albums, which had limited success. In 1985 she was discovered by Roland Orzabal and Curt Smith, founders of the famous English pop band Tears For Fears while performing in a Kansas City, Missouri, bar. They invited her to join their band as a singer for their album *The Seeds of Love*. The album appeared in 1989 and the single "Woman in Chains," a duet by Adams and Orzabal featuring Phil Collins on drums, became her first hit. Oleta launched her solo career in 1990 with her debut album *Circle of One*. The platinum album received much critical acclaim, topping UK music charts and the U.S. Top 20. Adams scored her biggest hit to date in 1991 with her cover of Brenda Russell's "Get Here." However, 1991 also saw Oleta contribute to the Elton John/Bernie Taupin tribute album *Two Rooms*, on which appeared her version of John's 1974 hit "Don't Let the Sun Go Down on Me." Her next album, *Evolution*, was also a commercial success. Oleta's 1995 release *Moving On* reversed the trend of smooth balladry to funky, up-tempo, dance-oriented numbers. During live performances in this phase of her career, Oleta moved away from the pop feel of her earlier shows toward the direction of R&B. For many R&B fans, Adams's sumptuous contralto voice became the vanguard in the R&B jazz segment largely vacant during Anita Baker's hiatus. Two years later she released the Christian-themed, Grammy-nominated *Come Walk with Me* (1997). In October 2006 Oleta released her first Christmas album, titled *Christmas Time with Oleta*. A longtime resident of Kansas City, Kansas, where she and her husband, John

Cushon (the drummer for Adams's band) have found sanctuary from the turmoil of the entertainment industry, Oleta's current album-in-progress showcases original prayer songs.

Selected discography
Circle of One (Fontana Island)
Evolution (Mercury/Universal)
Moving On (Polygram Records)
All the Love (BMG International)
The Very Best of Oleta Adams (Fontana Island)

Oleta Adams

LKB: In my background research on you, I ran across a couple of different dates of birth for you, but I couldn't find any dependable source that provides your birth date.

Oleta: [*laughter*] I know. That's on purpose. I really try not to divulge that. And the reason is because as soon as we find out how old someone is our minds trigger certain things. That is, we immediately begin to make certain assumptions about who that person is. And I firmly believe in the case of singers you listen in a different way. This way, if you're ageless, you just do what you do and people like you for that.

LKB: Where were you born?

Oleta: Seattle.

LKB: And you moved to Yakima when you were eleven?

Oleta: Yes.

LKB: Can you talk to me about some of your earliest musical influences?

Oleta: I'm a church girl. So those influences would have been

James Cleveland and the Cleveland Singers, Inez Andrews, and Shirley Caesar. That was from the church world. Obviously Aretha Franklin and Gladys Knight, but not many black artists made it to the radio in Yakima, where I was growing up. Matter of fact, in our household we listened to a lot of country-and-western music because that is what came in most clearly on the radio. Then, as I got into high school I was turned on to other music, like Barbra Streisand. I loved Barbra Streisand. And Cleo Laine. I got a chance to work with her last year at the Hollywood Bowl.

LKB: I saw Cleo Laine—I won't ever forget this because I was supposed to see her on September 11, 2001, but of course because of the World Trade Center attacks her show at the Regency in New York City was canceled. So a couple of months later, after being blown away by her performance—this ties into the comment you made earlier about age—I remember going to the Internet to find out her age. I couldn't believe that she was seventy-three or seventy-four, and that's a testament to the care she has obviously given her instrument. Her range is still incredible.

Oleta: You know what she said to me? She told me her age or made a comment about it, and then she said, "I've spread since my younger years, but for some reason age has not affected my voice." She still sounds amazing. You know, there are certain people that you really want to meet, and to perform with her was just an amazing experience for me.

LKB: How old were you when you began to study piano?

Oleta: I started taking lessons when I was about nine years old. Gracie Young was my first teacher.

LKB: You had a piano in the home?

Oleta: Yes, but not at first. My first lessons were not on a piano. You know what I had? I had one of these things that had piano keys on it—

LKB: Like a photocopy of the keyboard folded into sections.

Oleta: Exactly.

LKB: That's also what I had when I took my earliest piano lessons.

Oleta: Well, I used that and *John Thompson's Teaching Little Fingers to Play* books, and when I got to Gracie's basement I played on the real piano. But it was a full year before we got a piano in the house. Finally they got me a little spinet piano. I practiced as much as I could until Daddy got home. 'Cause then he'd say, "Let my y'ears rest. Let my y'ears rest." But later, when I got a little older, although he couldn't play chords, he would pick out melodies on the black keys to comfort me. I had menstrual cramps really bad when I was in school, so bad I often had to miss school. Dad, not really understanding what I was going through, would try to calm me down by playing "Jesus Keep Me Near the Cross" and some other songs. I never talked to him about that before he passed, but those were some really tender, tender moments. My daddy was a complex man, but I was a daddy's girl. My dad, who was my great-uncle actually [*pause*]—black people got a lot of them stories, you know—he was like a black Archie Bunker in every respect. My biological father, who is still living, is very famous in the black Christian world.

LKB: Archie Bunker was a misguided bigot. You said your dad was a minister.

Oleta: Oh, girl, please. He was from the country, too. I mean, he had reasons for feeling and thinking the way he did. "Trust no white man," he'd say. And when you brought white folks into our house, my people were very skeptical—very. I mean, they came from a different world. The things that they saw—horrid things that we don't even know about. And the things they lived through. These days they talk about people abusing their children because they spank them? My mama was put in a gunnysack in the smoking shed and smoked as a punishment for talking out of turn. A visitor had previously come to the house two weeks in a row—with two different women. The second time he came, Mama said, "Oh Mister So-and-So, that ain't the same woman you brought last week." And for that she was hung up and smoked like a piece of meat!

LKB: What did your parents do for a living?

Oleta: My father was a Baptist minister, and my mother was a preacher's wife, and she sang in the choir. Mom was a person who really loved words. She loved the lyrics in music. Remember that song—no, you're too young. You're far too young. There was a song called "If I Can Help." [*singing*] "If your baby needs a daddy, I can help. It would sure do me good to do you good, let me help." It was a bluesy-country kinda thing. And Mama really liked that song. Since I was a piano player, I would focus on the music of a song, so I was listening to the chords thinking, that ain't *that* cool. And I asked her, "Mama, how come you like that song so much?" She said, "It's the words."

LKB: Perhaps subconsciously that influenced you to consider songwriting even then.

Oleta: Completely. Words are key. So that's how I write songs. I write lyrics first. The story is most important for me. However, when you listen to someone like Ella Fitzgerald, you don't focus on the words. You hear and you focus on the melody, because she was an instrument. She was simply an instrument. Sarah Vaughan, too—words often got lost with her. I was actually pointed toward that direction by my vocal coach in high school since I had the same kind of vocal quality as she. But if you focus on the musical aspect of the song you're singing, that means you'll always have to do those vocal acrobatics because that's the main thing the audience expects. I focus on the lyric and the mood because I want the audience to become addicted to a feeling. What I want to say is, this is how I think you feel in this situation, and then I'm going to portray that with the words, and the music helps evoke the mood. But focusing on the words, as a listener you'll say she understands. She must've been there in my house when I experienced that. The recognition of that is going to pull you in so much because I understood your pain. And what do we do when we have a girlfriend or boyfriend who understands exactly what we were feeling when we were feeling it? The next time you get into trouble you call up that same friend and say, "Let me tell you what I'm going through." 'Cause you want to experience that again. So there's a way in which the audience becomes addicted to your thing because you lived it out, you enacted their situation through song on the stage. There's something very cathartic about that, both for the performer and the listener. You know, when we're feeling bad most people first want to feel worse.

LKB: Yes. I put on the saddest music when I'm down.

Oleta: Exactly. That's because you want to deal with it. You don't want to escape it. And that's what I feel my role is as a song-writer. I want to find a solution to the problem, but first I want the listener to know I understand. You can't just do that with music. If you want to float on top of an emotion you might turn to instrumental music—the saxophone or, say, one of Miles Davis's beautiful ballads. But it doesn't really help you deal with it, it just tells you there's a real problem. I like to use the lyric to state just what you were feeling—either find it in someone else's words or write my own and put the melody to it that helps to express that emotion. For me, though, the lyric always comes first, which is why I don't write a lot of songs. You have to have something to say.

LKB: What is your songwriting process like?

Oleta: If I'm going through something hard, sometimes in order to get over it I have to write about it. And other times, when things are really good, I'm not writing, which is why I don't have many albums. I get in that place often, when I'm just feeling really good. It's not a super-high, it's just a nice com-fortable place. However, there's always a voice saying, "You need to write some music." Rarely have I written songs about being at that super-high place, though. I only write about that kind of exuberant joy if I am experiencing it for the first time in a certain area of my life, because then I feel it warrants artic-ulation. My song "All the Love" was one of those times. I remember when I was rehearsing that at a sound check for the Turner Awards and the gospel singer Donnie McClurkin asked me, "Now is that a sacred song or a secular song?" For me, I do not separate. How can I? If I'm Christian then it is my skin, my bones; it's everything. So how could I possibly separate the sacred from the secular?

LKB: Some of the songwriters I've interviewed have lamented the difficulty of the songwriting process. More often this is not because the artist is in search of perfection but because of the deep reverence they have for songs themselves. I am wondering what your thoughts are regarding the ease or difficulty with which you write.

Oleta: Songwriting is often a daunting process for me. Since we allow music into our most sacred places, we have to be careful about what we say because people wear this music, they breathe it. It's an incredible responsibility.

LKB: What was the first song you wrote?

Oleta: I wrote an Easter cantata when I was very, very young. But another song that I do remember writing with sort of pop-ish lyrics was "Goodbye to a Friend." [*singing*] "Here I go again making the same mistake / Loving someone else's friend / Guess I'll never learn / Finding love striking out / Wondering what game I'm in / Can't live with you or without you."

LKB: I have all of your albums and I don't recall this song. Which album is this on?

Oleta: Oh, this is on the *first* album that I made locally in Kansas City called *Going on Record.* I did a benefit concert for the Women's Center of Exchange in 1983 and instead of being paid for it, I got a record out of it.

LKB: Is your songwriting process different when writing gospel music?

Oleta: I don't write gospel music traditionally. Right now I am writing a prayer album—it's meant to help people learn how to pray. So the words that I use necessarily have to be in line with the concept of praying. I have a few traditional worshipful prayers, like "Oh Lamb of God, which taketh away the sin of the world" . . . but then there are those prayers that a woman will have for her husband who dun' messed up. Now that has a little more poignancy and urgency. That's not going to be one of those sweet little chant numbers. There are many ways to pray. One way to pray is with the Bible. Sometimes we say what the psalmist said, like—

LKB: A personal favorite: "I will lift up mine eyes to the hills from whence cometh my help. My help cometh from the Lord who hath made heaven and earth."

Oleta: Exactly. You know, sometimes you get to a point in your life where you can't pray. Things can really get bad and you can lose your faith. It's a very sad place to be. That's why for tonight's show, I'm including a little preview. I'm going to do the prayer that I wrote from a mother's perspective, about her son. I performed it at a women's conference a couple of months ago and I had a woman come backstage and say, "My son just went off to college and your song is exactly how I feel. Thank you for saying that for me." I believe that musicians and poets are supposed to find ways to help the audience express themselves.

LKB: Oleta, if not music, what other career path might you have taken?

Oleta: I don't know what I would've done, probably teach. I probably would have taught music. I love doing what I'm doing. I've never done anything else. I have not waited tables or sold shoes or anything else—since I was eleven. When I was eleven

I played for four choirs in Dad's church. I was making twenty-five dollars a month.

LKB: How do you practice voice care?

Oleta: It becomes more and more difficult to hit some of those high notes. My voice is lowering. It only does what it can do. My husband will yell out sometimes, when we're watching people sing on television or listening to people's records, "Give the melody a try! [*laughter*] Give the melody a try!" When I first started out in the clubs, one night somebody requested "The Way We Were." When I finished that song you didn't know what it was. [*laughter*] Later on that night my mentor said, "You know, when people ask you for a well-known song like 'The Way We Were,' they want to recognize the song." One of the lessons for me there was not to abuse my voice, to let it do what it naturally wants to do. The other lesson, of course, was about doing the kind of improvisation which can render a song totally unrecognizable.

LKB: What do you say in a case like Betty Carter, though, who could not only get away with deconstructing a well-known song and making it something altogether different, but was a master at it.

Oleta: But then the audience gets used to that and then that means you have to do that for the rest of your life. What if you're not feeling that right then? At one point will you become honest and not hide behind vocal acrobatics or a gimmick? See, that's entertaining. And I'm not saying that there is anything wrong with that, but the thing is . . . that's not going to help me when I'm feeling down. Now, I don't want everybody to feel down, but the fact is that most people experience lows and they come out to your show with an expectation that you will lift them up. And you know, sometimes it's not even that people are feeling bad, they're just not feeling. I think it's my role to put you in touch with emotions and I really don't see how getting lost in vocal acrobatics can do that for the listening audience.

LKB: Before I ask you the inspiration behind some of your original songs, I'd like to know what attracts you to the songs of others. For instance, you've recorded songs by another songwriter included in this book, Brenda Russell. What attracted you to the songs "We Will Meet Again" and "Get Here"?

Oleta: "Get Here" suited my voice very well. I was in a dress shop in Norway when I heard it for the first time. I had sung many of Brenda's songs before, so I recognized her voice immediately. I stopped whatever it was that I was doing, listened, and thought, *Oh, I have got to find that.* My boyfriend at the time—who is my husband now—he was back home in America and he had heard it and sent me the tape with a note that said: "Check the new Brenda Russell out, especially 'Get Here.'" When I got back to the States we started playing it in the show every night. And we would place it later and later in the set so we could do variations on it in the key of B flat, which meant sometimes the song lasted ten, fifteen, twenty minutes. It was the same with "We Will Meet Again." When Roland Orzabal of Tears for Fears, who produced my first record, asked me what I wanted to sing I didn't hesitate before I said "Get Here." As I've said before, I'm really interested in the lyric, the story of the song. Brenda writes really good stories. If I have nothing to offer a song, though, I won't touch it. I have to be able to find room in a song to express myself, to make the song mine. I told Roberta Flack when she interviewed me on her radio show a number of years ago that as far as I was concerned they never needed to touch "Killing Me Softly." It was not broken. And she said, "Oh no, girl. I loved it! I just loved it! It needed to be done."

LKB: By saying, "It needed to be done," it sounds as though she is glad that the song was revised in a more contemporary musical form so that a younger, a different listening generation could relate to it, which is what Lauryn Hill's hip-hop version succeeded in doing.

Oleta: I'm sure, but I still think that with a classic like "Killing Me Softly" you don't have to touch it.

LKB: You mentioned Roland Orzabal of Tears for Fears, I have read that he is the reason you were signed to Universal.

Oleta: Yes, I had recorded with the group and he went to the label and said, "When our record comes out Oleta's going to get a lot of offers. You'd be smart to be the first one." Of course A&R commented, "But how do we market her?" And Roland said, "Just let her sing." You see, this is what a lot of record companies want to do—they want to mold you. But I was already middle-aged when this was happening. I was already grown and knew what I was about musically. So I was not about to be molded by a record company just to secure their idea of success. Furthermore, Roland was able to get across to them that I was versatile enough to sing with a British pop-rock group and sing jazz and gospel.

LKB: On your first commercially released album, *Circle of One*, you

penned five of the nine songs, including the title track, which
I would like to know the inspiration behind.

Oleta: When I first signed with the record company, they sent me
out to L.A. to write with this group of songwriters, including
some that are still writing today—ones that write with Brenda.
I found L.A. a very difficult place to be in. I was very lonely
and I felt that a lot of what the industry folk did made me feel
even smaller. I thought I was going out there to make music in
a circle of friends, but I found myself in a circle of one. So
while I was there feeling horrible and writing on my own,
Circle of One came about.

LKB: Tell me about the song that begins "Restless days of feeling
insecure makes it even harder to endure / There's a way that
you can make me smile / But only if you hold me for
while." I remember living in Shawnee Mission with my
lover at that time and when "Hold Me for Awhile" was first
played for me, I thought, *Now, there's a person with some true
understanding.* That was over ten years ago, Oleta, and I'm still
playing that song.

Oleta: You know what's funny about that? [*laughter*] I lived in
Shawnee during that time. That's too much. I wrote "Hold Me
for Awhile" in Kansas City a long, long time ago. We used to
play that in the clubs. And one of the principals from my husband John's school in Kansas City, he used to come in with his
lady friend and request that song again and again when I was
playing at the Alameda. "Hold Me for Awhile." [*long pause*]
Well, I'll tell you. What I found was that holding someone
without speaking was more intimate than sex. Listening to
each other breathe is very intimate. Anybody can be full of bull

and try to talk to you in a way—try to tell you what they think you want to hear to calm you or seduce you. And it's so easy to hide during lovemaking, which so many people confuse with love. Sleeping with somebody doesn't mean that you love them or that you even actually enjoy being with them. But to actually have someone hold you . . . to have time to smell each other, to listen to each other's heart beat and no words are being said . . . it's just intimate. Sometimes words get in the way. Sometimes they get in the air and they cover over what really needs to be communicated. I'm talking about just holding someone, letting them know you truly appreciate who they are. And I'm not talking about while the television's on or falling asleep during the holding. In the song, I'm talking about the healing that comes with holding someone. Mothers do it with babies, you know, that's our introduction to comfort—being held by our mamas. When you're a kid and you're afraid and Daddy holds you, the fear dissipates. This is what we're used to, so why do we stop it when we get older?

LKB: From your album *All the Love*, what inspired the song "Bump in the Road"?

Oleta: Well, with that song we had actually gone through a bump in the road in our marriage. And when we hit one of those I think our first reaction is to throw up both hands and say, "I don't want this at all." You know, we've become a fast-food society, a disposable society, so if things don't work—get another one. This has become our nature. With that song I was working out for myself, I was learning the difference in a love with no maturity and a love with maturity. I think when you've been blessed with the latter you can discern a big ol' mountain you can't get over from a bump in the road, but being able to do that depends on how deep your well is. How much you're able to give and *forgive*. I wrote a song called "Act of Forgiveness" along these same lines, but I haven't recorded it yet.

LKB: "My Heart Won't Lie."

Oleta: Whew . . .

LKB: I know a couple of folks who left marriages behind that song.

Oleta: Yeah, me too. Well, on a personal level for me this song had to deal with making up my mind about which marriage I was going to commit to. Because the man that people expected me to marry . . . I don't know if you have friends like this, friends who say to you, "You're so educated and you're so this, you need this kind of man." And I actually tried to really feel something for this other guy, the one who was good on paper. We tried and it just did not work. But the other one that I had been running from for years—because some folks thought he just was not worthy—that's the one that I really wanted. And in the end my heart just wouldn't lie. That song is very, very personal for me. I love that song because writing it helped me to decide that I was going to follow my heart because the heart don't lie. Wherever you are going to love the most—

LKB: Is really where you should be, because that is where you get your lessons, and your greatest rewards.

Oleta: That's right.

LKB: "Window of Hope."

Oleta: I wrote that song after reading an article in the newspaper about a teenage black girl who had leukemia. You know that the bone marrow bank for black people is minuscule compared

to other banks because it just isn't promoted or ever really
discussed in our communities. Plus which, it's a major opera-
tion to take the marrow from the bone and it's a very painful
procedure to donate bone marrow. Anyway, the young cancer
patient used to draw pictures of what was going on outside of
her hospital window and one of the pictures she drew was of
a tree bearing few leaves because it was winter. The nurses
called the picture "The Window of Hope." When I read this in
the newspaper I was inspired to write the song. And you know,
years later I met the young girl's parents? I met them at a
convention. Unfortunately, she died, but her parents were so
appreciative of the song.

LKB: I read that you were interested in writing for a Broadway
musical. Is this still a goal of yours?

Oleta: Yes, I said that in an interview some time ago, but I have
since decided that's it's not important for me to write a
musical. Actually, LaShonda, I'm not a really ambitious person.
I love what I do. I love performing live. I only make records so
I can keep working, so I can earn the invitation to perform live
at some venue. Even though I don't see myself doing this
forever—there are so many other things to doand we are
getting increasingly involved in the ministry at our church—I
do think that performing live is the meaning behind my life.

Fourteen
PAMELA MEANS
(JUNE 14, 1969)

Brooklyn-based independent artist Pamela Means believes strongly in not looking far afield for songwriting inspiration but keeping the practice close to home, drawing on her own experiences: "As the adoptive daughter of a white mother and black father, I learned about dismantling systems of oppression from the inside out." A native of Milwaukee, Means studied at the Wisconsin Conservatory of Music before moving to Boston, where she gained exposure on the highly competitive New England folk scene. Pamela Means is known for her politically charged lyrics embedded in complex rhythm guitar, of which fellow artist Ani DiFranco commented, "You've got such a deep, deep groove, I can't get out, and I wouldn't want to." Once landing in Boston, Means hit the ground running, racking up gigs at top listening rooms in Massachusetts like Club Passim and the Iron Horse. Nevertheless, it wasn't until 2000 that Means's performance schedule began to reflect her wide appeal. Promoting her fifth self-released album, *Single Bullet Theory*, which San Francisco's *Bay Area Reporter* reviewed as "one of the best musical summations of our current political situation," the artist's 2003 summer tour took her nationwide and also included a few international dates. A classical and jazz-trained guitarist, Means recently shifted her focus away from the folk idiom toward jazz. "It all started when I saw a [John] Coltrane documentary," Means says, "highlighting his lifelong obsession, like every serious jazz musician, to master his or her instrument. I decided to bring jazz back to the foreground and nurture that part of me as well, along with the folk singer." The artist's sixth recording, *Pamela Means Jazz Project, Vol. 1* finds the artist paying homage to the first ladies of jazz: Billie, Ella, Sarah, and Dinah, and features Pamela Means and her Gretsch, flying solo or fronting an upright bass duo or trio with drums. The natural timbre and tone of Means's voice fits the medium perfectly, breathing new life into timeless jazz standards. Pamela Means maintains a busy touring schedule, touring coast to coast and internationally. She performs over 150 shows a year at clubs, coffeehouses, colleges, and festivals both across the country and internationally, most notably at the Newport Folk Festival, Falcon Ridge Folk Festival, South by Southwest Folk Conference, Jazz Café Alto in Amsterdam, Stockholm Pride in Sweden, and Woodford Folk Festival in Brisbane, Australia. Pamela is also a favorite at innumerable regional Gay Pride events, Take Back the Night rallies, and Black History Month celebrations. Pamela has shared the stage with artists including Ani DiFranco, Joan Baez, Neil Young, Shawn Colvin, Richie Havens, Patty Larkin, Melissa Ferrick, the Violent Femmes, Pete Seeger, Janis Ian, and Holly Near. Means's music honors include being named Falcon Ridge Folk Festival's number-one Most Wanted New Artist, Outmusic's 2004 Outstanding New Recording award and both Wisconsin's Folk Artist of the Year and Female Vocalist of the Year awards. She has also been a Boston Music Award nominee (Outstanding Contemporary Folk Artist). Recently, the *New York Times Magazine* commented that Means's "stark, defiant songs" set the status quo and the stage afire.

Selected Discography
Bone Spurs (out of print)
Cobblestones (Phylorra Music/BMI)
Pearls (Phylorra Music/BMI)
Single Bullet Theory (Wirl Records)

Pamela Means
LKB: I was reading somewhere about your unusual background.

Pamela: I was adopted at three months by a biracial couple, but I looked for my birth mother a few years ago and she was found. Over the years, I would start the search many times and not finish. My partner, who is Alix Olson, has been encouraging me since 2003 to complete the search. My mother was found in Georgia but she declined to meet me. However, all of my records were released to me, like the transcripts of the interviews she gave at the time of my birth. I was born in a home for unwed mothers. Basically I was given up because I was mixed, but I was also adopted specifically because I was mixed.

LKB: For the most part, you grew up in Milwaukee, correct?

Pamela: Yes, and its suburbs. When my parents separated I moved with Mom to the suburbs and that was really difficult for me because it was an all-white suburb and I was the only kid of color in the school that I attended. So I had to put up with a lot. To make matters worse, I was attending a Lutheran school

and heard quite often about how homosexuals were going to
hell—this to a child who was already experiencing serious
crushes on girls when I was in the fifth grade. Later on, I
worked through a lot of this stuff in my music.

LKB: As you were growing up, were you thinking about becoming
a musician?

Pamela: I thought of becoming a foreign-language interpreter
even though I really loved music. At the Lutheran school I
attended and even later at the public schools I went to, I had
discovered a real love for Romance languages. I studied both
French and Spanish. And today, I have a desire to learn and
perform songs in other languages.

LKB: I know that one of the reasons that you moved to Boston,
which is where you broke into the folk music scene, is because
you were very inspired by Tracy Chapman. Who are some of
the other artists that you looked to as models professionally?

Pamela: Suzanne Vega and the Indigo Girls.

LKB: Thousands of people land in new cities with the dream of
making their living by their music and gaining a devoted following, but for many people it doesn't turn out this way. How
does a singer-songwriter new to a city break into the local
music scene? Once you landed in Boston, how did you get
started?

Pamela: A singer-songwriter breaks into the scene by getting at the
back of the line and going to all of the open mics, and that is
exactly what I did. I played in the subway. I got a job doing
sound and hosting the open mic at Kendall Café. That was
really great because I got a chance to meet a lot of good musicians. I also put out an album [*Bone Spurs*] as soon as I got

there, so I would have a product to sell no matter where I played. I was picked up by Goldenrod and Ladyslipper distribution, which helped a lot. And, when all of that did not provide enough to sustain me, I worked temp jobs. I really dreaded the idea of dressing up and working a nine-to-five, but my first temp position was with a law firm run by lesbians so I reevaluated and thought, "Well, maybe I *can* temp." [*laughter*] I also answered telephones at Harvard Divinity School, and they eventually hired me as a casual employee. So, if I said I had to gig on the road for a month they were very cool about it, they let me go.

LKB: So while working you slowly cultivated a fan base—

Pamela: I'm still slowly cultivating a fan base [*laughter*].

LKB: You played places like the famous Cambridge folk listening room Club Passim?

Pamela: Well, it took one year before I had my own gig there. At first I did open mics there. Then, after they went through the transition of being operated by the married couple who ran the place for over twenty years to being a nonprofit organization, I volunteered to do sound there. I was there quite a bit. I eventually got to do a gig there. My first gig there was a "reverse guarantee," where you have to guarantee the club. I had to guarantee fourteen hundred dollars to the club and if not enough people came I would have to pay them to make sure they made that amount. Luckily for me, enough people showed up.

LKB: Is the reverse-guarantee practice common among listening rooms?

Pamela: It's common for the club to keep a percentage, but Passim keeps a higher percentage than usual. Usually between 10 to 20 percent goes to the club; Passim keeps 35 to 40 percent.

LKB: When did you first begin to write songs?

Pamela: I started writing at a very young age, but those were crappy little songs full of clichés and usually with a "baby, baby" refrain somewhere in there. I think I was probably around the age of twelve when I started to write, but I was really, really shy. I couldn't sing in front of anybody. Music has always been a part of my life. I remember playing my Mickey Mouse toy drum set when I was three. It was a cool set. [*laughter*] And then, when I was about eight years old I got a hand-me-down toy guitar. It only had four strings on it and I didn't know you could restring it, so I played it with four. Then one broke and I played it with three. I remember playing that guitar with a broken pick and three little strings.

LKB and Pamela: [*laughter*]

Pamela: I played rock star in my room for years. Also during adolescence is when I started cultivating my own musical taste. Prior to that time I heard the B. B. King records that were my father's and I had stumbled across some of my older brother's Elvis Presley 45s, but when I turned thirteen and got my first stereo, I really started listening heavily to the radio so I heard a lot of eighties pop, groups like Wham, Culture Club. In tenth grade my classmate and I would skip class to go steal Boy George pictures out of the teen magazines at the convenience store. [*laughter*] When I was fourteen I borrowed my brother's guitar and took beginning guitar lessons at the YWCA in Milwaukee. But I had to give it back to him shortly thereafter so

I was without a guitar for a while. Then my mother died during the spring of my fourteenth year, and when I turned fifteen that June, I got a guitar for my birthday. For the next three years I taught myself how to play, and then I started at the Wisconsin Conservatory when I was eighteen.

LKB: You have to audition to be accepted into the conservatory, right?

Pamela: If you want scholarships you do, and I needed scholarships, so I auditioned even though I was primarily self-taught, and I won a few of them. One semester, I auditioned for a scholarship and didn't get it. Since I couldn't afford the tuition, I was preparing to drop out when the bursar's office called and said there had been an anonymous donation and I could continue. I still don't know where it came from. The classical guitar, the jazz, even though it was way over my head at the time, everything I do is still based from what I learned there. Another thing that happened around this time, though, is that I started working at a record store because I really wanted to surround myself with music and learn as much as I could. I also started frequenting used-album stores. I remember thinking on one of my first trips, "I'm gonna pick up a Joni Mitchell album to see what all the fuss is about." I bought *Court and Spark* and went home.

LKB: "People's Parties." "The Same Situation," "Car on a Hill," "Down to You."

Pamela: [*laughter*] You know it. You're listing all of the songs.

LKB: It was released the year I was born, 1974, so I came to it after you, in the midnineties. And yet it resonated with me as powerfully, I would bet, as it did with you in the eighties and the audiences who heard it a decade before you when it first came out. Her writing is timeless. I love that album. It is definitely one of my favorites.

Pamela: What other ones do you like?

LKB: I'm crazy about *For the Roses*, and *Mingus* is special, too. I also really like *Ladies of the Canyon*. You know, I should stop singling out her albums because I really like so much of what she's done.

Pamela: Well, of course I fell in love with her the first night I opened up and listened to that *Court and Spark* album. I remember reading along with her lyrics and I was just floored. Floored. She really inspired me to start looking into other singer-songwriters. So, I picked up Tracy Chapman, Bob Dylan, Patty Griffin, people like that.

LKB: I thought maybe you'd list another one of my favorites, Lucinda Williams.

Pamela: I remember working in the record store when her "Passionate Kisses" came out. I didn't like that song and I wasn't inspired to listen to that album, and I haven't picked up any of her subsequent ones.

LKB: It's interesting how as listeners we sometimes don't give artists a second or even multiple chances when exposing ourselves to new stuff. I'm always shocked when I'm talking about music with my friends and I ask them if they've heard so-and-so's new album and they tell me no because the album they had years ago left them cold. My response is always like, "Yeah, but that was five albums ago." Sometimes people don't go back—

Pamela: You're right about that, LaShonda. Often, you don't get a second chance to win a listener. I worry about that a little bit now with the jazz record I just released. I mean, who really follows jazz but jazzheads. Last night at Café Vivaldi, I had a huge cross-section—young women in their twenties; one old couple in their seventies stayed until after 11:00 P.M. But I'm aware that this is because I live and play in New York City. I don't think audiences as varied as this would be into following an indie artist who's doing jazz, especially if they've not heard of me. Most people will only go to see a live show of someone they've never heard of once—maybe twice. I think about this all of the time.

LKB: What inspires you, Pamela?

Pamela: Great songwriters, and I want to be one of those. So that means I have really high standards for what I produce and also for what pleases me to listen to.

LKB: What was the impetus for the Pamela Means Jazz Project?

Pamela: I was in Northampton, Massachusetts, at the time, feeling very restless. I was thinking about and looking for ways that would help me keep growing as a musician. Then I thought I should experiment with playing more jazz, because I felt like grown-ups play jazz. I wanted to become a strong enough musician to play jazz. I've never been satisfied with the strum-strum, C, F, G, just-get-by type of guitar playing that many folk artists manage to build careers with. I wanted to be a real musician. And yet, despite that I had real reservations about playing jazz. I was at the Michigan Womyn's Music Festival and talked to Tret Fure about it. I said to her, "I have this real fantasy of pulling together my own jazz trio." And she said, "You can do that." I guess I needed to hear that. I went home after that festival and started teaching myself a bunch of jazz songs—I took on thirteen songs that summer and at first the process was painstakingly slow, but it got better. Then I arranged for a gig at this place in Northampton called the Basement, which is about as big as this room.

LKB: Pamela, what can you accomplish, performance-wise, during an acoustic solo performance that you can't performing with the jazz trio? Or vice versa?

Pamela: I think the acoustic stuff is coming more directly from my heart because when I am performing in that vein I'm singing the material that I have written; and I get to play using a lot of alternate tunings, which I use to create different colors and textures in a song. Sometimes I perform other people's songs, but rarely. I remember my voice teacher telling me once that it's okay to do covers of songs. So I use them sometimes, especially when I need to gauge the audience. Playing jazz, I feel like I am getting the chance to develop my style and my confidence more as a guitar player. You know, jazz requires you to be loose enough to improvise, and this has been good for me on the electric guitar especially because I'm still growing with that instrument.

LKB: Describe your process when you are writing a song.

Pamela: I make up music a lot, but it won't stay unless I put a lyric to it. So I work a lot harder at lyrics. I really have to sit myself down and focus on the lyric, or I will sit around all day long just playing the guitar. I'll be making up music with no words. [*laughter*] I've learned over time that I can't wait for an inspirational moment—when the whole song, words and music, comes to me at once—because those moments don't come often enough. You know, at first I didn't think it was legitimate to work on a song. I thought they had to be magical. After a while I realized you have to really work on them. Crafting is involved. So I practice playing a lot and then I really try to hone in what needs to be said. Of course, even without words the music would have some kind of emotional meaning, but putting the lyric to the music is really an important part of my process because it's a way for me to get at my subconscious: What's really on my mind these days? What's really on my heart? Similarly, sometimes after I read a book, I will write a book report for myself. Just like a little essay so I can understand it in my own words, and it also cements what I have learned from the book. I didn't go to a normal college, so it's something I've never done. In fact, I would say that I didn't really start reading on my own until I was twenty-five because I thought reading was boring. Well, a lot of the stuff we had been given in high school was boring. After I moved to Boston, where I officially came out, my first girlfriend gave me a copy of Audre Lorde's *Sisters of the Yam* and that changed everything for me. Everything.

LKB: Can you delve deeper into that?

Pamela: After reading *Sisters of the Yam*, I realized that as a duty to myself and also the only way I could truly honor my creative spirit was to write songs that pertained to my life's experiences.

LKB: I want to go back briefly to something, your comment involving the disciplinary aspect of songwriting. Do you find that you are always able to write a song when you set out to?

Pamela: I have en expectation to myself to try to write but not necessarily to produce a song under a certain time constraint.

I have worked like that, I have worked with self-imposed deadlines, but I find that when I put that kind of pressure on myself,
I won't produce. But at the same time, I have learned that when
I make myself sit down and go through writing exercises, push
through and beyond those moments where it feels like
nothing's happening, that I will produce even if it does take
eight hours to come up with one verse. I've heard songwriting
described as fishing. You throw your line in and see what you
get, and it's always there; there's always something.

Fifteen
PATTI CATHCART ANDRESS
(OCTOBER 4, 1949)

Born in San Francisco to Texan parents who migrated to the Bay Area after the war, Patti Cathcart, who was born a twin, was fated to find her musical soul mate in Tuck Andress. Although Patti's parents divorced when she was four years old, she recalls a childhood full of happiness and music. These experiences have continued to abide with the vocal half of the duo Tuck and Patti, who claims, "Joy is the basis of our music and everything we do. Call it divine love, love of your mate, love of your planet; whatever you call it, joy is what it's all about." Now celebrating their twenty-fifth year together as partners and soul mates, Tuck Andress and Patti Cathcart continue to stoke the fires, not only of their own love, but also of their love of life and of the explicit joy they find in making music. For acoustic-music lovers familiar with Patti's mezzo-soprano and Tuck's astonishing guitar virtuosity, consider the two unequaled in converting that joy into memorable music. The two describe their 1978 meeting as musical love at first sight (and soon after, it grew into the real deal, sealed by their 1981 marriage). Over the subsequent six years, in clubs, steak joints, and lounges across the country, Tuck and Patti honed their highly individualistic style. Though label deals frequently came their way, Tuck and Patti passed on all offers until they were certain of their goals and ambitions. That day came in 1988, when Windham Hill came calling. Their first three albums, *Tears of Joy* (1988), *Love Warriors* (1989), and *Dream* (1991), plus a pair of solo albums from Tuck—*Reckless Precision* and *Hymns, Carols, and Songs about Snow*—established the two worldwide, leading the dean of jazz critics, the late Leonard Feather, to make his now-famous pronouncement: "Not since Ella Fitzgerald met Joe Pass onstage has there been so felicitous a mating as Tuck and Patti." In 1995, the pair recorded *Learning How to Fly* for Epic Records before returning home to Windham Hill to begin work on *Paradise Found*. And so it begins again, the cycle of writing, recording, touring, and communing with fans worldwide. Like the seasons of the year, each part of the cycle affords pleasure and rewards for Tuck and Patti. But, as always, most important to both is the steadfastness of their love. Sound corny? Just ask Tuck. "You find out a lot about the fabric of love over many years with somebody," he says. "People fall in love, and they think they couldn't experience that feeling any more deeply, but it turns out that's just the start. If you've got something good, and you hang in there, and you work real hard, the rewards are unbelievable. I feel we're experiencing those rewards on a daily basis."

Selected Discography

Love Warriors (Windham Hill)

Dream (Windham Hill)

Learning How to Fly (Epic Records)

Paradise Found (Windham Hill)

Taking the Long Way Home (Windham Hill)

As Time Goes By (Windham Hill)

Chocolate Moment (T&P Records, distributed by 33rd Street)

A Gift of Love (T&P Records, distributed by 33rd Street)

Patti Cathcart Andress

LKB: Did you grow up in a creative household?

Patti: You know, there was always music. We went to church—I grew up Baptist—and, of course, heard lots of gospel there. The radio was always on. All of us kids loved music, so there was always a record playing. Cleaning up the house on Saturday, we'd throw on some music while we worked. Music was just really part of the fabric of our lives. My mother and aunts loved music. One of my aunts was really into jazz and I remember that during the evenings she'd light the candles and play Sarah Vaughan, Count Basie, Joe Williams, people like that. My mother liked jazz, too, but she also liked Mario Lanza and Leontyne Price. Her musical taste was wide-ranging and so was mine. We all had little transistor radios by our beds and my radio was liable to be on the country-western station one night and the classical station the next.

LKB: Did you play an instrument or sing in a chorus while growing up?

Patti: I sang in the choir at church. Then, as soon as I was able to go to school, I started singing with the big kids. I started playing violin in the fourth grade. I played through high school, and then I stopped 'cause I really wanted to sing. I knew that I wanted to sing when I was quite young. I was about six years old when I really knew that singing was what I wanted to do.

LKB: Do you remember the moment—

Patti: Completely the moment. I realized later on that it was for me a kind of religious experience. I was on vacation with my grandparents, and we were up in Seattle. I was playing with a bunch of kids, having a good time. Later, I took some time away from everybody and was lying in the grass looking up at the clouds. It felt like the earth was breathing under my back. I was breathing, but then I became aware of this other breath that was happening. All of a sudden it got really quiet—everything became still, no clouds were moving, I didn't hear any birds chirping, and then I felt this voice move through me and it said to me, "You will sing, and everything will be all right." I was little, but I knew that that was really happening, number one, and, number two, that the message wasn't for anybody's ears but mine.

LKB: That story sounds very much like your original song "Lifeline" from the 2001 album *Taking the Long Way Home*. I remember hearing that song and wondering if it was autobiographical. Now I know that it is. One of the verses goes: "I was a child when I knew that a song would be my lifeline / I lay dreaming when she came and she sang her secrets to me / She sang about a love supreme, and a heaven she said I would surely someday see."

Patti: Yes.

LKB: You said you were six years old when you received the calling to sing, but when did you start to write poetry or something that you would consider a lyric?

Patti: Well, I always made up songs and lyrics. I was always writing. In school I started writing poetry in the fourth grade. I had volumes and volumes of books where I had written poetry and my thoughts, sometimes just a phrase of this, a snippet of that. Also, I used to hear other people's songs on the radio and make up my own words to go with the music. I was definitely on the singer-songwriter path, but at the time nobody was talking about that. I didn't really have language to describe what I wanted to do, musically speaking. I had always heard people interpreting other people's songs. Then, when the folk era came around, that was the first time I heard the phrase *singer-songwriter*. Keep in mind, though, when I heard this it was usually applied to Bob Dylan, who was writing his own music and singing it. But Joan Baez, for example, even though she played guitar, she was still singing other people's songs. So I still didn't quite know where I fit in, because here I was, this black woman doing this, and I didn't hear about Odetta for quite a while. I didn't even know she existed.

LKB: Who were the artists that made major impressions on you while you were beginning to find your voice in high school?

Patti: Nina Simone. Nina Simone was singing jazz, gospel, and she was also singing Leonard Cohen and Kurt Weill. Her repertoire was just so different. I loved the jazz singers Ella Fitzgerald, Sarah Vaughan, and Dinah Washington. And then I listened to Aretha and the girl groups; musically speaking it was just such a rich time.

LKB: Your own repertoire reflects that richness, too, Patti. You've covered jazz standards like "Stella by Starlight" and "On a Clear Day," but you've also recorded songs by the Beatles,

Goffin and King, and Stevie Wonder in addition to the songs you've written.

Patti: You know, the reality of the music business can sometimes force you into pigeonholing yourself, restricting yourself to one musical idiom, but Tuck and I have always been able to steer clear of that. I've had the confidence to perform music from different genres because I find it comforting. It comforts me and soothes my spirit to sing, period—despite the genre. I've always loved singing since early on because as a child I became aware that an adult would really notice me and perk up when I sang, and it seemed to me that they heard something in my voice. I realized that what they were hearing was what I was feeling, and what I was feeling was bringing me solace and comfort. Years later I met this wonderful pianist, Art Landy, and he used to say that the reason we're here is to serve the music. So if you're wondering if you're doing the right thing you have to ask yourself, is this serving the music? I think that's the way to look at it—just serve the music. And if the music wants you to do a rock and roll thing and it's a Tadd Dameron tune, you have to go with that creative impulse. Lucky for me, I had the amazing good fortune to run into a partner that believed the same things.

LKB: And that leads nicely to my set of questions involving you and Tuck, because I've always felt that the sound you and Tuck create melds so beautifully it's ethereal. I want to know what the process was like on the way to this incredible groove you two have found and had going for twenty years now. First of all, how did you find each other?

Patti: I was always searching. I had been in a couple of different bands and had sort of gravitated towards rock and roll. I also sang with a Top 40 band on the weekends and I sang with a jazz group called Midnight Sun. We used to do a lot of Brazilian music.

LKB: The bands that you were singing with, were they strictly cover bands or also performing original music?

Patti: We did some original stuff and then we'd do some rock, some Sly and the Family Stone, some funk. . . . It was a real mixture. The greatest similarity, across the board, with all the bands that I worked in was that there was always a lot of jamming, a lot of improvisation going on. That's what I always liked, because coming up in the church that's what it was all about. Yes, you learned a song, but then it was your testimony, what you brought to that tune that made the song really yours.

LKB: It's interesting to me that you moved away from all of the "big" sounds, if you will, of rock bands and jazz ensembles to a more open, earthy, acoustic sound.

Patti: Yes, for some reason I was starting more and more to want to hear less and less. So I started this little group with a percussionist conga player, a guitarist, and a saxophone player. I just didn't want the full band sound.

LKB: What was the impetus for moving in this new direction?

Patti: I wanted to explore the percussion aspects of the voice. I wanted to explore more of the textures of the human voice, and in order to do that you have to make room for it in the song. All of the space can't be filled with a horn section, a huge band, and all of that stuff. Then, too, LaShonda, I guess I wanted to take it back to the roots. It wasn't that I was going to give up bands, but I wanted to return to the roots, my root of the voice and then build around that—not build around some big sound.

LKB: And around this time is when you met Tuck?

Patti: Right in this moment is when we met. I went to audition for a band, and he was the guitar player in that band. We had heard about each other; in fact we had all been trying to get together—various people in the band—but our schedules had just been too crazy. It took about a year from the time when I first started hearing about Tuck until I finally met him, and then it was at this audition that we met. I came in and passed out my music and counted off the music, started singing, and then I went, "Who is *that* playing *that* guitar over there in the corner?"

LKB: How long after that where you two actually making music together?

Patti: We started instantly once we started playing together. The band only lasted a couple of months, so we came together and said, "We need to get some gigs. Okay, how many tunes do you know?" We were doing everybody else's songs but the same thing was happening. We'd start off playing one song and then it would take off in another direction and have its own melody, its own lyric. So, that would end up being the improv section, and then we would come back to the original tune and finish it. We were doing that for a long time and we never wrote anything down. It was just remarkable, because early on we both talked about—"Okay, what do you want to say? What do you want to do?" No band that I had ever been in had ever actually done that, had ever actually communicated goals and aspirations for the music. So, when

Tuck and I had this conversation he said he wanted to be positive and he wanted to create music that was uplifting, and I said so do I. And that worked for us, it really did. You know, it took us a little time to get used to the fact that we were a duo. We didn't have a percussionist or a bass player, so we would just explore, but what we learned was that we didn't have to make up for the instrumentation that was missing. We were already complete. When our minds switched that way, then the music was really able to grow.

LKB: At what point did you know you would remain a duo, that you would never include a bass player or other instrumentalists?

Patti: About eight or nine months in. By then we had started getting gigs as a duo, and we were loving it. We would play a two-hour gig and never take a break! We would literally play the whole night because we were so lost in the music. People used to say, "Do you guys ever take breaks?"

LKB: I'm sure performing in a duo pushed you as vocalist in new ways by giving you the opportunity and freedom to really explore your voice, which you mentioned earlier was becoming a real priority.

Patti: Yes, LaShonda, it gave me complete freedom but also complete terror because you're completely naked. Every single thing you do, every breath you take, everything is right out front and center—there's no hiding. That was really challenging for me as a vocalist because I was familiar with singers whose voices were really amazing instruments, singers like Jon Lucien, Leon Thomas, and then Al Jarreau came along. Then, right at the time Tuck and I were starting to get known in the Bay Area, Bobby McFerrin showed up in town and blew us all away with his solo gigs. It was an exciting time, and when you hear those voices as a vocalist yourself, you can't help but feel you have to step up because the bar keeps getting raised and you want to be a part of it. You want to be a part of the tradition of exploring the voice as far as you can possibly go.

LKB: What were the circumstances surrounding your and Tuck's first record deal?

Patti: Windham Hill was starting a record label called Windham Hill Jazz. Well, they had actually called us a few years earlier. A woman had called and said, "The president of our company, Will Ackerman, would like for you to send us a demo tape." And we were like, "Oh, thank you. We like Windham Hill a lot but we're not quite ready to record yet." We were just so naïve. So we thanked the woman and told her we would get back to her when we were ready.

LKB and Patti: [*laughter*]

Patti: They called back about a month later and asked us to send our demo tape again and we told them again that we did not have a demo tape. The woman said to us, "I don't think you understand. Record companies don't just call people on the phone and ask for their recordings." But we were still very much staying to true to the fact that we did not feel we were ready, because for the first time in my musical adult life the focus was really on the music—not on the business of music. We didn't want to sabotage that focus in any way. We both had the strong sense that we did not want to pollute it with industry worry. And, like I said, we were really naïve and hopeful, like little kids. We just assumed we would get a record deal at some point. Other companies called us, too, like Concord Jazz, but they wanted us to get a band. We continued to focus on our music and put together our own studio. When Windham Hill Jazz called back four years later and invited us to their Christmas party to play, it was perfect timing because we had just put out our first record.

LKB: Now, this is four years after you started playing together?

Patti: No, ten years! We didn't put out our first record together until ten years after we first met. We really took our time.

LKB: Generally speaking, when you and Tuck are composing a song, how does the process begin?

Patti: For me, most of the time it starts by me hearing a texture, you know, I'll hear a string part or some kind of percussive part.

LKB: Instrumental voicings?

Patti: Yes. And I tend to work from the middle out. It took a long time for Tuck and I to figure out that that's what I was doing. I don't start with a melody. I start with inner voicings and harmonies and I start writing from the center.

LKB: So, you get the story, the lyric, from the music you hear?

Patti: Yes. Most of the time I get the music and then the lyric comes. Sometimes I'll get a phrase first, and then I'll write the lyric without knowing what the music is going to be, but it's rare. I always have a little tape recorder with me, though, so when inspiration strikes I can just sing or hum into it and take it from there. Part of what Tuck calls our "secret weapon" is that I'm the writer. Since I'm not the guitar player, I'm not thinking about what he calls "the limitations of an instrument" when I write the songs. Now, the other part of that "secret weapon" is the fact that Tuck is an incredible musician and can play what to me are seemingly impossible pieces of music.

LKB: When you are planning an album, do you generally begin with a theme in mind or some plan?

Patti: Usually an album will begin by me having an idea of some songs written by other writers that I want to sing. And then I'd write three or four songs, and they just tended to come. Every song that I've really taken the time to sit down and write, we have recorded. Now, as the years have gone by I am really thinking of Tuck's style of playing when I write a song. The textures that I know he plays and also the textures that I love to hear him play are what really inspire my own writing. Like a song called "Rejoice" that I wrote a few years ago. I was really thinking about South Africa. It was like a celebration song for Mr. Mandela, and I wanted to hear that South African township-music energy in the song, and I could hear Tuck playing with that kind of feeling, which eventually brought the lyric from me. The process doesn't always start off smoothly, though. Like the *Chocolate Moment* album, which was post 9/11. I remember sitting down to write that album without the slightest notion of what I wanted to write or what I wanted to say. I didn't even know what kind of record it was going to be. But then I wrote this song called "Comfort Me," and after I wrote "Comfort Me," it cleared the air for me and made room for the spirit, and songs just started coming out. The next thing I knew, I had written all of the songs for the album. That was the second time something like that happened. The first time it happened was with the album *Taking the Long Way Home*. I was going to do a straight jazz-standards record, then I started to think about standards of my own that I'd love to write and I wrote a couple and then just kept writing, writing, and writing. Those are the first two albums that we ever recorded that include only originals, but they weren't initially conceived that way.

LKB: I'm really glad you brought up the album *Taking the Long Way Home*, because it's one of my favorites, and I wanted to find out the inspiration behind the song "This Light This Life."

Patti: With that one, I wrote the poem first. I had written most of the poem, and I had no idea what kind of music was going to go with it, and I was listening to some old rehearsal tapes we had from our first recording, *Tears of Joy*. At the end of the tape, Tuck was playing around on the guitar, going *da da da da da da da da*. And I kept listening to that, it was haunting me, so I thought, that's the music for "This Light." After I finished writing the song I took it to Tuck and said to him, "I don't even know what this song is about but it makes me cry." [*laughter*]

LKB: My absolute favorite song of yours is "Forgiveness"—

Patti: That song came after meeting Carlos Santana early one morning at the airport. I can't remember where we all were. Carlos was carrying this big beautiful book full of pictures of angels, so we started talking about the book. We were sitting on the ground in baggage claim waiting, and he was like, "You know, all of this injustice, deprivation, and murder going on in the world is really getting to me. I'm really an angry person. I carry these angels with me to keep me grounded." And it was from that that I started writing the

song "Forgiveness." You know, I believe that many singer-
songwriters sing not about the world we inhabit but the
world we dream of inhabiting. What a gift to be able to sing
a world into being.

LKB: A lot of your music creates a world rife with compassion,
truth, and understanding. "Knowing" is one of these songs.

Patti: We had fun making that song. When we finally got a take
where we had made it all the way through the song, we
weren't going to try for a second! [laughter] We have take after
take after take of us doing the song and every time we'd get to
that part, "We dive in," I'd get lost and be like, "Tuck, I don't
know where I'm going." And, he'd say, just, "I don't either, so
let's start again." [laughter] I was inspired to write that song
while listening to Tuck practice. I was sitting at the kitchen
table, and I just wrote the whole thing, and then I went to
record it and realized I had left no place to breathe. There was
absolutely no place in this piece of poetry where you could
take a breath. I think I could sing one note by breathing in and
there were a couple of places where I just had to catch a breath
wherever I could catch it.

LKB: That's the first time in our conversation that the process of
revision has come up.

Patti: Revision happens often—especially in the early days and
even when it's somebody else's tune, some revising happens
when you are arranging the tune. Tuck and I usually jam
around the kitchen table, and as we're doing this I start to hear
parts. But you know, you can't tell until you go in to record it.
You can't tell if your arrangement is really going to work until
it's recorded. Then you can go through the musical revision,

"Okay, I need more of a bass line. . . . I need it to be more legato here. . . . And I want you to play staccato here, but I need this part to be flowing at the same time." [*laughter*] During this process Tuck is looking at me like I'm crazy, but he goes back in and does it anyway, and it blows me away. So, yeah, I embrace revision. You have to.

LKB: Do you practice other creative arts?

Patti: I love to draw, and I love weaving. I don't have my loom set up now, because I don't have the time to do it, but I really love to weave. Gardening is something else that I love to do but since I've been on the road for the last . . . sixteen years. [*laughter*] My garden is lacking. At some point, I'll get back to gardening.

LKB: Who are some of the artists that you're listening to now?

Patti: I love Ledisi, and I think that Jill Scott is wonderful, what a voice.

LKB: I think it's very cool that you just cited two women from a different generation than yours. One of the topics that has come up a few times in my conversations with singer-songwriters is how intergenerational listening is not a phenomenon like it once was.

Patti: You're right, but it has to happen. We really need to listen to each other across genre and age differences. As singers, I think we hear certain voices and we are, in a sense, mentored by what we hear, but I think that one of the tragedies of singers is that we haven't really mentored each other the way we should.

LKB: I've never thought about that. You see it so much between male instrumentalists in the jazz world, for example, this mentoring of future generations.

Patti: I understand that it's difficult when you're trying to make it as a vocalist, because there's only that one slot to get, everybody's clamoring for the microphone, but just think of the vocalists that might have been if Sarah Vaughan, Dinah Washington, Betty Carter, had actually mentored a vocalist—took her under her wing and passed on all of her knowledge about performing and about the industry. I think all of us have to start doing this. I'm certainly going to start. Tuck and I are purposely making more time in our lives for teaching.

LKB: Patti, what specific thing or things are you striving for during a performance?

Patti: To get as close as I can to my creator. To get as close as I can to feeling like I am completely and totally submerged in an ocean of love, and to be able to shine that out to every corner of the room and to every person in the audience. I'd like for the music to have reach, to break past the boundaries of the walls and heal the universe. You're a singer, too, LaShonda, so you know that in addition to loving the physical aspect of singing a song there is this spiritual element— that's why singing, music is one of the healing arts. As a singer, I've found that you have to be where your source is in order to be able to facilitate that, in order to mediate that healing for others.

LKB: And when you say, "You have to be where your source is," you're talking about heeding the inspiration, not singing or performing material because it's the trend, it'll pay well, or what have you.

Patti: Exactly. I've always been very clear on this. In fact, it's never been a choice for me not to be true to my source, to the divine spirit that is music. It has been my guide since I was a child.

Sixteen
SHEMEKIA COPELAND
(APRIL 10, 1979)

Born in Harlem, New York, in 1979, Shemekia Copeland grew up in Teaneck, New Jersey, and came to her singing career slowly. "I never knew I wanted to sing until I got older," says Copeland. "But my dad knew ever since I was a baby. He just knew I was gonna be a singer." Her father, the late Texas blues-guitar legend Johnny "Clyde" Copeland, recognized his daughter's talent early on. He always encouraged her to sing at home and even brought her onstage to sing at Harlem's famed Cotton Club when she was just eight. At that time, Shemekia's embarrassment outweighed her desire to sing. But when she was fifteen, and her father's health began to slow him down, she received the calling. "It was like a switch went off in my head," recalls Shemekia, "and I wanted to sing. It became a want and a need. I had to do it." Shemekia's passion for singing, matched with her huge, blast-furnace voice, gives her music the timeless power and heart-pounding urgency of a very few greats who have come before her. The media has compared her to a young Etta James, Koko Taylor, Aretha Franklin, and Ruth Brown, but Shemekia, who was raised in central Harlem, has her own story to tell. With considerable experience under her belt, sixteen-year-old Shemekia joined her father on his tours after he was diagnosed with a heart condition. Soon enough she was opening, and sometimes even stealing, her father's shows. She stepped out of her father's shadow in 1998 when Alligator released *Turn the Heat Up* to massive popular and critical acclaim. Rave reviews ran everywhere from *Billboard* to the *New York Times*, the *Washington Post*, the *Chicago Tribune* and *Sun-Times*, the *Boston Globe*, and others. In 2000 she returned with *Wicked*. Almost immediately, the young singer was in great demand on radio, television, and in the press. The opening song, "It's 2:00 A.M." won the Blues Music Award for Song of the Year, and the album was nominated for a Grammy Award. With her Dr. John–produced follow-up, *Talking to Strangers*, Copeland's third release revealed the singer's eclectic taste and her penchant for blurring the lines between blues, soul, and rock and roll. The album debuted in the number-one spot on the Billboard Blues Chart and received critical praise all around the world. The Associated Press declared, "Copeland blazes through *Talking to Strangers* with fervor and grace. Her singing can be as thunderous as Etta James and as mellow as Chaka Khan." Copeland was featured in the Martin Scorsese–produced concert film *Lightning in a Bottle* and the PBS television series *The Blues*. She has played with Buddy Guy and B. B. King, and has shared the stage with Taj Mahal, Dr. John, Koko Taylor, and the Rolling Stones among others. Throughout her most recent album, *The Soul Truth*, Shemekia Copeland testifies her music to both seasoned music lovers, who appreciate her musical roots, as well as to new fans, who love her contemporary attitude. "I want people who love hip-hop to know where it came from," she told *Vibe* magazine. "My music is rooted in blues, but it's different. I'm singing about my era. I'm here and I'm singing about now and not yesterday." And that's the truth, nothing but the soul truth.

Selected Discography

    The Soul Truth (Alligator Records)
    Talking to Strangers (Alligator Records)
    Wicked (Alligator Records)
    Turn the Heat Up (Alligator Records)

Shemekia Copeland

LKB: Going back to your childhood, Shemekia, what do you remember foremost about your connection to music?

Shemekia: Oh, wow. My earliest memories of music are my daddy playing guitar around the house. When I was very young I didn't know what he was playing, but it was always music around the house. As I grew up I started to sing some of the songs Daddy played.

LKB: How old were you when you sang these songs?

Shemekia: About three. I started singing when I was three.

LKB: In addition to your father's music, what other music was in the household? What records did you listen to?

Shemekia: Girl, I remember Otis Redding. I used to force my mother to play Otis Redding over and over and over again. And Sam Cooke. I loved Sam Cooke.

LKB: It's interesting that you haven't listed any female singers.

Shemekia: Yes, it is. I would say my first impressions of music were black male voices, definitely. I didn't get into listening to women until much later.

LKB: What professions did your parents have?

Shemekia: My father was a full-time musician, and most of the time while I was growing up, my mother was a college student. I think she studied psychology and later she went on to work with crazy folks, which is good for her because her whole family's crazy so she's used to it. [*laughter*]

LKB: How old were you when you decided you were going to pursue music as a career?

Shemekia: I never wanted to sing. I thought it was a ridiculous profession.

LKB: Really?

Shemekia: Yeah, my father pretty much never came home with any money. He worked all the time, but he never had any money, so the musician's lifestyle didn't appeal to me. I thought that going onstage and having people watch you was demeaning in a way. But by the time high school came around, I knew that I was going to sing.

LKB: As you were breaking into music, who were some of the artists that were your inspirations?

Shemekia: At the top of that list is Ruth Brown, who recently died. Matter of fact, her funeral is today. She was so good to me. She was so sweet. She was very supportive of my career from the beginning. She'd give me clothes, you know, outfits to perform in, and advice, and the same goes for Koko Taylor. They have been my go-to girls. Anytime I had an issue or question they were the ones, they were my sister/mother/friend/confidantes.

LKB: When did you write your first song, Shemekia?

Shemekia: On my first album we did a song called "Big Lovin' Woman." That was the first one.

LKB: What was the process like?

Shemekia: Well, I came up with the title. Originally it was "Blues Lovin' Woman," but I liked "Big" instead, because I love big. And the cowriter liked the title, too. I think he thought it fit me 'cause I ain't never been little my whole life. I mean, I'm only five feet one, but because of my confidence I feel six feet tall.

LKB: There are a couple of songs of yours that I'd like to take you through to find out a little bit about your process with songwriting. First off is "Sholonda's," off your *Talking to Strangers* album.

Shemekia: "Sholonda's" was completely my idea. I grew up with a girl named Shewanda—changed the name a little bit for the song. Shewanda's a good friend of mine. She did hair; she was going to beauty school when I wrote the song, and I was always her guinea pig. She always wanted to try new styles out on me. I would end up with red hair, green hair, weaves [*laughter*]—girl, just all kinds of stuff. Anyway, I wanted to capture the very special experience of being in a beauty shop. I mean, when you go to one you end up being in there for hours and hours. And it's important to really let your hair down, no pun intended. You can get things off of your chest, laugh, learn something new, and, if you're not above it—gossip. [*laughter*] You're not just getting your hair done; you're part of a community. I wanted to share that feeling because it's something I've always appreciated. I've always appreciated what I learn when I go to Shewanda's.

LKB: The black beauty shop is definitely one of the most important and unique institutions in the black community. There are several scholars who have written about the social and cultural significance of beauty shops recently. Tiffany Gill's book *Civic Beauty* deals with this, and Maxine Leeds Craig's work *Ain't I a Beauty Queen* touches on this. Ingrid Banks's book *Hair Matters* also addresses this topic. When I listened to your song, I thought back on these works and thought what an interesting dialogue your song was having with their texts.

Shemekia: Wow, I had no idea there was so much out there on this.

LKB: You share coauthorship on many of your original songs.

Shemekia: Yes. I collaborate with John Hahn, who is a guy I have known since I was eight years old. When I was growing up in Harlem, we lived on 127th Street—right in the center of things—and it was very dangerous. People were getting shot up and everything. Well, John was the white guy who would brave all of that and come and have dinner with my family.

LKB: John's also your manager, right?

Shemekia: Yes, but because I've known him since I was eight, he's more than that. We also collaborate musically. Usually we write the lyrics together, and then we work with the musicians to build the song.

LKB: What inspired your song "Don't Whisper That You Love Me"?

Shemekia: That was about one of my first boyfriends. I didn't know any of his family or his mother or anybody in his life. I was quite a bit younger than him and I think for various reasons he didn't want to tell anybody about me. And, you know, that was tough on me. When you're young you want your lover to brag on you and to brag on the love, too. Anyway, all's well that ends well. His mother, Lord have mercy, she has become so supportive of me. She comes to all of my shows.

LKB: "It's My Own Tears," from the album *Wicked*.

Shemekia: My father, Johnny Copeland, is a singer-songwriter from Houston, Texas—the Third Ward. He's an amazing artist, and he wrote great songs, and that was one of them. He recorded it years ago, and I wanted to record it because I feel that that song is saying so much. My dad had a way with simple lyrics that packed a punch, like, "Don't worry about what I do because if you satisfy me it should please you." That just—uh, girl, it makes my liver quiver! [*laughter*]

LKB: "Miss High Sedity" is something else. *Sedity* is a word we use in the black community but, you know, if you look it up in the dictionary, it's not there.

Shemekia: Yeah, I know it's not really a word. I was sitting with John and his wife for dinner one time, and we were with another man and his wife. When that couple got up to go have a cigarette, speaking about the woman, I told John, "She just gets on my nerves. She's so high sedity." And John said, "We gotta write that song." I never would've thought to put that in a song, you know what I mean? So, I thought about all the high-sedity women I've ever known my whole life, wrote about them and had me a song. [*laughter*]

LKB: When you're writing a song, Shemekia, either with John or solo, does the lyric generally come to you all at once or—

Shemekia: Yes. When I'm writing it's just there—all of it comes together. I'm not one to sit down with a piece of paper and try to write a song. If it's there, it's there. However, just because it comes to me like lightning doesn't mean I don't work on it a lot. When I have a song I spend a lot of time polishing it, trying to get it just right. That's why, for me, collaboration is so critical and so helpful. It's really nice to have John to bounce ideas off of because I'm very, very honest—brutally honest, I've been told. Sometimes I'll say something kind of outright in a lyric, and John, [*laughter*] he'll say to me, "Are you sure you want to say it like that?" I don't mean to be offensive but sometimes it'll come out that way and I'm glad to have someone around who'll hold me back, give me pause, and encourage me to approach it another way.

LKB: From the album *The Soul Truth*, what inspired the song "It's All about You"?

Shemekia: [*laughter*] Girl, that's another one that's about a boyfriend. I was dating a guy and basically that was the demise of the relationship. It was all about him. It was a good revelation for me to realize that I couldn't love that guy, because I couldn't love him the way he loved himself. So I figured I needed to keep the hell away from him. I do draw from personal experiences for my songs but I feel that I haven't even begun to *really write*.

LKB: Why do you say that?

Shemekia: Because I feel on the past records I hadn't even begun to really explore my deepest feelings. Writing about what has passed, my history, doesn't really address my deepest feelings right now, if you know what I'm saying. Like, I can't write about my current boyfriend. We've been together three years and just bought a house and moved in together. He's the best thing that ever happened to me, but I can't write about that now. For whatever reason, it's been easier to write about the shitty men in my life—not this guy. Writing a blues like "I'm Giving Up You" comes easy to me, but writing a love song is the hardest thing I've ever tried to do. That might be the hook for my song . . . right there!

LKB: What? Writing a love song is the hardest thing I've ever had to do?

Shemekia: Yes! And I came up with it while talking to you.

LKB: You better jot it down.

Shemekia: Girl, I am. I am! [*laughter*]

LKB: Shemekia, do you have any practices, habits that you find help your songwriting process?

Shemekia: I keep a journal. I find that it helps me stay on top of my feelings. I am getting more and more in touch with them and it feels so good. I'm twenty-seven going on twenty-eight, and I've never felt so clear in my head. I'm an Aries woman, and we always want to control everything, but I've realized that I can't. I cannot change the economy. I cannot make our president just go away. [*laughter*] But seriously, the journal writing has helped me get over my control issues and given me some clarity. And that clarity definitely feeds the music. Matter of fact, now that I'm thinking about it, you could say that some of my blues lyrics are like a journal entry set to music.

LKB: Shemekia, I am intrigued by your youth and the fact that you choose to perform the blues, which many people equate with an older generation. I'm wondering if, when you were younger, other genres appealed to you. How is it that hip-hop or R&B didn't capture you?

Shemekia: Girl, 'cause it just did not get me like my Koko Taylor records. [*laughter*] I mean, back in the day I used to listen to a

little rap—back in the day, because now I think it has just gone
south. I used to love myself some En Vogue, Sounds of Blackness, Mint Condition, Tony Toni Toné. . . . Now, they were real
bands. And even though I grooved on this music, it just wasn't
the same as blues music. I also love soul and gospel, but again,
it's not the same as blues music.

LKB: Did you attend church growing up? And did you sing in the
choir?

Shemekia: I went to church, but I was never a part of any choirs,
mainly because to sing in a choir you have to be consistent.
You have to go to choir rehearsals, and at the time there was
no constancy in my life—with my dad traveling all the day
with his music and all.

LKB: Shemekia, what themes have you noticed in your songwriting that seem to surface again and again in your lyrics?

Shemekia: You know, I'm really glad you asked that question,
because I find that so many young women have no confidence
at all. And because they have no confidence they allow men,
or women, it doesn't matter, to just walk all over them. I'm
very sensitive to the stories that I hear and the scenarios I witness where young girls let people do anything to them because
they really believe they can't do any better. So I tend to tackle
songs about self-esteem a lot, songs that deal with questioning
women about how they feel about themselves and challenging
them to demand better for their lives. I have a niece who's ten
years old, you know, and I never want her to feel inferior or
like she can't be everything that she wants to be. At the same
time, I like to write songs that deal with the topic of respecting
men. Some women have to learn how to respect men. If I have

to be with a man that I have to call a motherfucker every five minutes. . . .

LKB: [*laughter*] Then you don't need to be with him.

Shemekia: You see what I'm saying. And I see it, or I hear it, so much—women who disrespect themselves also disrespect men. And I like to deal with this phenomenon in my music because it needs correcting, especially in our culture. That's why I said that hip-hop music has gone south, because a lot of those lyrics flaunt the ways we disrespect ourselves. I won't even go to the videos, where young women are dancing around with their asses out. I mean, no class whatsoever. No class. I worry about the generations that are going to come after us. . . . And I'm very grateful to my parents that they showed me a different way to go, that they brought me up to have a great deal of respect for myself and for others. You know, people say that I am always preaching in my songs, well, somebody's got to. I don't sing lyrics that I don't believe in! Sometimes I do just want to do a fun song and make people laugh, and I do perform those songs, but most of my songs have a message.

LKB: Shemekia, are there other arenas in which you'd like to take your music?

Shemekia: I would like to go back to school and take some acting classes. I think about doing musical theater or something like that.

LKB: If you weren't a singer-songwriter, what other calling would you pursue?

Shemekia: Well, recently I started disc jockeying on satellite radio, and I like that very much. I'm not in the studio; I do my show weekly from my computer wherever I am in the world. It's a lot of fun because I get to speak my mind and share my thoughts with many, many people.

LKB: Take me back to the period of your life right before you signed your first record deal. What were you doing and how did the deal come about?

Shemekia: For the first full year after I signed my record deal I was still working a job. I was working at a dry-cleaning plant. Matter of fact, the guy I used to work for was at my gig the other night. He was very proud of me, and he was very good to me when I worked for him. He let me go when I needed to go and do gigs. I like to tell people that I worked the whole first year of my record contract, because people have very grandiose ideas about what a record deal can do for someone's life. That said, it was still a great experience because for the first time I began to think, *Wow, maybe I will be able to make a living doing this.* Also, I think that people working in the blues genre approach their careers a little differently than people working in more commercial genres, like hip-hop. Some people get into hip-hop to make money. Some of them don't have any passion for the music or anything like that. It's just a "I wanna make that money; I wanna get the bling and sleep with big-booty girls" mentality. In the blues genre, we sing our asses off for every dime.

LKB: What's next for you, Shemekia? Are you cooking up a new album?

Shemekia: You know, the business has changed so much even since I've entered it. So much is changing about how people get music—I know you've noticed this. Record stores are closing down left and right. Record labels are dissolving. I've been thinking a lot about this. I used to worry about it, but my boyfriend said something to me that made a lot of sense. He said, "No matter what happens with the business aspects of music, there will always be music." And he's right. As long as I can sing and make a living, I feel like I have God's blessing. So, after the first of the year I am going back into the studio to cook up something new. And the rest—how it's going to get to people, how it's going to be received—I put all of that in God's hands.

Seventeen

SHIRLEY CAESAR
(OCTOBER 13, 1938)

Performing over 150 concerts a year and with more than thirty gospel albums to her credit, Shirley Caesar has earned the appellation "First Lady of Gospel." Born the tenth of twelve children to a homemaker and tobacco farmer and lead gospel singer in North Carolina, Caesar began performing professionally with her father's group, Just Come Four, at the age of ten. When she was twelve, her father died, yet she continued touring with evangelist LeRoy Johnson. While in high school, Caesar toured extensively throughout the Carolinas and Tidewater area (Virginia and Maryland). While studying business administration at North Carolina Central University, Caesar heard the Chicago-based female gospel group the Caravans. She sought an audition with the group, was immediately hired, and left school to devote herself to a life of singing and ministry. Several members of the Caravans, including Albertina Walker, Inez Andrews, and Sarah McKissick, made their mark in the annals of gospel music history. Making a name for herself on the gospel circuit during the sixties, Caesar's energetic and dramatic approach to music typically found her acting out the songs and walking among the congregation, engaging the members directly. Her forte is the sermon in the middle of songs that addresses the subject of the song and expounds on its theme. Her style of song and sermonette finds her exhorting listeners to reach out to God. Shirley formed her own group in 1966 called the Caesar Singers, but she would reunite with the Caravans and the Reverend Cleveland occasionally throughout the years. In 1971, she won her first Grammy, for the popular song "Put Your Hand in the Hand of the Man from Galilee." The story goes that on the night of the awards, Caesar had returned very late from an engagement in Homer, Louisiana. People began banging on her door, and when she eventually answered, her sister Ann, one of her backup singers, shouted, "You won!" It was the first Grammy for a black female gospel singer since Mahalia Jackson. Caesar went on to win the award in 1980, 1984, 1985, 1992, and 1994, for a total of seven Grammys. Between 1981 and 1985 Caesar received eight Dove Awards for Black Gospel Album of the Year and two Black Gospel Song of the Year awards for "He's Working It Out for You" and "Hold My Mule." In addition to leading her church in North Carolina and performing concerts nationwide, She has performed in off-Broadway productions of Vy Higginsen's popular musical plays: *Mama, I Want to Sing; Sing!: Mama 2; and Born to Sing: Mama 3.*

Selected Discography

Stand the Storm (Liquid 8)

Faded Rose (Liquid 8)

Be Careful of the Stones You Throw (Liquid 8)

No Charge (HOB)

Live in Memphis (Sony)

Jesus, I Love Calling Your Name (Sony)

Don't Drive Your Mama Away (Liquid 8)

He's Working It Out for You (Sony)

Live . . . He Will Come (Sony)

I Remember Mama (Sony)

A Miracle in Harlem (Sony)

You Can Make It (Word Entertainment)

Hymns (Word Entertainment)

Church Is in Mourning (Calvin Records)

I Know the Truth (Artemis Strategic)

Shirley Caesar

LKB: I'll begin by telling you a little story about the effect of your music on my personal life. In April of 1989 I was thirteen years old, and I was sitting in the backseat of my aunt Lena Faye's car with my sister. We were driving to the cemetery in Dallas, where we were going to bury my great-grandmother Roena. What I remember most distinctly about that day is that the gospel radio station played "I Remember Mama," and how hearing that song affected my aunt Lena Faye. First, she started humming, lowlike, in the tradition of the deacons devotional in the Baptist church. Then she started crying and hitting her hand against the steering wheel. Not long after that, we had to pull off the road because my aunt was getting happy. She was shouting in the car. As an evangelist and gospel singer, you're often the conduit for people's most spiritual experiences. As you well know, this is tremendous power. How has it been, accepting that?

Shirley: Well, LaShonda, I'm excited about the fact that God has chosen me to be able to touch so many lives. I often think back to when I was a little girl and some of the teachers, especially the music teacher, would tell me, Caesar, shut up with that old throaty voice. And yet if I had listened to that, it would have certainly destroyed me. I thank God that he not only put melody in my mouth, but he put the right lyric that would bless people. I just thank God for that.

LKB: What do you think was in you, Ms. Caesar, as a young child, that enabled you not to crumble? Because I could see a seven- or eight- or nine-year-old girl hearing, you know, "Shut up with that throaty voice," and just crumbling. But you didn't.

Shirley: Well, no. I didn't, because I had a very, very strong mother and a very supportive family. All of us were singers, and the very fact that out of twelve, God would just choose me to take care of my mom and take care of my family—well, I'm just in awe of God, if you really want to know the truth. He's a dynamo. He's just all right. I know that all of this is the Lord's doing.

LKB: Has there ever been a time in your illustrious career when you've been sort of overwhelmed by your calling? Has there come a time when you've thought, I *don't want to run this race anymore?*

Shirley: Well, yes, there have been times when I was weary, weary. But my mind and my heart always goes back to the apostle Paul's writings in Galatians 6:9, where he says, and I just add my name there: "Shirley, be not weary in well doing; for in due season you shall reap, if you faint not." And I thank God because God is so faithful to his word. You know I'm pastor of a church in Raleigh, North Carolina?

LKB: Yes, and it's a large church. I read somewhere that it seats fifteen hundred.

Shirley: Yes, but my congregation is up and down. Church people are transient sometimes. They come and go, come and go, but you know, I don't count numbers. I count those who I can count *on*.

LKB: You write many of your own song lyrics—

Shirley: Yes, I do. I've written so many of my songs: "You're Next in Line for Miracles," "Hold My Mule"; I could go on and on.

LKB: Tell me what inspired "Hold My Mule." That's one of my favorites.

Shirley: "Hold My Mule." My sister used to buy Avon from this lady who came by the house one day with some of her product. I got the story from the Avon lady. She told me the story, but not like I tell it. I had to kind of Caesarize it. But anyway, she was telling me about the story of "Hold My Mule." So every time I would see her I would call her "Hold My Mule." And finally, the Lord put it on my heart to record that song. He just gave me the right song to put with the story and everything.

LKB: Did you hear the melody as you were crafting the song?

Shirley: Yes, but let me just tell you this, though. We were recording live in Chicago. I think it was in 1988, the end of '88, like October or November. I was recording with the Tommys— and by the way I'm getting ready to have a reunion. I'm gonna recut a lot of my old stuff, and it's gonna take place at my church, too. I think it's June the second. Anyway, so there I am at the recording studio. We had all of our songs recorded, but we still needed one more. I said, "Lord, I need one more song."

Now I had the story of "Hold My Mule," but I didn't have the song. And so the young man who was producing the record encouraged me, tried to make me feel better about not having it altogether right. The group loaded up everything, put everything away to get ready to take it out and put it in the truck, like guitars and all of that. And I said, "Mike, come here"—Mike plays for me. I said, "Come back to the organ right quick." And while they were taking all the other instruments out I started singing, "I see you; I praise, praise him," just like that. And my backup voices joined me, which were the Caesar Singers. If you notice on the recording of the song, the choir does not come in right away, and that's because they didn't know it. I had not rehearsed it with them. And so you hear my singers coming in and then after I made one round of it, then the Tommys came in. Do you know that became the biggest-selling song on the whole CD, and it almost didn't even get recorded. I know it was spirit working.

LKB: In your own words, Pastor Caesar, what do you think accounts for the longevity and the newness of songs like "Sweeping through the City," "He's Working It Out for You," "Revive Us Again," "I Remember Mama." Every time I hear them, there is a freshness about them.

Shirley: Well, you know, I think that it is because we have so many contemporary songs today that do not bring the deliverance. Oh, they sell, because we have more young people today who are interested in gospel. But the old-timey songs bring deliverance. These other songs that have strayed so far away from the tradition; these songs don't bring the deliverance. These old songs are what caused your aunt to just let go. . . . It's why you guys had to pull over, because there was something in some of those lyrics that hit her right where she was. I will never ever stop singing my old songs.

LKB: Your listeners, we'll all hold you to that. You talk about the deliverance and I know that is a major part of it, but when I hear gospel music, I hear hope. Gospel music, at the end of the day, is such a gift to us because it bears hope.

Shirley: And you know, I also look at the fact that our baby boomers need these songs. I'll tell you, I'm getting ready to recut "No Charge" and "Hold My Mule." I don't know if I can do that again.

LKB: Did you write "No Charge"?

Shirley: No, I didn't. A husband and wife wrote that. But "I Remember Mama" is mine, and I wrote that from my mom's passing. I might do that one again. But "I Remember Mama," and I'm probably going to record songs from the Thomas album that I did, like "Never," and I'm going to do "God Don't Want No Coward Soldiers."

LKB: We need that one.

Shirley: I'm going to do "Teach Me Master"; I'm going to do "The Millennial Reign" again because this is a grand millennium. I've got a whole list of them that I'm gonna record. And all of this is going to take place at my church. And halfway through the evening we're all gonna put on old clothes, and that's when I'm gonna start singing those old songs.

LKB: Wonderful. Will this be ready for us to buy by 2008 or the end of this year?

Shirley: Yes, it should be out by that time.

LKB: And that will be on your own label, Shubop?

Shirley: Yes, on my own label.

LKB: What prompted you to start your own label, Pastor Caesar? A lot of artists are doing that.

Shirley: For years and years I kind of wanted to do that because for so many years I was mistreated by major labels. One of the main things that would always happen is that I would put out a two-for-one CD, and they would always have a changing of the guard right at the time when they should be out there working my CD. But what they would do is that something would come up and they would start firing their people and bringing in new folk, and when they'd bring in the new people . . .

LKB: You'd get lost in the shuffle.

Shirley: There you go. So this way . . .

LKB: You don't have to worry about anybody dropping the ball on your project.

Shirley: There you go. When the CD *I Know the Truth* came out, I sold more in the first six months than I had in twenty years.

LKB: Oh my.

Shirley: Right. More in twelve months than I had in twenty years on some of the other CDs.

LKB: You've already talked to me about the importance of the traditional gospel music, and when I interviewed Tramaine Hawkins last December, she echoed your sentiments. I'd like to know what you make of the transition in gospel music. When you entered the gospel singing in 1966 as a solo artist, things were very different than today's gospel culture, with music videos and dance-club remixes.

Shirley: What do I think of this new trend of gospel? When we compare it with yesterday's gospel, there is no comparison. None whatsoever. Absolutely. And here again it's selling because men and women in their hearts are growing less love for God, they're becoming weaker, not wiser. And secondly, nothing stays the same. If it does, then it's stagnant. It will sink and then bring forth disease. Nothing stays the same. So each generation becomes weaker, again, and wiser. So gospel music has certainly grown. In some respects it just does not give to the people what it once did. But at the same time, I'm grateful for the change because I also can enlarge my borders.

LKB: That's true. You can reach another generation. I'm thinking now about the title track off your forty-first recording, *I Know the Truth*, which was produced by Tonex. Now, this album is certainly a hybrid of traditional gospel and hip-hop. You're even rapping on this album.

Shirley: [*laughter*] Yes. And the kids connect to that. All of the kids do. Of all the songs on the album, that's the one that makes young people excited.

LKB: I'm wondering if you will speak a little bit about gender discrimination you've faced in the church, because I'm very interested when I look at female evangelists and ministers about how they have dealt with that.

Shirley: Well, you know, at first we were not allowed in the pulpit. We could not call ourselves preachers; they called us teachers and missionaries. One preacher told me, I got the *P* mixed up with the *T*. He said, "You think God told you to go *preach*, you got it mixed up with *teach*." And of course he's asleep now, that man that said that. I wish he were alive so he could see what God is doing through women, like Juanita Bynum or Georgia Meyers or Shirley Caesar. I wish he was alive to see this.

LKB: How did you respond to him?

Shirley: Well, it hurt because it came from a bishop, it came from a man of God. You know, he knew my life. I was young in the ministry. I was there with the Caravans, traveling and singing with them. It was Bishop Hightower who said that to me, and it really hurt to the point where I couldn't respond. Then, later I preached in a church in some part of New Jersey, I believe it was Neptune, and Bishop McKnight wouldn't let me in his pulpit. When they brought me in, they sat me on the floor over in the corner, along the side of the wall, and they pulled over a table for me to stand behind on the floor. But since then, the Church of God in Christ has changed. Thankfully, things are different now.

LKB: Can you tell me what you learned about gospel performance from Albertina Walker and your experience singing with the Caravans?

Shirley: Well, let me just say this. The thing that she did do was just gave me the platform. I went there with it in me. I got all of my know-how, I guess, as a chip off the block, which was my dad. I don't remember him very much, but the old people used to tell me about how he would sing, and be all out on the aisle walking up and down. Who does that sound like? And all my brothers sang in quartets, too. So, it's not that the Caravans taught me how to sing; I come by that naturally. And they didn't teach me how to work an audience so that my performances would touch the lives of people. The Lord did that. What Albertina did was she gave me a chance to be heard. And I said to the Lord, I said, "Lord, you don't have to open the door wide, just crack it and I'll kick it down for your glory."

LKB: How does your evangelism feed your performance? I mean, having your own flock, having your own congregation, how does that feed what you do on those albums?

Shirley: Singing and preaching go together like ham and eggs. I love prayer, and I'm a praiser. When I get up on Sunday morning, I get up with a song. Sometimes, like Sunday morning past, I got up singing "Nobody but You, Lord." I'm gonna recut that.

LKB: I don't know that one.

Shirley: Oh, it's easy. [*singing*] "Nobody but you, Lord, nobody but you, nobody but you, Lord," that one. Anyway, I got up singing that. And my choir, they didn't know anything about those old songs. Boy, when I go to singing [*singing*], "Teach me master, teach me," boy, those young folks really enjoy that music. I sing the old songs because I've got old members, too. Sometimes I'll get up and I'll sing, "In Thee Oh Lord I Put My Trust." Sometimes I'll sing, "I Can't Let a Day Go By without Praising His Name," and from there I will go right into prayer. Sometimes I will have everybody turn on their cell phones, and I tell them to call somebody. "Call somebody that you know that needs this prayer." When I do that and they're standing holding the phone up, and the prayer goes through their line right into the hearts of those that are in need, I just ask the Lord to feed me something different that will bless the people. It seems to be working.

LKB: Pastor Caesar, in an interview in 2000 you told Maureen Bunyan, a reporter on the religion-and-ethics newsweekly on

PBS, that you were interested in being mayor of Durham, North Carolina. Are you still interested in politics?

Shirley: Oh, no. But I really meant that at that time. But since then I moved to Raleigh, which is about twenty miles away. I kind of want to be close to my church. I'm through with politics.

LKB: I know that you eventually went back to school, to Shaw University, where you graduated magna cum laude with a BS in business administration. What prompted you to return to school?

Shirley: It was a career choice because of the fact that during my career so many of the promoters across the country have taken advantage of me because of my giving spirit. My mind goes back to my time with the Caravans, when Ronny Williams would give the group members two hundred dollars—not the members, the whole group. And they would come into the room and make us sit and wait for our money until like two or three o'clock in the morning.

LKB: That's terrible.

Shirley: And he would put his gun up on the counter while they were paying the singers. He did that one night and when they brought in one of the other groups, and one of those other quartet singers took his gun out and placed it right alongside his. I wanted out because of that, and I knew that God had something else in my future. Something better. I knew that God had more purpose for me. And I always wanted to make sure that I had the letter behind that. I wanted to make sure I had that degree. And lo and behold, I became a part of the city council. And all of them were either educators or whatever, but they all had degrees, and here I am with a degree. Hallelujah.

LKB: When you look back and canvass your years of experience in the gospel world, starting from your experiences as ten-year-old baby Caesar to the present, if you could pass some wisdom earned during that time along to someone entering the gospel-music world today, what would it be?

Shirley: One of the main things I would say—because they're going to run into some hard knocks out there—I would tell them not to allow anybody to make them bitter. Let whatever you go through make you better.

LKB: Better, not bitter.

Shirley: There you go. Not bitter but better. And I would tell them, remember that Saul threw a spear at David. Don't be a spear thrower. Don't allow the enemy to bring you down to his level. But you rise to a new and higher place. And I would also tell them to don't go out there and try to jump to the top overnight. Just know that if you come up the rough side of the mountain, if you happen to slip, just know that there's a twig or a rock or something that you can grab hold to and start back up on your journey. Don't expect things to just happen for you overnight. It's better when you pay some dues. That way you can look back from where you've come and know that had it not been for the Lord on your side, that you would have never made it. And above all, live what you sing.

LKB: What was the most recent song you wrote? And can you take me through the process of writing it?

Shirley: Let me see, it was "Every Day Is Like Mother's Day."

LKB: And how was the song born?

Shirley: A young man from Philly came down and we were writing songs together. I told myself I was going to write a Mother's

Day song. And I sat down, and I just started thinking and praying about that. I remember seeing my mom, like, on Christmas morning she'd be sitting over in a chair and all of the children, we would get all of the gifts and put them down around her. And Momma would pray, she would pray for us. And I just said I'll never forget on Christmas morning when our family would gather round, my momma would sit over there in an old rocking chair, and she'd speak so softly.

LKB: Was your mother Pentecostal?

Shirley: Oh yes, oh yes. She was a semi-invalid also. Momma said, "Lord, you know I thank you for all of my children." She would often say that because she never wanted the children, the others, to think she loved me more than them because I was taking care of her. She used to say, "Lord, you know I thank you for all of my children, every one of them. I've tried to be a good mother to them; I even forgot all about my needs." And she did. So many times Momma wanted a dress, so many times she needed shoes, but she sacrificed, as parents are known to do. I could go on and on telling you about my mother. Up until each one of us, the children, would turn eighteen, Momma would get like forty-five dollars for me, forty-five dollars for Ann, forty-five dollars for Solomon, forty-five dollars for Joey, and so on. That's what she would get each month to take care of us, until we turned eighteen, and then that small amount would drop off.

LKB: That's not a lot of money to raise a child on—forty-five dollars.

Shirley: Did you say that's not a lot of money?

LKB: Yes, I did. To feed and clothe and buy shoes for a person, let alone the things that they need for school.

Shirley: And rent and stuff had to come out of that money, too. But I knew that one day God was going to vindicate; God was going to bless Momma. I didn't know how he was going to do it, but when I turned twelve years old and I started traveling and singing, the people would raise an after-offering for me. The after-offering had nothing to do with the first offering. And every bit that they would raise for me, I'd bring it home and give it to my mom. Sometimes I'd be sitting at the bus station, and I'd be so hungry, but because I knew that my momma needed the money, I wouldn't dare touch it. Well, on one occasion I remember buying a cheeseburger and a cherry Coke, but every other time, I brought all the money home and gave it to Momma. Sometimes I'd bring as much as three hundred dollars. And I did that up until I was, like, seventeen. And then when I joined the Caravans, I sent money home. But we were not making that much. We'd make twenty-five dollars and God would stretch my money out to the extent that some of them would come and borrow money from me. That's the thing some people don't understand about money. It will come to you if you don't make a god out of it. In fact, a young man I hadn't seen in a long time called me yesterday, and he needed money, and I'm getting ready to close on a house that I bought for my nephew. And the Lord knows that I needed that money, but I sent it to him. He's the son of a dear friend, and let me tell you something. If I tell you that the Lord is so faithful, he is faithful. I want to say this to your readers, whenever you remember those that are less fortunate than you, you are blessed. And I know whereof I speak, because for thirty-five years I've had an outreach ministry, where I try to bless people and give them emergency shelter. This comes from 50 percent of my earnings.

LKB: Of your own money.

Shirley: That's right.

LKB: I've read about it. It's incredible.

Shirley: But let me tell you something. If you remember those that are in need, and I know we can't help everybody. I know you can't sweep the Atlantic Ocean for ten pounds of sugar, but you can sweeten it. And if you would just sweeten a small portion, if you would just bless somebody, then God will bless you. But above all, you must be a tither, and God will take that remaining 90 percent and stretch it out. I am a witness to this. I come from a long line of poor folk, but I'm a witness that when you bless God, God will allow the enemy to give you back all the stuff he's taken from you. And you'll look around and you'll be so blessed that you'll just look up and say, "Lord God, where did all of this come from?" God will touch the hearts of people, and you'll never have to buy clothes, he'll give you new clothes and new shoes. The lord blessed me with a brand-new Mercedes. Brand-spanking-new 500. If you'll be faithful . . . now there's a difference between faithfulness and having faith. You can have faith but still not be faithful. And God is calling for faithfulness. There is a difference.

LKB: Pastor Caesar, when writing a song, do you will yourself to sit down and write? Are you inspired by a melody or a lyric first? How does it usually happen for you?

Shirley: You know, I heard a statement on television this morning just before you called. The statement was "You might not be able to do everything that you planned, but you can plan how you can turn it around." Now, that's heavy. And you know that I'll put that in a song. I am inspired by simply listening to things that are happening. I listen to what different folks are saying on television. Sometimes I read something and get inspiration. My most favorite preacher in the world is Bishop T. D. Jakes, and maybe just one thing he'll say will inspire me to write a song. I'm not the only one who works like this, either. I remember Dad [James] Cleveland said, faith is stepping out on nothing and landing on something, and I mentioned that to the Williams Brothers, and they wrote a song from it. And they heard me say, "I'm just a nobody trying to tell everybody about somebody who can save anybody," and they took that and wrote a song about it.

LKB: I didn't know that came from you.

Shirley: Oh yes, oh yes. And back to this new song that was coming to me just before you called. I've got to remember this. . . . This little boy wanted to go out and do something with his mom, and the mother said, "Well, you know I can't do it, because I can't leave my job." And the little boy said, "But we had planned this." She said, "But you can't do everything that you plan, but you can plan how you turn it around." . . . or something like that. But . . . if you figure it out for me, call me.

LKB: Well, sounds like you already have your title, Pastor Caesar, it's "Turn It Around."

Shirley: Yes . . . yes. And if you figure the rest out for me, call me, 'cause there's definitely a song in that somewhere.

Eighteen
Tokunbo Akinro
(September 15, 1975)

Born in Helmstead, Germany, to a German mother and Nigerian father, Tokunbo Akinro, the lead vocalist and lyricist for the European acoustic soul band Tok Tok Tok, spent her formative years in Nigeria, where she was drawn to her own musician father's compositions and black American soul music. Inspired by her host-family experience as a foreign-exchange student in California during high school, upon her return to Germany she pursued her interest in music. Graduating from the University of Hannover with a degree in jazz studies, Tokunbo began performing in local nightclubs, gaining popularity for her quiet, supple singing style. Free of industry restraints and musical clichés, the sound of Tok Tok Tok fuses the improvisatory nature of jazz with the open, earthy feel of acoustic folk music. Their original lyrics, written solely by Tokunbo, are crafted in good storytelling fashion. Their live performances have thrilled audiences through much of Europe, including the North Sea Jazz Festival at the Hague, Netherlands. In 2003 Akinro and Morten Klein, a multi-instrumentalist, reached the Top 10 on the German jazz charts with their album *It Took So*

Long. In 2005, the jazz fusion group was awarded the prestigious SACEM Grand Prix Award in France, and once again the German Jazz Award for the album *About*. The group's 2006 album release is made up of twelve tracks created by some of their favorite musical influences. *From Soul to Soul*, Tok Tok Tok's most recent album (2006) honors the artists Erykah Badu; Stevie Wonder; James Brown; Santana; Herbie Hancock; and Earth, Wind, and Fire.

Selected Discography

50 Ways to Leave Your Lover (BHM Records, Germany)
Love Again (BHM Records, Germany)
Ruby Soul (BHM Records, Germany
It Took So Long (BHM Records, Germany)
About . . . (BHM Records, Germany)
I Wish (BHM Records, Germany)
From Soul to Soul (BHM Records, Germany)

Tokunbo Akinro

LKB: Recently, I read an article about you wherein you spoke candidly about the shock of racism you experienced as a youth in Germany. I believe this was when you returned here to live when you were ten years old. I believe you wrote a song about this experience called "About."

Tokunbo: That's right, because for me I had always identified strongly with Germany as my home. My parents divorced when I was small and my mother returned to Germany. Since she lived far away from me, I always wanted to see her and the part of my family that was still here. So until the age of ten when I moved here, I associated Germany with only positive things, mainly my family. When I moved here it was the first time I encountered hostilities and alienation. Yeah, it came as a shock, and with time I developed my own ways of dealing with it. In this particular song that you're referencing, "About," the title song of our previous album, it deals with my racism experiences and also the experiences of friends of mine with racism in the United States.

LKB: During your childhood in Nigeria, who or what were some of your musical influences?

Tokunbo: Living with my father in Nigeria, I grew up with a lot of soul—Motown, Stevie Wonder, the Jackson Five, Aretha Franklin. Also, my dad formed a duo with a singer—an amateur band. Really, it was the recordings of my father's duo that touched me so deeply ever since I was quite small. Their recordings have always stayed with me because they are such a true expression of music. On my mother's side, I have an uncle who's a sound engineer and a musician. And my grandfather was a music teacher and musician, so there's always been a lot of music in our family.

LKB: How old were you when you decided to become a singer?

Tokunbo: I was eighteen. Before the decision, I was sixteen when I went to the United States as an exchange student. I lived with a family in California who encouraged me strongly. The school system in Germany is very different from the U.S. school system. In the U.S. high school, the subjects that I could choose from were so much more interesting. I chose all kinds of arts like choir, drama, and that's when I started singing solo. When I got back to Germany I got the lead part in the musical *Kiss Me Kate*, singing the music of Cole Porter, and then I joined a band. Around this time is when it hit me—that I really wanted to go into music. So I started looking for academies where I could study jazz. I heard about the one in Hannover, and I applied there. That's where I met Morten Klein, who is my musical director and my partner in the band Tok Tok Tok.

LKB: How long did you study at the Jazz Academy in Hannover?

Tokunbo: For four years. We had all kinds of classes—music theory, of course, classical singing, piano, arranging, songwriting, and a class in recording, which was quite interesting. I received my degree in jazz vocal performance.

LKB: What were the circumstances surrounding the formation of your band Tok Tok Tok? And I wonder if you could talk about the band's name. I'm assuming Tok is short for Tokunbo.

Tokunbo: That's right. Well, basically the forming of our band was sort of an accident. I'd been in a show at this theater and this club owner saw me and invited me to do three shows in his club. So I put a trio together, with Morten on saxophone and a guitarist. We did one concert, and after that the guitarist couldn't come to the next gig. Morten and I had both been in our own duos with a double-bass player, and we'd always thought about working together with the bass player, the three of us. So we gave it a shot and realized that the sound was so interesting because there was no harmony—no piano, no guitar, no harmonic instrument. The three of us had to be everything. We had to develop the harmony of the song and be very precise with the rhythm. It was a big challenge and it made our sound very unique. So we pursued that path. Slowly we incorporated other instruments, like the Fender Rhodes.

Morten has been doing mouth-drums ever since he was a teenager—

LKB: When you use the term *mouth-drums*, are you referring to beat-boxing?

Tokunbo: No, it's not the same because usually with the beat box—well, the beat box is sort of an imitation of the drum machine. What Morten does is, he really imitates the sound of an acoustic drum.

LKB: Like he does in the beginning of your version of "50 Ways to Leave Your Lover"?

Tokunbo: Exactly. That was actually the initial start of incorporating mouth-drums. It was just an idea, you know. We thought, *Why don't we do this song because the groove is by Steve Gadden and the sound is so particular, so special.* But no one could ever come close to covering it by playing the normal drums. 'Cause no one could top it, of course. With mouth-drums it was a completely different direction. After that we incorporated Morten's mouth-drums into a lot of the songs, and it became very popular and then some of them grew too big. Morten was playing less and less saxophone, which is why we now have a real drummer in the band.

LKB: When did you begin to write your own songs?

Tokunbo: I started, I think, when I was seventeen. I started playing the guitar and fooling around with the chords. And later I started with the piano. Actually, when I was at the music academy I had one class that was very, very important to me because the teacher was so encouraging. He always said, "Write songs rather than just interpreting the songs of other people. It's the most important thing you can do as a musician because you get royalties for that and you can build up something for yourself." I used to have another group where I tried out my songs, but at the moment I am a lyricist for this band. Morten writes all of the music, and I write all of the lyrics.

LKB: Do you write the lyric after Morten has composed the music? Or does the lyric come first?

Tokunbo: Almost always the music comes first. It also depends on the concept. For this new album [*From Soul to Soul*] we've dedicated original songs to our favorite soul artists from the sixties and seventies, mainly. So naturally the music was the catalyst, the driving force behind all of the lyrics that I wrote. Writing this album, I tried to let myself be inspired by what the artist stands for and also what themes have appeared in their lyrics. With the previous album [*About*], we did it vice versa. I gave Morten poems of mine, and he wrote music for them. We've released four albums with our own material: *Ruby Soul, It Took So Long, About*, and *From Soul to Soul*.

LKB: Speaking of *From Soul to Soul*, there are two songs that really stand out for me on that album: "I Could Never Forget" and "How." Can you speak a bit about what inspired the lyrics of these songs, which are tributes to Carlos Santana and Erykah Badu?

Tokunbo: With "I Could Never Forget," I was really inspired by the tropical-music atmosphere Morten created. It just instantly took me back to these childhood places, places in Lagos, Nigeria. It was one of the easiest songs for me really, which was nice because I just had all of these pictures in my mind. I think that the tropical mood conveyed fits a lot of Santana's repertoire. With "How," I was really inspired by Erykah Badu, who is a very spiritual person. On her live album, she talks about how important spirituality is to her. When Morten and I were writing the album, we talked about what we wanted to say and what topics we wanted to spend time on. Basically, the song "How" is a question about why nations go to war. And why do people use religion to legitimate war. With this song I thought I would research the main religions just to see if they have a core belief system and if so, why can't we see it? In my research I learned about an organization that is really interested in bringing the religions of the world together. I'm Protestant and there's a church congress that we have in Germany every two years, and now they're having the ecumenic congress—putting together Catholics and Protestants. And they also include spiritual leaders of other religions. It's very interesting because we have Buddhist monks coming. One of my favorite spiritual leaders, Thich Nhat Hanh from Vietnam, maybe you've heard of him?

LKB: Yes.

Tokunbo: And they will have Jewish leaders and Muslim leaders and try to get a dialogue going in an attempt to come to peace.

LKB: Whose idea was it to have this character motif of Phyllis Jones on your latest album? Her presence is felt across the entire album, especially tracks two, "Tuxedo Junction" and ten, "Don't Mess around with Phyllis Jones." Having a narrator's presence, in some of the songs, that is distinct from the singer's voice in obvious ways is a very interesting approach, Tokunbo.

Tokunbo: Well, the song is for James Brown. It started with me thinking about James Brown, who, in my opinion, is this hypermasculine, supermacho personality. So the idea was, why not turn it around and spin a lot of Brown's perspective from a female point of view. You know, he says, "It's a man's world." Why not turn it around and develop a female character that is so strong, she just knows what she wants and she goes for it. Also with this song I was battling against the cliché that a woman has to be approached by the man, discovered, and picked up. This is a concept that I strongly disagree with.

LKB: So she's like a Superwoman character, or is she you?

Tokunbo: [*laughter*] No. Sometimes I wish I had more of her qualities. But I am somewhat like her. I'm also straightforward. I think, though, from what I experienced in the United States, that it can be rather hard for women to approach men because the men become intimidated. And the same can be the case here, but I've always believed that it's the best way, you know, not to be picked but to pick—for the woman to decide who she wants to be with.

LKB: [*laughter*] Yes, I totally agree.

Tokunbo: This song is really about encouragement for me. It's my way of telling women not to be ashamed of who they are, not to be ashamed of their sexuality and their high self-esteem.

LKB: Over the course of seven albums, you've maintained creative momentum, in part because of your eclectic choice of material, which includes jazz, soul, and pop covers from Bacharach and Jobim to Paul Simon and Stevie Wonder. When you are deciding on which songs to sing, what features of a song are you most interested in?

Tokunbo: Well, I must say that the music turns me on first. I think it's very unusual for a singer not to be interested in the lyric foremost, but I listen to the melody first. The way we pick

songs to cover is mainly based on the music. We've always been
on the search for good melodies, which is why we went back
to the sixties and seventies for our inspiration for this last
album. Because today it seems that a lot of artists are more
focused on the production and all of the technological devices
that can be employed when making music.

LKB: I tend to agree with you. A lot of the music has lost its
humanity, and by that I mean that it's more technological than
musical; it's harsh sounding to my ears. I've heard about and
witnessed recording sessions that are more about production,
using the technology, than actually capturing the personality of
the artist and the dynamic nature of the music.

Tokunbo: Yeah, and we just really like the idea that musicians like
Stevie Wonder—he wrote the songs, he sang them, he played
the instruments and produced the whole thing. You can really
see the profile of an artist and feel the person and you don't
just have someone who is impersonating something.

LKB: That's a very interesting statement and it explains why you
have covered the songs that you cover. I'm looking at the list
of musicians whose work you have interpreted and Paul
Simon, Antonio Carlos Jobim, Stevie Wonder, they all write,
sing, and play their own songs.

Tokunbo: Yes.

LKB: What are some of the elements that you are striving for,
Tokunbo, in a live performance?

Tokunbo: Well, I really like when there's a connection between the
band and the audience. It's not just trying my best to perform
very well, it's also to maybe give a part of myself. Sometimes it's
a bit hard because you don't want to reveal too much. Some

people can mistake that, and they'll approach you and talk to you as if you were friends with them. It can be very awkward. I try to reach people by sharing a part of myself. I often share anecdotes from our experiences touring. And I try to reach them by making them laugh. Sometimes that works, sometimes it doesn't. [*laughter*] We're a funny band, though. We're a funny band behind the scenes, and we're also funny onstage. I think people like that because we're not distant to the audience. We try to be who we are. I guess that's the most important thing to me. I could never impersonate someone who I'm not. I try to have entertaining qualities but still be natural; that's the highest goal for me. Of course, I also like to get the lyric across. It's a bit hard in Germany because some people don't understand English that well. But a lot of times they approach me afterwards having read the lyrics in the liner notes and then they may say that it touched them or that the lyrics mean something to them, and that's, of course, very gratifying.

LKB: You sing songs solely in English, correct?

Tokunbo: Yes, but depending on where I am, I will talk to the audience between songs in their language. We perform mostly in our home country, Germany, so I speak German most of the time. But when we perform in eastern Europe I try to use a little Russian, but mainly I'm speaking English. In France, I speak French. In Spain, I speak Spanish.

LKB: Are you fluent in Spanish and French?

Tokunbo: Quite fluent in Spanish and doing quite well in French, too.

LKB: Did you pick up the languages in school or during travels or both?

Tokunbo: I studied French in school, and Spanish was a hobby of mine. I was invited to Spain, I don't know, thirteen years ago, and I completely fell in love with the culture and the language and I started traveling to Spain all the time after that. And I had a partner here in Germany, it's called a tandem—like the double bicycle. You meet every week and you practice and you teach each other your own language. I did that for four years.

LKB: Where in Nigeria did you grow up?

Tokunbo: In Lagos, in the former capital. That was a completely different life than here in Germany. It's very interesting because it was only a few years ago that I realized what a culture clash it was for me as a child.

LKB: When I studied abroad in Germany in the early nineties, I didn't experience racism in Göttingen, the town where I lived with my host family. But I do recall a somewhat scary incident when I traveled to Hamburg to attend the opera with a friend one weekend. This elderly woman, who I could tell was from the former East Germany by her dialect, followed me from the train station for several hundred yards yelling at me, "*Geh zurück nach Afrika! Geh zurück nach Afrika!*" ["Go back to Africa!"] Any bystander could've observed that and thought I had done something to the woman, and anything could've happened. It's very harrowing when I read about the difficulties that immigrants are facing in Germany, which, after the USA, has the second-highest immigrant population for a nation its size. I bring this up because I know one of your hit songs happens to be an original song on the topic of race and ethnic injustice. I wonder if you might talk about your song

"About" and how it relates to the current climate for people of color in Germany.

Tokunbo: Well, I think, for one, we have to differentiate. There is a real problem in the former East Germany because of social issues and poverty. There is no perspective for the majority of people.

LKB: They perceive the immigrant population as taking jobs away from native Germans?

Tokunbo: This is the excuse they use. There is a high unemployment rate in Germany at the moment, so everyone is looking for a scapegoat. There are communities that are completely deserted, where everyone is unemployed. So, naturally, these people—most of them are young people—are frustrated, and it's very easy for certain groups to recruit these people for hate crimes. Also, Germans just weren't used to people who aren't white for many, many years. It's not until the last forty years that the society has become truly multiracial. I'm very happy when I go to cities like Berlin and Hamburg and I see that there are more and more Asian people, Turkish people, Indian people, African people. Our country is becoming more and more multicultural, and as a child of a white German woman and Nigerian man, this obviously makes me happy. I moved to Freiburg, [in] the south of Germany, six years ago because I feel very, very comfortable here. It's an international city, there are loads of students like [in] Göttingen, where you lived. Since it's a big university town there are many, many young people who are generally open-minded. Also there are loads of tourists. A lot of times when you walk through the streets here, the language that you hear isn't German but French. It is a quaint town, and I like it very much.

LKB: Have you thought about writing or recording songs in German?

Tokunbo: I have never sung in German, but I have thought about it. I haven't done it because, well, I must say, it's quite hard. Until a couple of years ago, when German hip-hop was born, and emancipated itself from American hip-hop—

LKB: Do you mean German hip-hop groups that make a form of the music that is distinct from American hip-hop, like the group Brothers Keepers?

Tokunbo: Brothers Keepers is exactly what I mean. So, until groups like this emerged, I would not have even thought it possible to make popular music singing in German and not sound harsh. Now I've heard more artists who are doing it, and it's easier for me to imagine. But I have to say it intimidates me a bit because it's in German and people really, *really* are now listening to the lyric, you have to have very strong lyrics that are very well written. Recently I listened to a German R&B record. It was good, it was American in the way it was produced, and the singer was singing in an American-soul style but the lyrics were in German, but you could tell that the lyric was originally written in English and then translated into German. And it just didn't sound right.

LKB: From your earlier album *It Took So Long*, I love the songs "When You're Far Away" and "I Cannot Sleep."

Tokunbo: "When You're Far Away" is basically about a long-distance relationship. My boyfriend and I are not living in the same town, so I wrote that when I was in one of my moods wishing that he was here. And, again, this is a case where Morten had written the music first. The nice thing about the way that he

composes music is that it really inspires me very quickly. When
I listen to his songs, it's like they take me into a certain mood,
and most of the time I find the story, or the lyric, when I am
in the mood.

LKB: Now, the song "I Cannot Sleep" is sort of deceptive.

Tokunbo: Yes. It starts out with the cliché of how parents tell children to count sheep when they cannot sleep—it's sort of a
joke—but later in the song you realize that what lies behind
the child's insomnia is a serious reason. It's serious things happening in the family that cause the nightmares to come. It's a
very personal song for me.

LKB: Does Morten ever contribute to the lyric-writing process?

Tokunbo: We talk about the direction in which we want to go with
the song, but the lyric writing is 100 percent me. Over the last
four albums, I would say that our process has become more
homogenous.

LKB: Would you say that your songs are largely autobiographical?

Tokunbo: Yes. Like on the earlier album, *Ruby Soul*, there's a song
called "Always an Excuse"—the last song on the album and at
that time I was really searching for a way to live my life very
consciously, and that song projects this journey of mine to
work toward being in the here and the now, because I am
really a control freak and quite often have to remind myself
that not everything is in my hands.

LKB: From your first album *50 Ways to Leave Your Lover*, the song
"Day Tripper" is so rich in imagery, the listener is pulled in
right away. It meshes great descriptive with a groove à la Cassandra Wilson's "Go to Mexico" and Jill Scott's "A Long Walk."

Tokunbo: Thank you for that. I was a student at the academy at the time we recorded that album. Sometimes I had a hard time at the academy, because of course they have their curriculum and they want you to perform certain things so that they can measure you. But I felt unrecognized for the kind of musician I was becoming, the quality of my singing. This was a time when I realized that I really had to come back to myself. I listened to a lot of Billie Holiday during my studies because she was so . . . so authentic, and that was my highest goal and still is. To be authentic when I sing.

LKB: Do you ever experience writer's block, and if so, what do you do to nudge yourself along?

Tokunbo: Basically, when I start writing for an album I stop sleeping [*laughter*]. Because what happens is I begin to brood over the songs. Usually Morten gives me a song every week, or two songs a week, and I write the lyrics continually until the album is finished. The exception was with the album *Ruby Soul*, when Morten gave me eleven songs at once because it was a hectic time for him, he and his wife had just had their second child. Once I'm onto an idea about a song I can't think of anything else. We don't have any concerts during the writing time. I remember working on the song "Oh Lord."

LKB: That's from the new album, *From Soul to Soul*—the tribute to Ray Charles?

Tokunbo: Yes. We were thinking about Ray Charles, what he stands for, and we started thinking about the work song atmosphere of his singing and his music. So, "Oh Lord" was supposed to be a modern work song. I wrote it when I was on the Nordsee. Do you know the North Sea?

LKB: Ah, yes. I vacationed there with my German host family the summer of 1991.

Tokunbo: Many Germans go on holiday there. I was spending New Year's Eve there with my boyfriend, and it was cold. So it wasn't the southern climate that you imagine when you think of work songs—that hot and humid atmosphere. But for some reason I was just really into that song, really brooding over it, and it came to me. Sometimes if I'm having a hard time with a song, it will come to me when I'm just about to fall asleep because that's when I'm relaxed and open enough to receive it. When we're on tour, there's no time to write. It's just the tour, organizing the next concert and the next steps. So I really love the times that we spend writing because it's so nice to create something new. If something comes to me when we're on tour, I will always write it down. But I don't sit down and try to make a song happen while we're touring because there is really too little time for it. I guess as a writer, you have a certain schedule? I suppose you sit down at a desk and devote a certain number of hours each day?

LKB: Actually, I can't write like that. At least, not originally. For me, the first writing, what I like to call the spirit writing, happens at any time, and the duration of the writing spell can be just as unpredictable. However, I can be disciplined when it comes to revising, polishing up the writing, because I find that I'm exercising more of the control in that type of writing. I have a close friend who awakens every morning around 6:30 A.M., and she turns her telephone off and writes until about 2:00 P.M. This is her schedule every day, or at least it was until she became a new mother. Now, I seriously doubt I will ever have that kind of relationship to writing. I can't go to a blank computer screen unless I have something to say. I consider myself a channel, and I absolutely have to receive the inspiration first.

Tokunbo: That's very interesting, but sometimes deadlines can be problematic, right?

LKB: It's true, it's true.

LKB and Tokunbo: [*laughter*]

LKB: Your last album, *From Soul to Soul*, is very much a concept album. Was it a successful approach for your band? Is Tok Tok Tok planning to make future concept albums?

Tokunbo: We really want to. We found that having a concept before writing the album was very triggering for our inspiration. So we do want to make more concept albums. When you give your work a theme, in a way it makes things easier.

LKB: It's interesting that you say that because I've had conversations with artists who have commented that structuring their albums around a concept or a theme is restrictive. Some artists have posed the question of what you then do with song ideas that fall outside of the concept. But it sounds as though you find the concept approach more conducive to working because it forces you to harness your creative energies in one direction.

Tokunbo: I can see what they mean, but then again, it's in your hands. You're the person who has created the concept, so you can always modify it. That's what we've always lived by. We can have an idea, but if it doesn't work, then why not create a little loophole. In the arts, I don't think there is such a thing as burdening oneself with a strict idea. As soon as the situation starts to feel limiting, that's the moment to loosen it up!

LKB: What do you think you would be doing if you weren't a singer–songwriter?

Tokunbo: I would love to be a writer. A novelist. I love to read, it has always been a real passion of mine because, as I said, I tend to be controlling, and reading provides me with precious moments in which I can really fly away to another world of my design.

LKB: Who are some of your favorite writers?

Tokunbo: John Irving, definitely. I like the Japanese writer Haruki Murakami. Do you know him?

LKB: No. I'm not familiar with any of his work.

Tokunbo: Very interesting. He wrote a book called *Hard-boiled Wonderland*; it's crazy, but crazy in a fascinating way. His books mix reality with fairy–tale qualities. One of my favorite books is *The Physician* by Noah Gordon.

LKB: Tokunbo, before we end I wonder if you would share with me the meaning of your name.

Tokunbo: *Tokunbo* means: the child who was born overseas and then returns home. It was given to me by my grandfather on my paternal side. It's a male and a female name. The people who carry the name are of the Yoruba tribe, so it is a name generally given to Yoruba born outside of Africa, like me. And I did return home to Nigeria after I was born, so the name turned out to be prophetic, too.

Nineteen
TOSHI REAGON
(JANUARY 27, 1964)

Atlanta native singer-songwiter Toshi Reagon can take any style, update it, and make it her own with incredible ease. Her genre bending has earned her legions of fans, who can catch Toshi anywhere from onstage at Carnegie Hall to a rock club. Whether playing solo or with her band, BIGLovely, Toshi's fusion of styles and forms draws listeners in, and as one review from the *New Yorker* put it, "showers retro funk, urban blues, and folk on the audience with evangelical fervor. Her performance roster is as eclectic as the shows themselves, whether a Central Park Summerstage benefit/Joni Mitchell tribute with artists like Vernon Reid and Chaka Khan, a tribute to Prince, the Smithsonian Folklife Festival, or the Blood on the Tracks concert in New York City celebrating the twenty-fifth anniversary of the Bob Dylan album *Blood on the Tracks*, you know you've seen a Toshi show if you still have a groove hours after the show and are thinking hard on how to instigate some social change. The sociopolitical messages prevalent in most of her songs are a natural carryover from the artist's upbringing. Both parents belonged to SNCC's (Student

Non-Violent Coordinating Committee) the Freedom Singers, a folk group that sprang up from the civil rights movement and toured the country to teach people about civil rights through song. Bernice Johnson Reagon, Toshi's mother, is also the founder of the world-renowned a cappella ensemble Sweet Honey in the Rock (she retired in 2004 after thirty years with the group). Toshi's rich musical heritage led her to become saturated in many traditional styles of music, feeding her desire to explore a range of music that was not as accessible, from blues to Kiss. Admittedly, Toshi says that she attempts to "take whatever I'm really into and try to learn it and put it into music." This trait results in a musical style that not only transcends classification, but also expresses a political consciousness that is as ingrained in her music as the multiple genres she embraces. Believing music is the way she deals with her political energy, Toshi once told *Curve* magazine, "From where you are, from who you are in your everyday life, that's where you make change. . . . Whatever your gig is, make change through your strength." Toshi is a recipient of a 2004 NYFA award for music composition.

Selected Discography

    Justice (Flying Fish Records)
    The Rejected Stone (self-released)
    Kindness (Smithsonian Folkways)
    The Righteous Ones (Razor & Tie)
    Africans in America Soundtrack, with Bernice Johnson Reagon, various artists (Ryco)
    Toshi (Razor & Tie)
    I Be Your Water (limited self-release)

Toshi Reagon

LKB: The musical knowledge, the musical experiences, and the musical products that came out of your childhood home, namely from your mother, the founder of Sweet Honey in the Rock, Bernice Johnson Reagon, are astonishing, Toshi. Can you speak to the influence of that rich musical heritage and its impact on you as a child?

Toshi: I think that the biggest way that my mother influenced me was to leave me alone to make discoveries and connections for myself. I have to say, though, that one advantage I had while growing up was that I got to be in the living room when she was having rehearsal. [*laughter*] My mom was a very good parent in that she created a learning atmosphere and opportunity. She took my brother and me to lots of musical venues, not just concerts, but if she was working at a festival we went along with her. So we absorbed a lot of different kinds of music and experienced lots of different people representing different cultures. Now that I'm an adult, I see how valuable that was to my life. It totally made me feel like I didn't have to walk down only one road, and I learned early that life is quite varied. It's a great lesson for any child to learn. Also, when I was growing up, if I liked something that my mother didn't like, her response was never that it was something wrong with my preference. When I was four, I loved Jimi Hendrix, so she bought me a Jimi Hendrix record. When I was twelve I was in love with Kiss, and she bought me tickets to go see Kiss in concert. [*laughter*] When I wanted to play drums, she bought me a drum set, and my two hours on the drums every day was built into the family schedule. No one ever said I was playing too loud or tried to discourage me. So those are the things that really helped to shape me.

LKB: I have always been enamored of the fact that your music traverses multiple genres, and from your first comment it's clear now that this is something that organically happens based on the musical freedom you experienced as a child.

Toshi: Exactly, LaShonda. It's very important for me not to place restrictions or confines of any sort on my music. My approach and my experience with the music should always feel and sound limitless, because it is about freedom for me.

LKB: You're just coming off of a recording project with the songstress Lizz Wright, who I wanted to interview but her recording schedule prevented it. Did you cowrite any of the material that will be on Lizz's third album?

Toshi: Yeah, Lizz is my girl. You know who she reminds me of? I was just listening to her last night, too: Roberta Flack. You know, I was too young when Roberta first came out to actually remember this, but the cultural memory is there. When Roberta first hit the scene, people would say they just never heard anybody sing like that. She opened her mouth and everybody—no matter what kind of music you liked or what race you were or how old you were—everybody just stopped and listened. We were listening to *First Take* in the house last night, and I was like, "Just listen to that. It's unbelievable." Her voice is incredible. And though Lizz doesn't sound like Roberta Flack, that same energy, that same power is there.

LKB: A friend of mine gave me a copy of *First Take* a few years ago, and my first listening of that album was truly an unforgettable experience. I was familiar with some of the songs, like "Ballad of the Sad Young Men" written by Fran Landesman, because I'm such a jazzhead and a few of my favorite jazz vocalists have recorded that, but Roberta interprets the song so differently. She evoked such strong feelings for me—just hearing the album was intense.

Toshi: See, you know what I'm talking about. Lizz is that kind of vocalist to me. She's a real one of a kind. And, to answer your question, Lizz and I did do a lot of writing together for her upcoming album. I don't know how much of it, or which songs, will make it on there, but we did do a lot of writing. I'm really excited about it and can't wait to hear it.

LKB: The main reason I brought up the recent work with Lizz is because I wanted you to sketch for me your musical journey from 1990's album *Justice* to your most recent songwriting efforts. I want to know your perception of the major ways your approach to songwriting has changed over the years.

Toshi: Well, I think the biggest way my approach has changed is that I'm much more relaxed about it. Through experience I know and trust now that the songs will come to me if I give myself the right energy and atmosphere. I'm one of those people who always has a recording device on me. When I was a teenager, a melody would come to me, and I could keep that melody in my head, but as I grew older that wasn't the case. So now I immediately record anything that I feel is a great groove or has potential to be a great song. I'm very, very inspired by good singers. For example, when I heard Lizz's voice I started writing immediately, just from hearing the sound of her voice. I could just hear stories. Another major change between writing songs then and now is the foundation of openness that I've built for myself over the years. I feel really comfortable singing any kind of style or writing any kind of style of music—be it folk, country, hip-hop, rhythm and blues, or gospel, or hymn-inspired. I didn't have that comfort twenty years ago, but I have it now and it's really fun. The benefit of having a career that people label eclectic is that I feel I can say what I want and do what I want musically. I have a lot of musician friends who are very famous, and I see them struggling with business entities that want them to collaborate on projects and write music a certain way just to create a ripple or a splash in the marketplace. I feel lucky to be free from that. You know, when you get an advance for a record that is thousands and thousands of dollars and they want to make millions in sales, they don't want you to have an idea for a record that is not easily categorized. I don't have thousands or millions invested in me by a record company. I operate in a small but fierce market. I collaborate with enough interesting and talented people, and musically I get to do what I want to do. All of this and I get to pay my bills, which is always the mark for me: can I pay my bills making music? What more can I ask for?

LKB: One of the things that you said harkens back to something very important that I learned from Abbey Lincoln. During one of my first conversations with her years ago, we were sitting in her living room and I commented on the little Post-it notes and other scraps of paper that I saw around. Abbey explained

to me that when a line or a lyric came to her she always wrote
it down—she never took anything for granted. I remember her
saying, "The spirit of music does not need me. I need it. If I
don't catch it, it will go on to another person. And it doesn't
even really need people, either. The spirit of music can whistle
through the trees or babble in the brook. Birds have the gift of
song, too."

Toshi: Wow, that's deep.

LKB: Abbey was talking about the humility that distinguishes
artists who have a spiritual awareness or relationship to their
craft and those who feel that the process is really only about
them. When you mentioned the recording device that you're
never caught without, you reminded me of that humility,
which, it seems to me, is a byproduct of the "openness" you
talked about creating for yourself. I do think it's really
important for creative people to learn not to leave their
inspiration to the prowess of memory.

Toshi: Yes, I don't take it for granted. Listening to that, you made
me think of another thing that I do now that I didn't do years
ago. Now I make regular appointments to go into the studio
and record, regardless if I have enough material for a record or
if I have a record deal. I will not let myself go more than two
or three months without going into the studio and recording
songs. I don't even tell myself what the songs are intended for.
I don't say it's for a record or a movie soundtrack, I just go in
and record songs. It's a way of exercising myself as a songwriter
and a musician. You know I was able to meet—maybe you've
talked to her—Nona Hendryx.

LKB: Yes, I spoke with Nona. She's fantastic.

Toshi: Well, growing up she was one of my favorite artists. I was a huge Labelle fan as a kid because I was a big rock fan, a big funk fan, and their music incorporated all of this. I remember my mother went to see them in concert, and I couldn't go with her—I'm still mad at her for that. [*laughter*] I just have so much respect for Nona.

LKB: Have you ever worked with her?

Toshi: Yes. When I was on Elektra Records for half a second, as the deal was falling apart they said to me, "Who is somebody that you would want to work with?" And I had just read in a magazine article where Nona had said she wanted to do some producing, so I spit out, "I'd love to work with Nona Hendryx." They set up a meeting between Nona and me. She listened to all of the songs that I had recorded—she had basically been brought in to do a fix because Elektra didn't feel comfortable with my record, and she was going to help me reshape the songs and maybe add a few more. I did this songwriting session with Nona, and I remember her giving me a great bit of advice. She said not to edit yourself as you're writing, just get your idea out, get it done, then you go back and assume the critical gaze. Then you go back and ask the tough questions: Are you making lines? Are they the most obvious choices? Is there a better way to say that? Can you use other words to say what you've said? And I didn't have that before I met Nona. I just spit out whatever I had; I never went back in and really honed.

LKB: I'm so glad you brought that up, because in discussing the title of this book with some people, believe it or not, there has been some question about my usage of the term *craft*, as if writing a song never requires revision or honing.

Toshi: Certainly it does. Crafting is exactly what songwriting is about. Even beyond the lyric writing, arranging entails quite a bit of crafting. When do you put solos in? When do you put bridges in? What can you do to make a song pop a little bit more? These are all craft questions, and craft involves a work ethic. If you don't have a work ethic, your music will be sloppy and repetitive, and nobody will buy it 'cause it'll stink! [*laughter*] So yeah, you're on the right track using the term *craft*. Anything else would be doing a disservice to a long line of artists who possess natural gifts but who also observe and respect all of the technical aspects of music.

LKB: Toshi, do you remember the first song that you wrote?

Toshi: Yes. I was in the seventh grade and I wrote this terrible, very mushy song called "I Love You," around the time when I first started playing the guitar.

LKB: So you started to play the guitar around the age of twelve, thirteen?

Toshi: Yes. My mom tried to get me interested in the piano, but it didn't work. I wasn't feeling the piano at all. Interestingly enough, and I may have alluded to this earlier, I felt like a drummer before I started to play the guitar. My brother actually got a drum set, and I would play his all of the time. One of the first songs I would play along to was "Lady Marmalade." Later, in high school, I picked up the bass. You know, back in the day high school bass players were rather unreliable. We had one guy and he got high all of the time—he was a chew-tobacco kind of guy—so he always had this big trash can, and he'd be spitting in it while we were rehearsing. [*laughter*] Anyway, I taught myself how to play the bass so I wouldn't have to use that guy.

LKB: You were the leader of your high school band?

Toshi: Yeah. We did a lot of cover tunes, not so much the songs that I was writing. We'd cover Crosby, Stills, and Nash; and Zeppelin. We were very much a rock band. It was fun.

LKB: In interviews conducted with the singer-songwriter Cassandra Wilson, she often talks about the ways her native Jackson, Mississippi, influenced her musically. I'm curious about whether or not Atlanta or D.C. were in any way influences on your musical development.

Toshi: Well, we left Atlanta when I was seven, but I was very much influenced by living there because the civil rights movement was happening, and we were right in the midst of it—the Black Panthers used to march outside of our front door in formation. During this time, my mom was in her mid- to late twenties and she had a group called the Harambee Singers. I remember going to concerts and meetings with her where people would always be singing. Also, there'd be these black band parades all the time. It seemed like every weekend you would see a marching band, though I'm sure it wasn't that frequent. And at the same time, black radio was exploding! You could hear the Temptations, Sly and the Family Stone, and Rufus Thomas back to back. My mom says that when I was three I was singing "My Girl," so, yes, all of those things had an important influence on me. I think early on I knew I was going to be an instrumentalist even though the music my mother devoted herself to was a cappella, as it was with Sweet Honey. I remember seeing Tina Turner on television when I was five and I was like, "Oh my God!" By the time we got to D.C., I remember listening to the black radio stations there and feeling like it had settled down a bit. By that I mean, there was a lot less variety; you kind of heard the same thing. When I was about twenty, though, it occurred to me that I couldn't do musically what I wanted to do in Washington. That's why I moved to New York.

LKB: And you've been a New Yorker for over twenty years now, right?

Toshi: Yes. I love this city. New York is a place where you can play every night at a different venue and get a completely different audience. Here, you can collaborate so quickly with someone who does film or works in theater or has a dance company or does spoken word. New York is just so much on another level than any other place I've ever lived. If you want to be a musician you come to New York, because right away you can go to work. Now, that doesn't necessarily mean you're going to make a lot of money, but you can go to work, you can find any café that will let you sit out in front of people and start singing, start honing your craft. And New York will influence anybody. It's just an amazing, amazing cultural phenomenon.

LKB: Yes, it is. You know, Toshi, I've noticed that a sociopolitical aspect is foregrounded in a lot of your music. Considering your lineage—I know that both parents sang for the Freedom Singers—this isn't surprising to me, but I'm nevertheless very interested in your obvious commitment to giving voice to social issues.

Toshi: Well, firstly, I believe that there is a social movement going on, even though we might not be able to see it or hear a lot about it. Part of our struggle is this war on information. You know, back in the day we were fighting segregation and that was literally black and white, and seen on television in black and white. There were black and white signs posted everywhere, you know . . . *White Only* and *Colored Only*. It was so in-your-face. Today there is so much going on but at the same time we're not so privy to the information, not unless you go out and purposely seek it. I feel that it is part of my job to make some of this information known, to voice the struggle, the various struggles that so many people are engaged in on so many different levels. I'm a real believer that if you have a thought, an idea, a feeling about how your community or country should be run, you say it all the time. You don't only say it when you have people marching with you in the street, or if you have a hundred thousand people listening to you, or just because Imus said something stupid; you say it all the time. Last night I listened to a music video that Mos Def did and I'm telling you, this song is crazy. Basically he wrote this song saying that Bush blew up the Twin Towers. He breaks down in the song how bin Laden was funded by the CIA. The whole video is a montage of truth-telling images that are just staggering. It's an amazing video, it's an amazing work of art circulating all over YouTube. Now, is MTV ever going to play that? No. But that doesn't mean that a hundred thousand or a million people won't see that video. I just think that we all have to be aware of the kind of work being done by artists and we have to seek it out, we have to get the information. All of these mainstream entities that people relied on for information during the civil rights movement, like the CDF footage of Martin Luther King giving a speech, well, it's not going to happen like that this time. We are not going to be informed in the same ways. The mainstream entities are so late, they're so far away, they so don't want to tell you anything that is going on that if you look to them for markers on where society really is, you're going to get a whitewashed consumer report. You're going to be told what new thing you can buy; you aren't going to get any real information that can turn things around and over. You're not going to have at your disposal the work of revolutionary-minded artists. That's not going to happen unless you consciously seek them out because they're not good for business.

LKB: Whew—

Toshi: And that's why I do what I do. You know, I really care about the people who are going to come along after me. I have a twelve-year-old daughter and a five-year-old goddaughter. I am always thinking about the kind of world they are going to inherit.

LKB: Toshi, I came to your music in the summer of 1996. I was working at Barnes & Noble Booksellers in Kansas City, not an area well-known for having lots of purveyors of independent music, but at the bookstore I got ahold of a Putumayo World Music compilation CD. On the CD was your song "Kindness." To this day it remains one of my favorites, so of course I want to know what inspired that one?

Toshi: I wrote that song when I was working with Urban Bush Women on this piece called "Bones and Ash." There was this little group of us that would hang out all the time, and it was just such a solid group of women. They seemed to be constantly lifting each other up at all the right times, and it just inspired me to write that song. "Kindness" is also one of my mother's favorites; she's always asking me to sing that song. She's done a vocal arrangement of it that's just bananas—it's so beautiful. We're actually doing a project this summer where we put together a band and collaborated with these Sufi musicians—they play a set, and then we play a set, and then we're supposed to create a project together. We're traveling to four or five cities in Europe together. Now, we're working out of African-American sacred music, and one of the songs my mother picked for that was "Kindness."

LKB: "Down to the Water," from your album *Have You Heard*, is another very fine example of a song with a social-justice core.

Toshi: That's another one of my mother's favorites, LaShonda. You're picking all of her songs. You know, the thing that I've never understood about corruption . . . well, let me start off by saying I understand greed because I've been greedy before, and I understand wanting to have something badly and bending a few rules to get it. But I don't understand the kind of corruption that wipes out any possible future for anything else to grow or happen. I was really upset when I wrote "Down to the Water." I wrote that song around the time that we first bombed Iraq and started destroying all of their artifacts, like one of their museums, which people then looted. Anyway, I traveled to Israel and Palestine shortly after the Gulf War. I had a girlfriend there who told me that after they were bombed they had been instructed by the government to go down to the water in the likely event that it happened again. They were all supposed to put on these gas masks that didn't really protect you from any atmospheric damage, and run to the Mediterranean Sea, and when the sirens went off they could come back home. So I started thinking about the resource that water is to our planet and how we're calling on it to save us from manmade destruction. The essence of life is water, this is something we've always known as reflected in songs like, "Gonna lay down my burdens down by the riverside . . ."

LKB: ". . . And study war no more."

Toshi: Yeah. And when you think about how close we are coming to losing it as a natural resource, it's a frightening thing. So I used this song to direct my anger at Bush. Usually, I don't harbor such strong feelings for presidents because I tend to think they represent a movement, but I actually can see the individuality of Bush's decisions. It *is* about his personality; it *is* about his lack of intellect and his disregard for many of the different cultures of people around the world. His decisions have brought us to the place where we are.

LKB: I've had you so long, Toshi, and I really appreciate this time with you, but I want to ask about "Building Blues" because I feel this song reflects well the unfortunate trend of urban planning that displaces whole communities.

Toshi: That song was essentially about all of the things that were changing in this neighborhood in Brooklyn. For a while, you really couldn't see much from the apartment building that features in the song—especially after the Twin Towers fell—but the Williamsburg Bank building and lots of cranes and other construction equipment. Recently they put up this mall. It's the worst mall than any developer could make. And it's specifically an insult to the people of that neighborhood because they designed the mall so they could catch you easily if you steal. None of the stores connect. Outside of the stores, there's a walkway that forms a circle, so if you tried to steal something you'd have to run that walkway. It's just ugly. It has an Old Navy and a bunch of other stores in it. Then they built a Target and a Starbucks and a Wing Wagon, and it's across the street from that that they want to build the Nets stadium. So if you look outside of the apartment building that I'm talking about in the song, you see all of that stuff happening. I'm a part of this group Develop Don't Destroy Brooklyn, and I'm going to do a benefit for them in December because they've had to fight, and are continuing to fight, this billionaire developer that really seeks to destroy their homes. You see, for me, ultimately my music is about creative documentation of my life and my community. You know, long after I'm gone, people should be able to listen to my records and hear a truthful story about what it was like to be here. And also, they should get validation for their experiences, whatever they may be. When I read about my ancestors they validate my experiences now because they did things for me. Harriet Tubman did something for *me*. Mahalia Jackson did something for *me*. When I read about how Dinah Washington formed her own booking agency and how she was one of the first artists to get ahold of the vast majority of her publishing, I know that she did something for me!

Twenty
TRAMAINE HAWKINS
(OCTOBER 11, 1951)

Granddaughter of Bishop E. E. Cleveland, a founding member of
the Church of God in Christ, the largest black Pentecostal organization in the United States, Tramaine Davis was born in San Francisco and raised in Berkeley, California. On the cusp of high school
graduation, she joined the Edwin Hawkins Singers, fortuitously
performing on the 1968 revolutionary recording "Oh Happy Day,"
the first million-selling gospel single. Later Tramaine moved to the
Los Angeles area, where she joined Andraé Crouch and the Disciples. During her tenure as the first and only female Disciple, she
sang lead vocals on the Grammy-nominated single "Christian
People." In the early '70s she wed Walter Hawkins, who went on
to lead the Berkeley Love Center Church of God in Christ. She
sang lead soprano and made several live recordings with the Love
Center Choir during the 1980s. She is one of the first gospel
singers to be signed to Columbia Records (1994); a short list of
classics recorded by the artist include "Goin' Up Yonder,"
"Changed," "That Kind of Friend," "Potter's House," "Justified by
Faith," "Trust and Obey," "What Shall I Do?," "He Brought Me,"

"It's Right and Good," and "Praise the Name of Jesus." Her song "Fall Down (Spirit of Love)" made history when it climbed to the number-one spot on dance charts, where it remained for weeks and is credited with ushering in a more techno-rhythm-based sound as heard in urban contemporary gospel music by artists such as Fred Hammond, Hezekiah Walker, John P. Kee, Kirk Franklin, Montrel Darrett, Trin-i-tee 5:7, and Erica and Tina Campbell, better known as Mary Mary. *I Never Lost My Praise*, issued on Zomba Records and recorded live at Reid Temple in Glenn Dale, Maryland, marks Tramaine's tenth solo recording. She is the recepient of numerous awards, including two Grammys, and Dove, American Music, and CEBA (Communications Excellence to Black Audiences) Awards. Tramaine is also a Gospel Hall of Fame inductee. She resides in the Sacramento area with her husband, Tommy Richardson Jr., a retired educator.

Selected Discography

Joy That Floods My Soul (Sparrow Records)

The Search Is Over (A&M Records)

Tramaine Hawkins Live (Sparrow Records)

To a Higher Place (Sony Records)

Tramaine Treasury (Light Records)

All My Best to You (Sparrow Records)

My Everything (Light Records)

Still Tramaine (Gospocentric/Zomba Records)

I Never Lost My Praise (Gospocentric/Zomba Records)

Tramaine Hawkins

LKB: Tramaine, you not only were brought up in the church, I read that you were almost born in one. Is it true that your mother left a church concert—

Tramaine: Yes, my mother left a broadcast at my grandfather's church. She was known at the time as the Songbird of the Bay Area. She was a lyric soprano. Of course it was her dad's church, Ephesian Church of God in Christ, where she was one of the featured soloists for the choir—especially at broadcast time. So she was actually singing when she went into labor and had to leave the broadcast and go to the hospital to have me. I came into not only a spirit-filled house but a music-filled house as well.

LKB: Was your father a vocalist or musician?

Tramaine: My father had a nice voice, but he was known as Deacon Davis, not a musician.

LKB: What did your parents do while you were growing up?

Tramaine: My mother and dad owned a restaurant called Lois the Pie Queen—named after my mother.

LKB: A soul-food restaurant?

Tramaine: Oh yes, and we still have it. We've been in business over fifty years. My brother is now the proprietor of it. My father did a lot of the cooking. He made the pancakes. He made excellent pancakes. Of course, we started off selling nothing but pies, but then gradually included breakfast and finally went on to offer lunch and dinner, too. It's a very well-known establishment in the Bay Area.

LKB: I bet I could get a nice peach cobbler there, my weakness.

Tramaine: Yes, you could. Come on through next time you're in the Bay Area, and tell them I sent you.

LKB: How old were you when you started singing?

Tramaine: I was four, and I can remember exactly the first song I sang. It was "I Come to the Garden."

LKB: I'm not familiar with that one.

Tramaine: It goes [*singing*]: "I come to the garden alone while dew is still on the roses . . ."

LKB: And you sang while matriculating through school?

Tramaine: Absolutely. I was in the glee club and I had the opportunity to go to Camp Cazadero. I was the only black student chosen by the music teacher at my junior high school to go to this special music camp. Matter of fact, I was the only black kid at the entire camp and the only one who didn't know how to swim. I learned how to swim that summer because I didn't want to be the only black and the one who couldn't swim. When I look back, I'm really proud of that camp accomplishment because—now this is going to really date me—I was heard by a folk group called the Lettermen—you're too young to know about them. Anyway, we were to sing for them. I was chosen to do a bit solo in one of the songs and because of that I won a scholarship to the camp. I was superexcited to be at the camp. We recorded an album there and I was featured on the album.

LKB: Was this your first recording?

Tramaine: Yes. I was twelve and the song was "Three Little Maids from School."

LKB: The operetta from Gilbert and Sullivan's *Mikado*?

Tramaine: [*laughter*] Yes. It's kind of funny, my mind has been going back to those times. I was really, really excited and so in love with music. I think I was too happy to feel lonely or ostracized because I was the only black.

LKB: I'm wondering if you had the notion then that music was your calling.

Tramaine: Oh, absolutely. I knew when I was eight years old, because at age eight I traveled to many different churches with my auntie, who is now a bishop, Bishop Ernestine Cleveland Reems. She took me on the road with her during her preaching dates all over the country. At that time, we would lodge at some of the church members' homes. It was nothing like what we do now—staying at all of these wonderful hotels.

LKB: By dint of these experiences, you knew that you would sing gospel professionally?

Tramaine: I thought I would. You know, my parents worked very hard in the restaurant business. Long hours, too, so that most of the time I stayed with my grandmother at what we called the Big House. Big Dee Dee, Big Mama is what we called her. Anyway, we were always, I mean always, at church. I ate, slept, drank, everything was church. On Sunday mornings there was Sunday school, of course. We went from there to children's church and then from there to YPWW and finally on to regular service.

LKB: What is YPWW?

Tramaine: Young People's Willing Workers.

LKB: Is that something that all Church of God in Christ congregations have? I was brought up Baptist and I've never heard of it.

Tramaine: Perhaps. I think so.

LKB: And is it like BTU, the Baptist Training Union?

Tramaine: Yes, exactly.

LKB: After all of that, it must've been seven or eight at night when you were finished with all of your Sunday services.

Tramaine: Yes, it was. Exactly. But after evening service, we came back for broadcast at ten o'clock. Later, after I got to be a teenager, after evening service, we'd go down to San Jose, which is about an hour away from Berkeley, to another church. So church was all I knew. All I knew. You know, nowadays kids have a fit if they can't go to this party or this club. Back then I would have a hissy fit if I couldn't go to church.

LKB: Were there other musical influences in your childhood home besides your mother?

Tramaine: My grandmother on my dad's side used to listen faithfully to the Staple Singers, so I loved them also. Keep in mind, the Staple Singers weren't singing secular music at that time. They were strictly gospel and that's all that my grandmother listened to. I remember Mavis singing [*singing*], "Oh they tell me of a home . . ."

LKB: "Uncloudy Day."

Tramaine: Yes, you know it. And then, later on, as a teenager I fell in love with the Caravans, of course. I also remember really liking the Roberta Martin Singers. And I'll never forget Mahalia. I remember my mom taking me to the Oakland Coliseum to see Mahalia Jackson sing. She wore a gold and white robe. She had her hair off her face and up—you know how she used to wear it—and she got on her knees and sang as if she were praying. We were in the second or third row in the auditorium, and in my mind's eye I can still see all that perspiration when she started to sing "Precious Lord." I was so moved by that as a youngster that I turned to my mother and said, "That's what I want to do." All of those influences have been very important to my life.

LKB: Do you play an instrument?

Tramaine: I started off at a very young age taking piano lessons, but I didn't stick with it. It's kind of unfortunate. I look back on that now and wish that I had had the fortitude to hang in there. I was taught by a woman who lived about two blocks away from our restaurant. I remember her today because anytime you made a mistake, she would hit you across your knuckles with a red wooden stick. I got hit so many times coming up I eventually told Mama I didn't want to go back to her. I wish my mother would have said, "Well, you don't have to go back to her; we'll find somebody else." Every now and then I piddle around on the piano.

LKB: By the time you graduated from high school, was the plan to venture into the professional gospel-music scene?

Tramaine: Oh yes. In fact, right after I got my diploma at the high school graduation I gave it to my mama and I went on the road that night with the Hawkins Singers. I didn't even go to my senior prom because we had an engagement, and we were traveling out of the country. I remember that so vividly because I was only seventeen but there was absolutely no hesitation on my part. I had no remorse over missing my prom or any postgraduation festivities.

LKB: As a teen were you ever interested in performing secular music?

Tramaine: Not really, not in high school. In high school—now listen to this—I was a part of a group called the Heavenly Tones and I also helped to form a group called the Black and White Keys. We named it that for what would have been obvious reasons back then; we were the first interracial choir at Berkeley High School. We sang gospel music. We were doing four-, five-part harmony back in the sixties. So it wasn't really new to me when I started performing with Edwin and Walter Hawkins. My interest in secular music came later.

LKB: I'd like for you to talk a little about that transition from touring and performing gospel music with the Hawkins Singers to singing R&B, which I know you did for a very short time.

Tramaine: I guess it came with my tie to Andraé Crouch and the Disciples, because before we went to Europe I'd gone on a little tour with Andraé. In fact, I was the first female to be a Disciple. I was before Sandra, and of course I was before Danibelle. I did one album with Andraé Crouch and the Disciples. It was a studio album. I think perhaps working with Andraé brought me to the consciousness of the lead singer of the Honey Cone, because she was also one of the COGICS—that was Crouch's female group. And of course COGICS means Church of God in Christ. Anyway, she [Edna Wright] got in touch with me and asked me to consider being one of the Honey Cone. I can't remember at this time why I would even entertain anything like that, but it must've been at a time in my life when I was interested in singing as much as I could. I'm sure I was also enticed by them having a number-one record. "Want Ads," one of their singles, had just made a huge splash. I mean, that song was a hit! So, I'm sure I was like, "Wow. These people calling me?" You know what I mean?

LKB: You weren't with the Honey Cone for long. What cut short your tenure with the group?

Tramaine: When they asked me to join, they did so right as they

began to rehearse for tour. I rehearsed with them for about
three weeks, maybe four. I was being fitted for outfits and
learning all of the steps because we were dancing while performing the songs. I remember one night, after I'd gone to
bed. . . . [*long pause*] Well, I believe it was the holy spirit
coming to me in my dreams and shaking me and dropping in
my spirit a warning of some sort. When I woke up the next
day, I felt nervous, terribly upset, and worried. And I knew
that I could not continue performing with the Honey Cone.
So I went to the lead singer and resigned. I never returned to
secular music after that.

LKB: And yet, years later your song "Fall Down" [1985] crossed
over to the secular world. It was a number-one dance hit and
played in black clubs and on black radio stations from coast to
coast. I know also that you received a lot of flack for the song
in the gospel community.

Tramaine: I believe that the same thing that happened to me with
"Fall Down" happened earlier around the song "Oh Happy
Day." The rhythm, the tempo, the style of that song and the
contemporariness of it just made "Oh Happy Day" catch like
a wildfire. Even people who knew "Oh Happy Day" was originally a hymn were in love with the song because it was such
a completely different sound for gospel at that time. I was a
part of "Oh Happy Day" and they really ridiculed us for the
success of that song in the Church of God in Christ. They
actually felt that it was encouraging bad behavior. And years
later, sure enough, the same thing happened with "Fall Down."
I remember going into my own department store at home in
Oakland and being on the elevator and hearing "Fall Down."

It was pretty spectacular. [*laughter*] I remember people telling me they loved the beat, all the percussion and that bass line. Some people said when the song came on their car radios they would stop the car, get out, and start dancing to it. See, and I think that's what really turned off the church, because people were dancing to what was supposed to be sacred music.

LKB: The uproar surrounding the song was of course not the lyric, which is obviously sacred, but the techno-funk arrangement. What was your feeling about the song's arrangement, Tramaine?

Tramaine: First of all, I don't know if it's known that I recorded that song with one take. When I actually heard the music for the first time I thought it was such a fresh sound. It was such a departure from the norm, and to me that was exciting. You know, it started off just as an instrumental, and the songwriters said, "Tramaine, we hear you doing something on this." They wrote out the lyric spontaneously, and I just went in the vocal booth and went for it! But what is most memorable to me about the whole thing is that it just sounded like it was my song. It sounded like it was written for my voice. I'm sure there are a lot of people who will say things like this to you while you put together this book. There are some songs that you just click with.

LKB: It's interesting to note that Kirk Franklin, while he received some criticism for his gospel-dance music, did not come under attack to the extent that you did. And this, I'm sure, reflects the changing times, the black church's struggle to regain its youth population and gospel music's major hand in helping to bring youngsters back into the fold, so to speak. But people like

Kirk, Tonex, and Mary Mary, they were ushered in through a door that you opened with "Fall Down."

Tramaine: Thank you for pointing that out, because I agree with you. I am sure Kirk felt the freedom to perform the way he does because of what we did.

LKB: Have you written some gospel songs?

Tramaine: I have written or cowritten some songs, but I wouldn't call them gospel by today's standards. I'd call them inspirational.

LKB: And what is the process of songwriting like for you?

Tramaine: I tailor lyrics to the experiences of my life. And even if a songwriter comes to me with a song, I like to go and sometimes change the song a bit so that it really matches my life. I don't like to sing songs that aren't really me. Maybe when I was younger I would have, but at this point in my life I only sing songs and record songs that I have experienced, songs that truly call out to me because I've found that that is the way for me to offer the song the best interpretation. See, I know Tramaine's story, so it's up to me to sing the songs that are my story, and I think having done this accounts for the longevity of my repertoire. Because to one extent those songs were and are true to my life, and to a larger extent, you know, the glory is God's. It has to be God.

LKB: I'm interested by your comment on knowing your own story and feeling like it is a duty to sing songs that reflect it, because I find that for many gospel singers this is requisite. Whereas in other musical genres I've had singers tell me they will purposely shy away from singing material or writing material that is too personal because they feel it somehow makes them too vulnerable or too accessible to the audience, and they want to maintain some distance. The element of the testimony, "This is my story, this is my song," is what makes gospel music so dynamic and so moving.

Tramaine: It is a duty to testify because we have a higher calling. It's not about me. At my best, I'm being used by God. I'm living this life, but it's really about Jesus Christ. So the duty, the responsibility to be true to that and to minister that in your music is enormous. And it's a duty I didn't take lightly as a youngster and I don't take lightly now. I'm very honored and excited about this new album featuring songs written by my son, Jamie Hawkins, Walter Hawkins, and my producer Kurt Carr, who has just done a fabulous job.

LKB: And the album you're referring to is *I Never Lost My Praise*, which will be out by the time this book is published.

Tramaine: Yes.

LKB: While preparing for the interview, I checked out one of the songs from that forthcoming album. I heard "Excellent" on your Myspace page.

Tramaine: That was written by my son and his wife.

LKB: And what about future album projects with some of your original tunes? You know where I'm going with this. . . .

Tramaine: [*laughter*]

LKB: I'd like to hear the *Tramaine Sings Tramaine* album.

Tramaine: Wow. Well, hopefully that will materialize. I'm working in that direction. You know, God has kept this voice intact for over forty years. It's amazing to me.

LKB: When recording, Tramaine, do you have a preference? Studio album or—

Tramaine: I love singing live. I'm really going to be challenged as far as getting into this new way of recording, which people say is much easier and more economical. I haven't felt it yet. But my forte is live; that's who I am. That's why it was something that I had to do at least one more time with this most recent recording. I was fought back and forth about it quite a bit. First it was a great idea, then it wasn't. I knew within my heart that it had to be live. A "live" album to me means a choir, an ensemble, but also a few songs that are just Tramaine. I mean, I love the call-and-response that I experience with a choir. It's not just the energy I feel from the choir, it's the actual presence of a great spirit moving through all those voices.

LKB: Speaking of live recordings with choirs, I've wanted to personally thank you for a long time for "Potter's House," Tramaine. That song has gotten me over more than a few humps. In fact, around this time last year I was having a dark mood, and when I couldn't find my *Tramaine Hawkins Live* CD, I went online and purchased it from the iTunes store. Actually, a short story evolved from my hearing the song during that moment. So it has inspired me both spiritually and creatively. Tell me the story of that song.

Tramaine: Tell me the title of the short story so I can look for it.

LKB: "Ezekiel Saw the Wheel," and it is about a minister's last sermon at a church where he has led the congregation for thirty years.

Tramaine: Okay, thank you. "Potter's House" was written by V. Michael McKay, who is well known for writing songs specifically for certain artists; he really has a talent for doing that.

LKB: Was "Potter's House" written especially for you and Mr. Hawkins?

Tramaine: That's a whole 'nother story because when Michael sang the song to me, I just knew it immediately, because I've been there. As soon as I heard it I knew that song would bring release to me and countless others. After hearing it, I presented it to Walter, who you probably know was my producer on that album. I believe the song was supposed to be a solo, but two or three nights before the recording, V. Michael McKay and I were at the piano rehearsing it together, and we taped it. I shared the tape with Walter, who heard the two of us and liked the idea of a duet, but Walter said, "That sounds good but V. Michael McKay can't sing it like I can." [*laughter*] And that was it.

LKB: Of course, you recorded numerous times with Walter; are there other gospel artists whom you'd like to record with?

Tramaine: Yeah, matter of fact, there are. BeBe's one of them. I love BeBe's voice. And, believe it or not, I would still like to do something with the Clark Sisters. In fact, Dorenda wrote a song that we wanted to put on this live recording, but we couldn't get our schedules together. But, yeah, I think singing with the Clark Sisters would be pretty powerful, you know what I'm saying? [*laughter*]

LKB: What music inspires you?

Tramaine: Some of the music that really inspires me are songs that are twenty, twenty-five years old. One of them is "He Cares." It's just a song that yet ministers to me, and it just so happens to be a choir song. I love the young lady's voice on there. A lot of the songs that lift me up were recorded back in the day by the Tommys. Those songs yet hit home with me. It's just something about those songs to me that are yet relevant. I don't care what you're going through. And I say that not because there's nothing out there now that is relevant but because so much that is out there has gotten so far away from the traditional sounds. It's not even so much that gospel has gotten very contemporary, it's that everybody is trying to sound unique. We have complicated the music too much. You know, there is something very healing about a simple melody line and someone telling the story of how they got over.

LKB: So you think that contemporary gospel music has different aspirations?

Tramaine: Oh, yes, definitely. Everybody is trying to sound different—

LKB: In order to carve a niche for themselves.

Tramaine: There you go. To me, though, the purest of songs still work. They *still* work.

LKB: Gospel is going, has gone, glam.

Tramaine: There you go! That's one of the reasons why it took me so long to make this last live recording, because I kept waiting—

LKB: For the tide to change, for the return back to a more traditional sound.

Tramaine: There you go. And you know, LaShonda, even though the tide hasn't changed and some artists have achieved just amazing status in gospel music, I'm not worried about the reception of this new album. And you know why I'm not worried? I love the music on this album and I gave it my all, and when you do that you have no regrets.

About the Author

A lover and scholar of black music, LaShonda K. Barnett has hosted her own jazz radio program on WBAI (NYC), recorded two independent CDs, taught courses on black music, and consulted and taught at New York City's Jazz at Lincoln Center. Generally talking nonstop about music around seminar and dinner tables and at invited lectures domestically and abroad, Barnett has engaged audiences on the subject of black music in Austria, Brazil, France, Germany, and South Africa. She teaches at Sarah Lawrence College and lives in Manhattan. She may be found online at http://www.lashondabarnett.com.

Index